THE 'DOUBLE DEMOCRATIC DEFICIT'

The 'Double Democratic Deficit'
Parliamentary Accountability and the Use of Force Under International Auspices

Edited by
HANS BORN and **HEINER HÄNGGI**
Geneva Centre for the Democratic Control of Armed Forces (DCAF)
Switzerland

GENEVA CENTRE FOR THE DEMOCRATIC CONTROL OF ARMED FORCES (DCAF)

Routledge
Taylor & Francis Group

LONDON AND NEW YORK

First published 2004 by Ashgate Publishing

Reissued 2018 by Routledge
2 Park Square, Milton Park, Abingdon, Oxon OX14 4RN
711 Third Avenue, New York, NY 10017, USA

Routledge is an imprint of the Taylor & Francis Group, an informa business

First issued in paperback 2018

A Library of Congress record exists under LC control number: 2003066255

Notice:
Product or corporate names may be trademarks or registered trademarks, and are
used only for identification and explanation without intent to infringe.

Publisher's Note
The publisher has gone to great lengths to ensure the quality of this reprint but
points out that some imperfections in the original copies may be apparent.

Disclaimer
The publisher has made every effort to trace copyright holders and welcomes
correspondence from those they have been unable to contact.

ISBN 13: 978-0-815-39765-6 (hbk)
ISBN 13: 978-1-138-62091-9 (pbk)
ISBN 13: 978-1-351-14712-5 (ebk)

Contents

List of Tables

List of Tables

List of Contributors

Dr. Giovanna Bono is a post-doctoral Research Fellow at the Department of Peace Studies at the University of Bradford, UK. She is a member of the research and training network project on Bridging the Accountability Gap in European Security and Defence Policy.

Dr. Hans Born is Senior Fellow at the Geneva Centre for the Democratic Control of Armed Forces (DCAF). He coordinates the DCAF working groups on parliamentary oversight of the security sector and on legal aspects of security sector governance.

Prof. Dr. Lori Fisler Damrosch is the Henry L. Moses Professor of Law and International Organization at Columbia University in New York City. She is Co-Editor-in-Chief of the American Journal of International Law and a counsellor of the American Society of International Law, of which she was Vice-President in 1996-98.

Dr. Willem F. van Eekelen is Alternate Member on behalf of the Netherlands' Senate to the European Convention. He has been a Member of both Chambers of the Netherlands' Parliament (Senate and House of Representatives), Netherlands' Minister of Defence, Secretary-General of the Western European Union (WEU) and Vice-President of NATO Parliamentary Assembly.

Catriona Gourlay is the Executive Director of the International Security Information Service, Europe (ISIS Europe), a Brussels-based independent research organisation. She is a member of the research and training network project on Bridging the Accountability Gap in European Security and Defence Policy.

Dr. Owen Greene is Research Director at the Department of Peace Studies, and Director of the Centre for International Cooperation and Security, Bradford University, UK. He is a Co-Director of the research and training network project on Bridging the Accountability Gap in European Security and Defence Policy.

Dr. Heiner Hänggi is Assistant Director and Head of Think Tank at the Geneva Centre for the Democratic Control of Armed Forces (DCAF); concurrently, he is a lecturer in political science/international relations at the University of St. Gallen, Switzerland.

Jan Hoekema is Ambassador for Cultural Cooperation at the Netherlands' Ministry of Foreign Affairs. From 1994 to 2002, he was a Member of Parliament (House of Representatives). He was President of the Defence and Security

Committee of the NATO Parliamentary Assembly and a Member of the Board of Parliamentarians for Global Action.

Dr. Charlotte Ku is Executive Vice-President and Executive Director of the American Society of International Law. She is Co-Editor (with Harold K. Jacobson) of *Democratic Accountability and the Use of Force in International Law* (Cambridge University Press, 2003).

Christ Klep is a historian specializing in Dutch contemporary military history and peace-support operations. From 1982 to 2000, he was a researcher at the Military History Department of the Royal Netherlands Army. He is currently a freelance writer and part-time lecturer at the University of Utrecht, The Netherlands.

Dr. Roman Schmidt-Radefeldt is Assistant Professor at the Institute of European and International Law, University of Leipzig, Germany. He is Legal Adviser to the German Armed Forces and a member of the International Law Association and the International Society for Military Law and the Law of War.

Marlene Urscheler is Deputy Head of the Coordination Office for Humanitarian Law EAPC/PfP at the Swiss Ministry of Foreign Affairs. From 2001 to 2003 she has been working as a Research Assistant and Research Associate at the Geneva Centre for the Democratic Control of Armed Forces (DCAF).

Prof. Dr. Donna Winslow holds the Chair of Social Anthropology (with special emphasis on development studies) at the Vrije Universiteit (Free University) in Amsterdam. Concurrently, she is an Adjunct Professor at the Royal Military Academy in Breda, the Netherlands.

Preface

Javier Solana[*]

The debate about the use of force in managing international order today is essentially about the perennial question of the relation between power and legitimacy. Law and power have historically been two sides of the same coin. Power is needed to establish law, and law is the legitimate face of power.

The new globalised world offers both a brighter prospect than mankind has ever known and at the same time a more terrifying future. Which of these comes about will depend partly on our actions. The European Union is committed to build an international order based on effective multilateralism which aims to tackle both causes and symptoms of instability.

The fundamental framework today for international relations is the United Nations Charter. It provides the framework for a rule-based international order and for action to confront the violation of rules and threats to international peace and security. In a world of global threats, global markets and global media, strengthening the international order requires commitment to equip and enable the United Nations to act effectively in order to fulfil its responsibilities. This is a key European priority. In support of effective multilateralism the European Union needs to develop a strategic culture that fosters early, rapid and when necessary, robust intervention. This applies particularly in efforts to deal with the new threats of terrorism, proliferation of weapons of mass destruction and failed states and organised crime.

International order however also depends on building a world of well-governed democratic societies. Spreading good governance, dealing with corruption and abuse of power, establishing the rule of law and protecting human rights are the best means of strengthening the international order. A world seen as offering justice and opportunity for everyone will be more secure for everyone. The European Union is committed to global partnerships to tackle causes as well as symptoms. For example, looking at causes also means addressing the political environment from which terrorism grows with the same vigour and determination that we address acts of terrorism. Because while no cause can justify terrorism, there is no justification for ignoring the causes of terrorism.

---

[*] Secretary General of the Council of the European Union/High Representative for the Common Foreign and Security Policy and Secretary General of the Western European Union (since 1999). Previously Member of the Spanish Parliament (1977-1995), Spanish Cabinet Minister (1982-1995), including Minister for Foreign Affairs (1992-1995), and Secretary General of NATO (1995-1999).

In conclusion, international order depends today on a shared responsibility across the globe to deal effectively and legitimately with the challenges to peace and security. Law and international norms have to be backed by force, while, if it is to have lasting effect, force needs to be backed by legitimacy. Navigating the perils of using force under international auspices with the aim to promote international order requires today, as in the past, a balanced commitment to effective and legitimate action operating in an inclusive multilateral framework and in a world based on rules.

Acknowledgements

The idea for this book has its origins in discussions at the Geneva Centre for the Democratic Control of Armed Forces (DCAF) on new challenges of parliamentary accountability for established democracies in an era of globalisation. These discussions resulted in a DCAF Think Tank publication project on parliamentary accountability and the use of force under the auspices of international institutions, which was launched in the Spring of 2002 and involved a number of outstanding international experts, including the contributors of this book.

A number of debts have been incurred in the implementation of this project and we are delighted to acknowledge them here. Ingrid Thorburn and Marlene Urscheler provided invaluable administrative, organisational and editorial assistance in the course of this project. Herbert Wulf and an anonymous reviewer of Ashgate Publishing as well as our colleagues Alan Bryden, Marina Caparini, Eden Cole, Robert Diethelm, Rafal Domisiewicz, Alain Faupin, Charlotte Ku and Dorina Nastase provided a number of incisive comments and useful suggestions on earlier drafts of the manuscript or parts of it. Wendy Robinson diligently undertook the language editing of the contributions which have been written by non-native English speakers, and Oliver Wates did the final copy-editing. Kirstin Howgate, Irene Poulton and Pam Bertram at Ashgate Publishing steered us through the publication process with patience and encouragement. We would like to thank all of them and to express our special gratitude to the contributors of this book who did a wonderful job in meeting the great many demands the editors made on them.

Hans Born, Heiner Hänggi
Geneva, 30 July 2003

List of Acronyms

ACTORDS	Activation Orders (NATO)
ARRC	Allied Rapid Reaction Corps (EU)
AWACS	NATO Airborne Warning and Control System
CARBG	Canadian Airborne Regiment Battle Group
CF	Canadian Forces
CFE	Conventional Armed Forces in Europe Treaty
CFI	European Court of First Instance
CFSP	Common Foreign Security Policy
CINCSOUTH	Commander-in-Chief Allied Forces Southern Europe
CIS	Commonwealth of Independent States
CIVCOM	Committee on the Civilian Aspects of Crisis Management
CJTF	Combined Joint Task Force
COREPER	EU Committee of Permanent Representatives
CSBM	Confidence and Security Building Measures
CSCE	Commission on Security and Cooperation in Europe
CWC	Chemical Weapons Convention
DND	Department of National Defence (Canada)
DPC	Defence Planning Committee
EAPC	Euro-Atlantic Partnership Council
EBRD	European Bank for Reconstruction and Development
ECJ	European Court of Justice
EDC	European Defence Community
EEC	European Economic Community
EP	European Parliament
ESDP	European Security and Defence Policy
EU	European Union
EUMC	EU Military Committee
EUMS	EU Military Staff
EUPM	EU Police Mission
FYROM	Former Yugoslav Republic of Macedonia
GNSS	European Global Navigation Satellite System
HG	Headline Goal
IFOR	NATO Implementation Force
IISS	International Institute of Strategic Studies
IPTF	UN-led International Police Task Force
ISAF	International Security Assistance Force
JSDF	Japanese Self-Defence Forces
KLA	Kosovo Liberation Army
MAP	Membership Action Plan
MC	Military Committee

MEP	Member of European Parliament
MNC	Major NATO Commander
NAC	North Atlantic Council
NATO	North Atlantic Treaty Organisation
NATO PA	NATO Parliamentary Assembly
NDHQ	National Defence Headquarters
NGO	Non-Governmental Organisation
NIOD	Nederlands Instituut voor Oorlogs Documentatie (Netherlands' Institute for War Research)
NPT	Non-Proliferation Treaty
OAS	Organisation of American States
OAU	Organisation of African Unity
OCCAR	*Organisme Conjoint de Coopération en Matière d'Armément*
OECD	Organisation for Economic Cooperation and Development
ONUC	1960 UN Operation in the Congo
OSCE	Organisation for Security and Cooperation in Europe
PAP	Police Action Plan
PfP	Partnership for Peace
PPEWU	Policy Planning and Early Warning Unit
PSC	Political Security Committee
PSO	Peace Support Operation
QMV	Qualified Majority Voting
RRF	Rapid Reaction Force
SACEUR	Supreme Allied Commander Europe
SACLANT	Supreme Allied Commander Atlantic
SFOR	NATO Security Force
SHAPE	Supreme Headquarters of Allied Powers Europe (NATO)
SILT	Somalia Inquiry Liaison Team
TEU	Treaty on European Union 1992
UN	United Nations
UNEF	First United Nations Emergency Force
UNIFIL	United Nations Interim Force in Lebanon
UNITAF	Unified Task Force
UNMEE	United Nations Mission in Ethiopia and Eritrea
UNOMUR	United Nations Observer Mission in Uganda-Rwanda
UNOSOM	United Nations Operation in Somalia
UNPREDEP	United Nations Preventive Deployment Force in the Former Yugoslav Republic of Macedonia
UNPROFOR	United Nations Protection Force
UNSC	United Nations Security Council
UNSF	United Nations Security Force
UNSG	United Nations Secretary General
UNTAET	United Nations Transitional Administration in East Timor
UNTSO	United Nations Truce Supervision Organisation
WEU	Western European Union

PART I

INTRODUCTION

Chapter 1

The Use of Force Under International Auspices: Parliamentary Accountability and 'Democratic Deficits'

Heiner Hänggi

Introduction

The US-led war in Iraq in spring 2003 was a clear reminder that the use of force is still very much a part of life in international relations. What made it disturbing for many was not so much the use of force, nor in particular its use against a 'rogue' regime, but the use of force without authorisation by the United Nations (UN) or another international institution. However, this relapse to 'unilateralist' practices should not divert our attention from the fact that the use of force under the auspices of international institutions has dramatically increased since the end of the Cold War, both in terms of frequency and in scope. Moreover, given 'post-Iraq' developments in other parts of the world, particularly in Sub-Saharan Africa, one may speculate that this trend will continue in spite of the counterfactual argument, which the war in Iraq appears to posit. This trend is first of all reflected by the substantial increase in the use of military forces authorised by the UN since the late 1980s. Two-thirds of these instances, ranging from monitoring missions to peace enforcement operations, took place in the period after 1990. The trend of using force under the auspices of international institutions has been further accentuated by the fact that regional organisations, such as the North Atlantic Treaty Organisation (NATO) and the European Union (EU), have begun to authorize the use of force outside their own territory. NATO's 1999 Kosovo intervention, its 2001 Operation Essential Harvest in Macedonia and the 2003 EU operations in Macedonia and the Congo are good cases in point. The causes of these developments are certainly manifold but, in a general way, they may be viewed as resulting from the internationalisation of security affairs in the broader context of globalisation and regionalisation.[1]

While the use of force under international auspices has increased substantially, the same does not necessarily hold true for its democratic account-

---

1   On internationalisation of security affairs see Chapter Two; on globalisation see Clark, 1999, pp. 107-126; on regionalisation see Fawcett and Hurrell, 1995, pp. 309-328.

ability.[2] Traditionally, the decision regarding both the internal and external use of force has been a crucial feature of the modern nation-state, and consequently accountability to citizens for the use of force was viewed as a central component of democratic governance. This is illustrated by the fact that adherence to the principle of democratic control of armed forces and the security sector[3] in general has become a basic requirement for membership in international organisations of democratic states (Greene, 2003). With decisions on the use of force increasingly being made by international institutions, even established democracies, where the democratic control of armed forces is usually taken for granted, are struggling to adapt established national mechanisms of accountability to new situations. Since the early 1990s, the deployment and use of national military forces under the auspices of international institutions has repeatedly provoked heated debates in a number of troop-deploying states such as the US, Germany, Canada and the Netherlands – with each of these cases reflecting deficiencies, but also offering new prospects of enhancing democratic accountability for these international engagements.[4]

This book looks at an important but under-researched aspect of democratic accountability, namely the role parliaments play in ensuring democratic accountability of the use of national armed forces under the aegis of international institutions. It discusses the problems and challenges facing established democracies, above all from the Euro-Atlantic area,[5] with regard to parliamentary accountability of the use of force under the authority of the UN, NATO, and the EU. This chapter sets out to establish an analytical framework for the discussion of the aforementioned problems and challenges by taking up the notion of the 'double

---

2   *Accountability* is viewed as a key requirement of good governance. As well as governmental institutions, the private sector and civil society organisations must also be accountable to their institutional stakeholders and to the public. Who is accountable to whom varies depending on whether decisions or actions taken are internal or external to an institution. In general, an institution is accountable to those who will be affected by its decisions or actions. *Democratic accountability* means that those who have the authority to decide and act are accountable to the elected representatives (representative democracy) or to the people directly (direct democracy). *Parliamentary accountability* refers to the former. See Behn, 2001, pp. 62-80.

3   The security sector includes all the bodies whose main responsibilities are the protection of the state and its constituent communities. It includes core structures such as armed forces, police and intelligence agencies as well as those institutions that formulate, implement and oversee internal and external security policy. Caparini, 2003, p. 2.

4   See Chapters Five (Netherlands), Six (Canada), Eight (United States and Germany) and Nine (Germany).

5   As a matter of fact, the comparative and case studies in this book concentrate on NATO and/or EU member states, with the exception of Chapter Three (which also covers India, Japan and Russia).

democratic deficit' in terms of parliamentary accountability at both the national and international level.[6]

'Democratic Deficit' – Outside In

The problem of ensuring democratic accountability in the case of international engagements is not a feature unique to the deployment and use of military forces. On the contrary, the role of international institutions in the system of governance and their influence on national policies tend to be much larger in other – perhaps less sensitive – issue-areas such as trade, finance, development, and the environment. The disparity between the growing power of international institutions and the absence of democratic scrutiny of their activities is widely viewed as constituting a major challenge for democratic polities.[7] When institutions of accountability and responsibility which are rooted in the democratic nation-state are no longer co-extensive with the affairs over which they have oversight, 'democratic deficits are (…) set to become the global norm' (Clark, 1999, p. 147). The issue of 'democratic deficits' of international institutions and decision-making first emerged in the context of the ever widening, ever deepening European Union, which has become an international entity in its own right.[8] In recent years, and in particular within the context of the anti-globalisation movements, the United Nations and UN-related multilateral institutions such as the International Monetary Fund (IMF), the World Bank, and the World Trade Organization (WTO) have increasingly been criticised for their 'democratic deficits'.[9] In contrast to the EU, these bodies have no state-like features but are of a purely intergovernmental nature and composed of both, member states with democratic forms of government and those with non-democratic ones. In the context of international security, and more specifically the use of force under international auspices, 'democratic deficits' are mostly associated with the UN Security Council, NATO, and particularly the EU's emerging European Security and Defence Policy (ESDP).

No consensus can be found in the relevant policy and academic discourses on how to tackle the democratic deficiency at the global and regional level of governance. Considering this from a sceptical perspective, one finds Robert A. Dahl, whose question 'Can international organizations be democratic?' is meant to be rhetorical. In his view, it is highly unlikely that international organisations could be democratised – '[i]f democratic institutions are largely ineffective in governing the European Union, the prospects for democratizing other international systems

---

6   Focusing specifically on the European Union, the notion of the 'double democratic deficit' has been discussed by a number of authors, for example, Schmitter, 2000; Lodge, 1996.

7   See McGrew, 2002; UNDP, 2002, pp. 101-122; Clark, 1999, pp. 146-166.

8   See Harlow, 2002; Hoskyns and Newman, 2000; Schmitter (2000). For a systematic discussion of the alleged 'democratic deficit' of the European Union from a theoretical perspective, see Schmidt, 2000, pp. 424-438.

9   For an overview see UNDP, 2002, pp. 101-122.

seem even more remote' (Dahl, 1998, p. 115).[10] On a more optimistic note, one finds a number of scholars and practitioners who are engaged in the search for possibilities to address the 'democratic deficit' suffered by international institutions. From a normative perspective, three theoretical approaches or 'models' can be distinguished: liberal-democratic internationalism, which aims at reforming the current international institutions; radical communitarism, which promotes the creation of alternative structures based on transnational participatory governance according to functionalist rather than geographical patterns; and finally, cosmopolitanism, which posits the reconstruction of global governance on all levels based on a cosmopolitan democratic law transcending national and other sovereignties (McGrew, 2002; Chapter Two). These normative models inform the global policy discourse on ways and means to strengthen the democratic credentials of global and regional arrangements. In this discourse, two general thrusts can be distinguished: proposals for the gradual 'democratisation' of international institutions on the one hand, and the call for greater pluralism in terms of actors involved on the other hand. Proposals for the gradual 'democratisation' of international institutions tend to focus on increasing representation, transparency, and accountability in the decision-making of these intergovernmental bodies. Calls for greater pluralism tend to emphasise the importance of non-state actors and civil society in influencing policy and holding international bodies accountable.[11] In terms of practical reforms, the participation of civil society actors in international institutions seems to be the standard attempt at narrowing the participatory gap in global governance (Brühl and Rittberger, 2001, pp. 34-35).

The discourse on the subject of reducing the 'democratic deficits' of international institutions concentrates on governmental and non-governmental actors, whereas references to the role of parliaments in ensuring democratic accountability are rather modest with some calls for the creation of a parliamentary dimension of the UN, a strengthening of the European Parliament or a greater involvement of national parliaments.[12] This is rather striking given the fact that

---

10 However, Dahl's harsh statement has to be qualified given the fact that the problem of the 'democratic deficit' has been recognized within the European Union and, since Dahl made his statement, the role of the European Parliament has been strengthened (though not necessarily in the field of security and defence policy). Furthermore, the draft European Constitution put forward by the European Convention would bring about a number of additional improvements in parliamentary accountability of the EU.

11 See, for example, UNDP 2002, pp. 101-122.

12 A number of proposals have been made to create a parliamentary dimension of the UN either by way of establishing a second 'Peoples' Assembly (Bienen, Rittberger, and Wagner, 1998, p. 297; Held, 1996, p. 358), or by way of including parliamentarians in national delegations to the General Assembly and other UN organs (Parliamentary Assembly of the Council of Europe, Resolution 1289, 2002, para. 8). Apart from numerous proposals for strengthening of the European Parliament, there is also the idea put forward by the Parliamentary Assembly of the Council of Europe of introducing an inter-parliamentary chamber to the European Parliament as a body of representatives of national parliaments to form a second chamber (Parliamentary Assembly of the Council of Europe, Resolution 1289, 2002, para. 10).

parliaments are the central locus of accountability and legitimacy in democratic polities. Parliaments articulate citizen's preferences (though not exclusively), they translate these preferences into policies through enacting legislation and adopting budgets, and they oversee governments once a law or a budget is passed. Though institutions and practices of democracy are an evolving phenomenon and vary from country to country, it is an undisputed tenet of democracy that the parliament, being the representative body of the polity, must exert oversight over every element of public policy, including the security sector and, in particular, decisions on the deployment and use of force. According to Lori F. Damrosch (1996), during the past decades there has been a general trend in democracies towards greater parliamentary control over 'war-and-peace decisions'. Whilst this trend may be welcomed from a democratic theory perspective, the extent of actual parliamentary accountability of security affairs, and more specifically international security affairs, should not be overestimated. In spite of differences in national constitutions, institutions and practices, parliamentary oversight often tends to be weakest when it comes to foreign and security policy of democratic states – both policy areas, which have traditionally been more government-oriented. This state of affairs reveals a second 'democratic deficit' on the national level – quite separate from the deficiencies of democratic accountability on the international level. It fits with Clark's general observation on 'the reciprocal manner in which democratic deficits on the inside have been necessary accomplices of globalization' (1999, p. 166).

The issue of parliamentary accountability of the use of force under international auspices, which constitutes a poorly mapped terrain in scholarly analysis, is a good case in point to study the internal (or national) and external (or international) dimensions of what could be termed the 'double democratic deficit'. There is an expanding body of literature on the problem of the 'democratic deficit' of international institutions, but the respective publications tend to address the issue from a general perspective, hardly ever touching upon the 'democratic deficit' in terms of security issues or even the problem of the use of force.[13] Despite the existence of ample literature on international security institutions such as the UN, NATO and the EU,[14] the majority of these publications do not discuss issues of democratic governance relating to security affairs, and least of all its parliamentary dimension.[15] Furthermore, there is a small, albeit rapidly growing, body of literature on democratic governance of the security sector as well as its parliamentary dimension, but these publications consider parliamentary accountability of the security sector largely in the context of the nation-state and

---

13 See Aksu and Camilleri, 2002; Anderson, 2002.

14 See, for example, Diehl, 1995 (UN); Yost, 1999 (NATO); Bronstone, 2000 (EU).

15 Reference is made to two research projects which study the parliamentary dimension of the European Union's evolving common security and defence policy: 'Bridging the Accountability Gap in European Security and Defence Policy, ESDP Democracy', see http://www.esdpdemocracy.net/2_the project.htm; 'The Parliamentary Dimension of ESDP', see: http://www.politik.uni-koeln.de/wessels/forup/Parliamentary_Dimension/Parliamentary_Dimension.htm [accessed 15 July 2003].

for the most part solely in new and transitional democracies.[16] Finally, reference is made to a recent publication on democratic accountability and the use of force in international law (Ku and Jacobson, 2003b), which addresses many of the issues raised in this study from an international law perspective. With this book, we aim to fill a remaining gap in the literature by exploring the aforementioned 'double democratic deficit'. That is, it examines challenges to parliamentary accountability of the use of force under the auspices of international institutions.

The Use of Force Under the Aegis of International Institutions

The use of force under international auspices refers, in its narrow definition, to the deployment and use of armed forces from more than one country in a third country under the authority of one or more international institutions. As mentioned above, the number of instances in which the national military forces have been used under international auspices has grown dramatically over the past decade and a half, but so has the number of international institutions which have authorised the deployment of military forces. Beyond the UN, regional organisations such as NATO, the EU, the Organisation for Security and Cooperation in Europe (OSCE), the Organisation of American States (OAS), the Organisation of African Unity (OAU), now re-named the 'African Union', and the Economic Community of West African States (ECOWAS) have provided authorisation for the collective use of force. This book concentrates on the use of military forces under the auspices of the UN, NATO and the EU. The focus on the former is obvious given the universality of its membership, the uniqueness of its legitimacy under international law, and the number of instances in which military forces were used under its authority (see Chapters Three, Four and Five). NATO embodies a traditional (collective) defence alliance which, since the end of the Cold War, has metamorphosed into a more activist security organisation capable of, and willing to deploy and use military forces 'out of area' (see Chapter Seven). The EU constitutes a regional organisation of a hybrid supranational-intergovernmental nature which, towards the end of the 1990s, has accelerated the development of its own security and defence policy including the creation of a Rapid Reaction Force to be deployed in external engagements (see Chapter Ten). All three institutions, the UN, NATO and the EU, pose challenges for democratic and in particular parliamentary accountability when it comes to using force under their authority. This applies even to NATO and the EU which, in contrast to the UN, are composed exclusively of democratic states.

The way these institutions utilize force may be of central importance from the perspective of democratic accountability. Some countries have constitutional or legal prohibitions or follow traditional norms of behaviour such as neutrality, precluding participation in certain forms of military operations under the auspices of international institutions. These prohibitions most commonly reflect two

---

16 See Born, 2003a; Trapans and Fluri, 2003; Born, Caparini and Fluri, 2002; Cottey, Edmunds and Forster, 2002; Van Eekelen, 2002; Desch, 2001.

distinguishing features, firstly, the way in which the use of force under international auspices is legitimised and, secondly, the type of force used in international military operations (see Table 1.1). As to the former, the use of force can be categorised according to the source of authorisation (Damrosch, 2003, pp. 40-41). If the UN Security Council is the authorising body, international military operations would be viewed as legitimate by virtually all countries, thus paving the way for national authorisation as well (see Chapters Three, Four, Five, and Six). The same would apply to situations in which a regional organisation has been mandated by the UN to use force on its behalf. This differs considerably from situations in which a military alliance such as NATO is the source of authorisation. Even for member states, it matters greatly whether the contemplated use of force would qualify as collective self-defence in support of an alliance partner who has been attacked or as an enforcement action 'out of area', and whether such action has been authorized by the UN Security Council or not (Chapters Seven, Eight, and Nine). The use of force under the auspices of a regional organisation such as the EU – which does not qualify as a military alliance but is capable of collective military action beyond its borders – poses new challenges in terms of legitimisation, which merits further exploration (Chapters Ten and Eleven).

Table 1.1   Use of military force under international auspices

International Institution	Authorisation for use of force	Type of use of force (as discussed in this volume)
UN: *Collective Security* (Universal organisation with a broad collective security mandate). *See Chapters 3, 4, 5 and 6*	Authorisation by the Security Council composed of 15 member states, including five permanent members with veto powers.	• Monitoring and observation. • Traditional peacekeeping. • Peacekeeping plus state-building. • Force to ensure compliance with international mandates. • Enforcement.
NATO: *Collective Defence* (Military alliance with integrated military command structure). *See Chapters 3, 7, 8 and 9*	Authorisation by the North Atlantic Council composed of all member states with veto powers.	• Projection of use of force e.g. through expansion of membership. • Stationing of foreign troops and armaments. • Creation of bi/multinational integrated military forces. • Deployment of troops 'out of area'. • Enforcement.
EU: *Security Integration* (Regional organisation developing a common security and defence policy including a rapid reaction force). *See Chapters 10 and 11*	Authorisation by the Council of the European Union composed of all member states with veto powers (in most cases).	• Humanitarian and rescue tasks. • Peacekeeping tasks. • Tasks of combat forces in crisis management, including peacemaking.

As far as the type of force used is concerned, the categorisation largely depends on the international institution which authorised the collective use of force. In the context of the UN, it runs the whole gamut, from monitoring by military observers, to full-scale war such as in the case of Korea (1950-53) and Kuwait (1990-91). Following Ku and Jacobson (2003b), the use of military force under international, and mostly UN auspices can be placed in five broad categories:

- Monitoring and observation;
- Traditional peacekeeping;
- Peacekeeping plus state-building;
- Force to ensure compliance with international mandates; and,
- Enforcement.

This categorisation is reflected in Chapters Three, Four, Five and Six, which all examine the use of military forces under the auspices of the UN and, though only marginally, also NATO from different perspectives. Chapters Three and Four discuss all five categories of using force from a comparative perspective, whereas Chapters Five and Six stay within the confines of peacekeeping.

In the context of NATO, the deployment of troops 'out of area' and their use for enforcement purposes appears to be the most challenging one from the perspective of parliamentary oversight, as illustrated by the case of NATO's Kosovo intervention (1999), which is used in Chapter Eight as a comparative case study on the US Congress and the German *Bundestag*. Applying a much broader conception of use of force would include activities ranging from the stationing of foreign troops and armaments (including nuclear weapons) to the projection of force through enlargement in membership and expansion in strategic reach. Such a perspective, as applied in Chapters Seven and Nine, enables a number of fundamental challenges which military alliances may pose to parliamentary accountability, to be discussed.

Finally, in the context of the EU, a broader perspective on the definition of the use of force is crucial in order to capture all the facets of an evolving ESDP (Chapters Ten and Eleven). In a narrower sense, however, the so-called 'Petersberg Tasks', which are being undertaken, among others, by the EU's Rapid Reaction Force, define the Union's room for manoeuvre when it comes to the use of force. These include:

- Humanitarian and rescue tasks;
- Peacekeeping tasks; and,
- Tasks of combat forces in crisis management, including peacemaking.[17]

---

17 The 'Petersberg Tasks' were originally set out by the Western European Union (WEU) in June 1992. The tasks have been introduced into the Treaty of the European Union under the Amsterdam Treaty of 1997 as a new EU competence. These tasks do not require an explicit UN mandate.

Though the terms 'crisis-management' and 'peacemaking' are not defined precisely in the context of the 'Petersberg Tasks', they may involve military operations, which ultimately fall into the category of enforcement.

In sum, from the perspective of democratic accountability, the use of force under the auspices of international institutions very much depends on the nature of authorisation and the type of force used. The UN, through its Security Council, is still the principal provider of legitimacy to the use of force under international auspices even for regional organisations such as NATO and the EU. As regards the type of force used under international auspices, there is a broad spectrum ranging from military monitoring and observation missions to war-like enforcement operations. Generally speaking, parliamentary accountability of such international military endeavours is more an issue of concern the weaker the international authorisation and the greater the degree of force used (see Chapter Three).

Providing Democratic Accountability through Parliaments

In a democratic polity, parliaments are the central locus of accountability for any governmental decision-making concerning the use of force, whether under purely national or international auspices. As democratic polities properly speaking have not (yet) evolved on the supranational level, the point of departure for the study of parliamentary accountability for the use of force under the auspices of international institutions has to be located in national political systems. These differ strikingly, particularly in terms of the relationship between parliament and government.[18] Consequently, the roles of parliaments are quite different in presidential, parliamentary or mixed systems of government. Beyond these constitutional differences, the role played by a parliament is contingent upon its powers, capacity, and willingness to hold the government to account for its actions.[19] Bruce George, member of the British House of Commons and President of the Parliamentary Assembly of the OSCE, referred in this context to a triad of 'authority', 'ability' and 'attitude' (George and Morgan, 1999). Thus one may speak of a triple-A criteria for parliamentary accountability.

---

18 In this Chapter, the term parliament is preferred to legislature, and government to (political) executive because the traditional division of 'government' into legislative, executive and judicial institutions, sustained by the doctrine of separation of powers, is misleading. In most modern democracies, the parliament is not the only legislative power nor is it a legislative power only: governments possess some ability to make law through devices such as decrees and orders, and – as spelled out in this section – the enactment of law is only one of the functions of parliaments, and not necessarily their most important one. See Heywood, 1997, pp. 294, 297-298.

19 See Born, 2003a; George ad Morgan, 1999; *A Concept Paper on Legislatures and Good Governance* (Based on a Paper prepared by John K. Johnson and Robert T. Nakamura for UNDP), July 1999, see: http://magnet.undp.org/Docs/parliaments/Concept%20 Paper%20 Revised%20MAGNET.htm [accessed 15 July 2003].

Authority Parliaments derive their powers from their constitutional and legal framework as well as from customary practices. The powers of parliaments can be categorized according to their standard functions. Although the role of parliaments varies from state to state and from system to system, in every case it fulfils a complex of functions which include:

- Legislative function;
- Budgetary function;
- Elective function;
- Representative function; and,
- Scrutiny and oversight function.[20]

These functions also apply, to a greater or lesser extent, to the decision-making on and the execution of the use of force under the auspices of international institutions (see Table 1.2).

Table 1.2   The powers of parliaments in overseeing international use of force

Function	Instruments
Legislative function.	• Codification of new legal powers, e.g. authorisation of the use of force under international auspices.
Budgetary function.	• Approval of budgets of military missions under international auspices ('power of the purse').
Elective function.	• No-confidence vote in case of disagreement with government's decision to deploy forces under international auspices.
Representative function.	• Facilitation of political consensus on or voicing popular disagreement with the government's decision to deploy forces under international auspices.
Scrutiny and oversight function.	• Information on the use of force under international auspices (e.g. through the main techniques of oversight such as questioning, interpellation, emergency debates, hearings, inquiry, and visits of troops abroad). • Consultation by the government on the use of force under international auspices (but no binding vote). • Co-decision on, i.e. authorization of the use of force under international auspices (legally required or politically required; decision to be taken *a priori* or *a posteriori*).

---

20 This categorisation as well as the description of the respective functions draw on Hague, Harrop and Breslin, 1998, pp. 190-196; Heywood, 1997, pp. 297-300; Brunner 1979, pp. 236-258.

Legislation has traditionally been viewed as the key function, but parliaments rarely monopolise legislative authority. Furthermore, most governance activities do not involve law-making, but rather traditional governmental functions such as making regulations, drawing up policies, and allocating money. In some countries, parliament and government may work closely together on the initiation and passage of legislation, but in others the legislative function of parliament may be limited to the 'rubber stamp' type of endorsement. In the context of the use of force under international auspices, there are instances where the parliament is asked to enact a law on multinational peace support operations (PSOs) or, as in the case of the Netherlands, succeeds in obtaining the right to authorise such operations as they are recognised as a new legal power (see Chapter Five). In other instances, such as in the case of Germany, it may be the judiciary which confers the same powers on parliament rather than the parliament itself (see Chapters Eight and Nine). But, by and large, the legislative function is marginal in this area.

Authorising expenditure is one of the oldest functions of parliament, but in many democracies the 'power of the purse' has become purely nominal. More often than not, parliament can only approve or reject spending proposed by the government, but cannot modify it, nor initiate its own expenditure proposal. In the context of the use of force under international auspices, one of the strongest tools of parliament is the power to approve or reject the budgets of PSOs. If this power does not exist, parliament could still have an indirect say by way of approbation or rejection of supplementary defence budget requests which are often triggered by unexpected PSOs (see Chapters Four, Eight and Eleven).

The elective function refers to the fact that, in parliamentary systems at least, parliament makes, and sometimes breaks, governments. This applies to those systems in which elections are held under proportional representation, mostly resulting in coalition governments, rather than those using plurality electoral systems, which tend to produce a one party majority. In the context of the use of force under international auspices, this function is marginal indeed. The elective function may work in a rather negative manner, i.e. through a no-confidence vote in the case of disagreement with the government's decision to deploy forces under international auspices or by the government's handling of the deployment. No such instance is discussed in this book, though the study on the fall of the Dutch Government as a consequence of the report on the Srebrenica affair presents a comparable situation (see Chapter Five).

The representative function of parliament refers to the ideal of providing a link between government and the people. The parliament has traditionally been conceived as the political body which stands for the people and represents the latter's interests vis-à-vis the government. One way or another, this may be true for powerful assemblies in weak party systems, but in most cases the ideal of representation is hampered by party discipline. The representative function is quite often reduced to the deliberation of national issues in plenary debates which, in the Westminster type of political systems, has become one of, if not the most important functions of parliament. Questions of war and peace in particular lend themselves to emotional public debates. In the context of the use of force under international auspices, the representative function is an important one.

Deliberations in parliament may voice popular concerns on, or disagreement with, the government's decision to deploy PSOs (see Chapters Five and Six); they may also provide a potential for consensus-building, particularly in instances where the level of force used is high and international authorisation is lacking (see Chapters Three and Eight); finally, they may or may not provide a means of coming to terms with a national crisis related to the use of force under international auspices (see Chapters Five and Six).

Scrutiny or oversight of the government is one of the most meaningful functions of parliament in modern democracies. It enables parliament to hold the government accountable for its activities, thereby helping to improve the quality of governance. Effective scrutiny is often viewed as a means to compensate for the relegation of parliament's traditional legislative and budgetary functions. Parliamentary oversight remains a contested function which most parliaments are still struggling to develop. This holds particularly true for issues that have traditionally been, or in many countries still are, the prerogative of the government such as foreign and security policy. In the context of the use of force under international auspices, the oversight function provides for the broadest range of instruments for ensuring parliament's ability to hold the government accountable for its activities. This includes the main techniques of parliamentary oversight such as questioning, interpellation, emergency debates, hearings and inquiries which are all designed to extract information from the government. These techniques reflect the fact that, without full and accurate information, meaningful oversight is impossible. Although applied *post hoc*, parliamentary inquiries constitute a major device to hold governments accountable for the use of force under international auspices (see Chapters Three, Five and Six). Beyond these legal means or customary practices to extract information from the government, parliaments may also have the right to be consulted by the government on its decisions regarding the use of force under international auspices. The strongest means of parliamentary oversight by far is, however, the constitutional or legal right to approve or reject such use of force (see Chapters Three, Four, Five, Eight and Nine).

Ability In addition to formal authority, parliaments must have the capacity of holding the government accountable for the use of force under international auspices. For this to happen, parliamentary representatives have to possess sufficient resources (and given sufficient opportunity) in order to develop their own expertise. In order to be able to pass legislation, to scrutinize the budget, to engage in informed debates and to oversee governmental activities, parliaments need to work through specialised committees which have their own budget as well as expert and support staff and have access to internal research and documentation services as well as external expertise provided by organisations independent from bureaucratic influence such as research institutions and non-governmental organisations. Although this applies to all sectors of government, it is particularly relevant as regards the security sector because of the latter's closed nature. This tends to further aggravate the asymmetrically dependent relations between the parliament which, in most cases, only has a very small support staff and infrastructure, and the government, which can rely on the ministerial bureaucracies. In the context of the use of force under international auspices, lack of resources may prevent parliaments from collecting first-hand information on their own by way of holding hearings and inquiries, requesting expertise from international experts, visiting troops abroad – rendering their efforts to develop the sufficient personal expertise and administrative capacity needed to judge the relevant governmental decisions more difficult (see Chapters Four and Six, Ten and Eleven).

Attitude Unless the members of parliament have the political will to hold the government accountable for its decisions, no amount of authority or resources will do the job for them. The political will to use the constitutional and legal powers vested in the parliament and the human and financial resources at its disposal is the *sine qua non* of effective parliamentary accountability. This also applies to parliamentary accountability for the use of force under international auspices. More often than not, parliamentarians belonging to political parties which are represented within government, are not eager to oversee their governmental counterparts in a critical manner. As a result, instruments of parliamentary oversight are often not applied, or left to the discretion of the opposition parties to scrutinize the government, except when scandals or emergencies occur (see Chapters Five and Six). Another limiting factor may be the fact that only a few members of parliament are willing to pay much attention to the security sector. The security sector does not often figure high on the public agenda and is therefore viewed as not being of great importance from an electoral point of view (see Chapter Six). On the other hand, the political willingness of parliamentarians to hold the government accountable for its decisions on the use of force under international auspices may be strengthened under heavy pressure from public opinion voiced though the media (see Chapter Five).

In sum, parliamentary accountability of the use of force under international auspices depends to a great extent on the formal and informal oversight powers vested in the parliament. To get timely and accurate information on the international deployment of military forces and to debate, authorise, and review such missions appear to be the most powerful instruments to ensure parliamentary accountability in this area. The relevance of these powers, just like all powers of parliaments, is contingent on the resources and expertise at the disposal of parliaments and, last but not least, on the political will of the parliamentarians to hold government accountable for the use of force under international auspices.

Parliamentary Accountability – Inside Out

Parliamentary accountability of foreign and security affairs tends to be weak in most political systems. This fact coupled with uneven national systems and practices, renders the analysis of parliamentary accountability of the use of force under international auspices particularly problematic from a comparative perspective. Given the wide variety of political systems even among established democracies, providing for strong and weak parliaments alike, the lowest common denominator tends to be at a point short of any parliamentary accountability at all. Even within the European Union there is no 'minimum standard' of parliamentary accountability (see Chapter Eleven). This leads to the existence of 'democratic deficits' on the national level, which does not preclude the existence and indeed an increase of instances in which parliaments effectively hold governments accountable for the deployment and management of national armed forces abroad.

As for the 'democratic deficits' on the international level, parliamentary accountability is largely absent when it comes to the use of force under the aegis of international institutions. This should not come as a surprise given the fact that, except for the EU, all relevant international institutions are of a purely intergovernmental character. The UN lacks a parliamentary or even an interparliamentary dimension at all. Interparliamentary assemblies such as the NATO Parliamentary Assembly (NATO PA) and the interim European Security and Defence Assembly, the former Western European Union (WEU) Assembly which now figures under the auspices of the EU, lack any of the functions that are characteristic of national parliaments (see Chapters Seven and Eleven). Even the role of the European Parliament, which has few powers, but considerable resources and a strong political will to exercise parliamentary accountability, is at best marginal when it comes to foreign and security affairs (see Chapters Ten and Eleven). We are reminded of Dahl's harsh statement that the prospects for democratising other international organisations are fairly remote if democratic institutions are largely ineffective in governing the European Union. This seems to suggest that the 'democratic deficits' which exist to a greater or lesser extent on the national level and the prevalence of 'democratic deficits' on the international level, appear to reinforce each other in worsening parliamentary accountability of the use of force under international auspices.

This book looks at this specific 'double democratic deficit'. The first part sets out the conceptual and empirical framework for the analysis of the subject matter. The three parts that follow discuss general and specific aspects of parliamentary accountability of the use of force under the authority of the UN, NATO and the EU. The book concludes with a review of concrete ideas and proposals intended to contribute to the reduction of what is viewed as the 'double democratic deficit' regarding the parliamentary accountability of the deployment and management of national armed forces under the auspices of international institutions. It shows that there are opportunities for improving the situation, but for this to happen depends on progress being made in all aspects of effective parliamentary accountability – authority, ability and attitude – and on both levels, national and international.

PART II

THE GENERAL CONTEXT

Chapter 2

Democratic Governance and the Internationalisation of Security Policy: The Relevance of Parliaments

Owen Greene

Introduction

Notions of 'democracy and 'democratic accountability' are complex and contested. However, there is no doubt that the development and effective operation of parliamentary institutions are critical issues for democratic societies. This is true for security issues and the 'security sector',[1] as it is for all other sectors such as education, health, trade and the environment. In many democratic countries, national parliaments have had relatively weak oversight or control over military and other security policies and programmes. In recent years, there have been determined and moderately successful efforts to strengthen the role of parliaments in these issue areas, both in established democratic countries and in transition countries, such as in Latin America, Eastern Europe and the area of the former Soviet Union.[2] Over the same period, multilateral coalitions and institutions have become increasingly central for security policies and operations. Since the end of the Cold War the United Nations (UN), North Atlantic Treaty Organisation (NATO), European Union (EU), Organisation for Security and Cooperation in Europe (OSCE) and several other regional organisations have become actively engaged in a range of military and police operations and interventions.[3]

---

1 The definition of the 'security sector' continues to be debated. In this chapter it refers to those institutions and organisations to which the state has allocated a legitimate role in the use, or threat of use, of exercise of coercive force in society to tackle external or internal threats to the security of the state and its citizens. It thus encompasses: military and para-military forces, intelligence services, national and local police services, border guards and customs services. The security sector is also often considered to encompass the judiciary and penal systems, and those civil structures mandated to control and oversee these agencies (e.g. see Born, 2003a; Caparini, 2003).

2 See, for example, Olson and Norton, 1996 and Norton, 1998.

3 Because of the book's focus, this chapter deals predominantly with the Euro-Atlantic area. Therefore, however important, the functioning of parliaments in other parts of the world, e.g. developing countries, will not be discussed.

This internationalisation of military and security policies is not simply a transitional phase. Some of the multilateral security institutions noted above are developing new capabilities, doctrines and roles. NATO and the EU member states are continuing to embed and shape their national military policies and programmes within the framework of multilateral security institutions – long after the supposed 'glue' of the Soviet threat has gone. Moreover, most newly independent 'transition' countries in Eastern Europe are determined to join NATO and the EU, and to integrate their own security policies and plans within their structures. Particularly in the Euro-Atlantic area, a well-developed complex of international and regional security regimes (such as the Non-Proliferation Treaty (NPT), Chemical Weapons Convention (CWC), Conventional Armed Forces in Europe Treaty (CFE), Vienna Document on Confidence and Security Building Measures (CSBMs), and the Wassenaar Arrangement shape and constrain most aspects of national security activity.

If they are to remain meaningful, processes of democratic oversight and control must therefore effectively engage with international security institutions and with the development and implementation of multilateral security policies. This is much easier said than done. In addition to all of the 'normal' obstacles to democratic oversight of the security sector with which we are familiar in a national context, the internationalisation of democratic processes poses new (some would say fundamental) challenges. The scope for oversight by parliamentary institutions must be considered within this broader framework.

This chapter identifies and discusses some key frameworks, issues and priorities for enhancing democratic oversight over internationalised security policies, to clarify the actual and potential role of parliaments in this context.

The Internationalisation of Security Policy

Military alliances have a long history. However, the key international security institutions in the early 21st century are not the traditional ad-hoc coalitions of states formed in response to a specific threat. This is particularly true in the Euro-Atlantic area, which is therefore the main focus for this chapter. NATO and the EU, for example, are highly institutionalised, and are associated with well-developed transnational networks of officials, decision-makers, politicians, opinion-formers and experts. These institutions have their own elaborated norms, principles, decision-making procedures, programmes and so on. They are embedded in a set of relatively well-developed clusters of security regimes. The same comments apply to other institutions including the OSCE and the UN.

This trend of internationalisation of security policy has developed strongly within the Euro-Atlantic area since the Second World War with the UN in 1945, NATO in 1949, since the 1970s the CSCE and later on the OSCE. Bi-polar confrontation stimulated the development of Euro-Atlantic institutions and transnational networks informed by shared liberal democratic values, on which NATO has continued to draw and build since the end of the Cold War. Important security regimes were developed as part of Detente processes, leaving a post-Cold

War legacy in the form of the OSCE and particular regimes such as the Confidence and Security Building Measures (CSBMs) agreements and the Conventional Armed Forces in Europe Treaty (CFE Treaty). Global security regimes were developed, particularly those dealing with control and non-proliferation of weapons of mass destruction, in response to the immense risks posed by these technologies.

Since the end of the Cold War, the process of internationalisation of security policies and institutions has intensified in the Euro-Atlantic area – not declined as many 'realists' predicted.[4] OSCE and NATO have, for example, been institutionally strengthened as well as re-oriented towards new security challenges (see Chapter Seven), and the EU has substantially developed its defence and security dimension (see Chapters Ten and Eleven). There are continuing tensions, for example, about possible competition between OSCE, the EU and NATO. These tensions have been highlighted by divisions over difficult decisions, such as were exposed around the US-led coalition's intervention in Iraq in spring 2003. However, even with the Bush Administration in power in the US, which has given relatively low priority to developing multilateral institutions, the wider process of internationalising security policies and practices has continued, particularly for all other Euro-Atlantic countries.[5]

In part, the maintenance and further development of multilateral security institutions after the Cold War can be explained by the determination of some powerful political leaders to avoid a 're-nationalisation' of security policies in Europe, to reduce the risks of a resurgence of security dilemmas and arms racing posed by an 'anarchic' structure of sovereign states independently trying to maintain national security. Such concerns played a powerful role, for example, in decisions to maintain and strengthen the EU, NATO and other multilateral institutions alongside the process of German unification. However, it is now widely recognised that the internationalisation process is part of more fundamental societal transformations associated with 'globalisation'.

Globalisation broadly refers to powerful trends including: the increasing transnational integration of economies, particularly production and financial processes; the development of technologies that dramatically widen global access to information and communications; and the increasing importance of transnational

---

4   The 'realists' referred to here are the adherents to the so-called 'realist' schools in the literature of international relations. These emphasise the centrality in international affairs of power-seeking sovereign states, which are reliant solely upon themselves for survival in an insecure, structurally anarchic, world. 'Realists' tend to regard international institutions and alliances as secondary reflections of coincidences of state interests, lacking influence in their own right and highly vulnerable to shifts in constellations of power and interest (see for example Dunne and Schmidt, 2001, and references therein). Several 'realist' authors predicted that regional security institutions relating to the Euro-Atlantic area would fade as interests shifted after the end of the Cold War (for example Mearsheimer, 1990 and Walt, 1998).

5   For example, the EU multinational peace support operation in Democratic Republic of the Congo, mandated by the UN and under French command, is a case in point (see *Guardian*, 13 June 2003).

or global policy issues, such as the environment, migration, security threats (Scholte, 2000). Associated with these trends are processes such as the rapid growth of transnational social, cultural and economic networks and organisations, and the declining significance of national borders.

In this context, the ability of political institutions at the level of individual states to effectively address key policy issues has been increasingly questioned, (Scholte, 2000) and international and local levels of governance have become more prominent. The dispersion of authoritative decision-making across multiple territorial levels – or 'multilevel governance' (Scharpf, 1994; 1999) – is increasingly the norm, if not globally at least in the Euro-Atlantic area and amongst Organisation for Economic Cooperation and Development (OECD) states.

Security, nevertheless, is increasingly recognised, particularly in the Euro-Atlantic area, as a paradigmatic issue area where sustained international cooperation is required. Indeed this principle is central to the norms of the OSCE, with its principles of 'cooperative security', 'indivisibility of security', and recognition that each OSCE state has a legitimate security interest in the internal affairs of other OSCE countries (in issues such as human rights, the rule of law, treatment of minorities, openness, democracy, etc), not least in the interests of conflict prevention (see Ghébali, 2003).

Countries in the NATO/EU security community, for example, recognise that their military operations outside their area must as far as possible take place within a multilateral framework. This partly reflects concerns with the legitimacy of the operation and appropriate burden-sharing with others in the international community. But it also reflects a lack of capacity of almost any countries to achieve their objectives alone: few countries have the capacity to conduct effective military operations independently far from their borders.

Only the United States (US) can realistically pursue substantial military operations independently across the world, and only in the US is there any substantial dispute amongst policy elites about the extent to which it should or needs to maintain and develop international security institutions. Even in this case, US Administrations have consistently sought to work within multilateral frameworks where they can. In practice, if they are to function effectively, even the US-led ad-hoc coalitions of the willing that are presently favoured by some US 'neo-conservatives' need to be able to draw extensively upon the consultation processes and standardised operating procedures of NATO.

In the Euro-Atlantic area, in particular, a complex of overlapping security institutions and regimes has developed in recent years. This means that their overall impact on processes of policy-making and implementation is much more than the sum of their individual impacts. For example, each NATO or EU member state has a choice of institutions through which to pursue issues of concern, and has to take into account the agendas and constraints of several institutions in formulating its national policies and programmes. In the Western Balkans, NATO, EU, OSCE and UN agencies, operations, programmes and mandates are deeply intertwined, working within frameworks of security regimes (such as CFE, CSBM, Convention against Transnational Organised Crime) and alongside other inter-national institutions (such as the World Bank, European Bank for Reconstruction and Development [EBRD], Council of Europe, Stability Pact, and Interpol) and transnational civil society groups (non-governmental organisations, church organisations, ethnic groups, etc).

Although there is some division of labour between security institutions and regimes, in practice this is often more at the micro-level than at the macro-level in areas of operation such as the Balkans. Thus, several institutions and organisations are involved in the most important elements of policy and operations, such as combating arms trafficking, dealing with displaced peoples, or police reform. Decision-making processes are thus often diffuse, with complex lines of accountability.

Democratic Governance and the Internationalisation of Security Policy

Many commentators have regarded the increasing internationalisation of policy making and implementation as a device which political leaders use to avoid appropriate democratic oversight and accountability to national parliaments, or at least as a process that is inexorably undermining democratic accountability (see for example Walker, 1988). It is not hard to find evidence to support such suspicions.

Decisions made through international institutions or in international negotiations are often made in private. Parliamentarians and ordinary citizens often do not have sufficient access or information to enable them to effectively either influence the decision or assess the outcome. With some justification, governments argue that national parliaments must allow them flexibility while engaging in international negotiations. After decisions are made within an international institution, national parliamentsare generally faced with a 'take it or leave it' option, and have little scope for insisting on adjustments. Moreover, virtually no international institution includes elected representative assemblies with powers of oversight or control. Similar comments apply to the EU in its present form: the European Commission is generally opaque in its work; the European Parliament has weak powers and low legitimacy; and most (until recently, all) meetings of the EU Council are closed.[6]

However, it is argued in this chapter that it is wrong to approach the trend towards internationalisation of policy-making, in security or any other sphere, as if it were an unwelcome and intrinsically anti-democratic development. It is in fact an essential development, if systems and institutions are to develop in a way that enables effective governance in a world of powerful transnational and global processes. Legitimacy depends on effectiveness ('output legitimacy') as well as on democratic process ('process legitimacy').[7] There is no real prospect of maintaining wide popular respect and legitimacy for democratic governments if they are seen as being profoundly ineffective in addressing the key problems because they are restricted to policy-making at the purely national level.

---

6   At the EU Council Summit in June 2002, in Seville, the Council decided to make some
     of its deliberations public.
7   See, for example, Elster, 1998.

It is often argued that politics in an era of globalisation faces a fundamental dilemma; between effectiveness of international governance on the one hand, and citizen participation and democratic control on the other (Dahl, 1994). Decision-making systems that involve wide participation of all citizens and stakeholders in complex policy decisions, and also involve procedures requiring specific parliamentary mandates or popular referenda, can be extremely cumbersome and vulnerable to blocking or populist campaigns. The decisions that emerge (if they do) may be legitimate from the point of view of democratic process, but poorly designed for actually tackling the problems they aim to address.

The tension between effectiveness and 'deep' democratic process in policy-making certainly exists. This is true in all spheres, but particularly in the security area with the special issues of secrecy, timeliness and the need effectively to manage risks to deployed forces in combat situations. But this tension is not strictly associated with globalisation or internationalisation of policy-making. It would exist in any case in developed industrial societies engaging in challenging security environments. Moreover, well-designed democratic processes can improve the effectiveness of decision-making.

The challenge is to design democratic systems so that involvement of parliaments, stakeholders and citizens is achieved in a way that will generally enhance policy outputs and respects the requirement for the executive and for professional armed forces to have appropriate scope for autonomous decision-making. This requires sophisticated rules and institutions (formal and informal) of information-sharing, access, consultation, decision-making, and accountability for the various branches of government, parliament, civil society and citizens.

These systems will inevitably have distinctive characteristics in each democratic society, due to the implications of differing constitutional arrangements, laws and traditions, and because each 'demos' has peculiar expectations and requirements for democratic legitimacy. Most democracies still have serious work to do to develop such systems for democratic oversight, control and accountability for security sector policy-making and implementation, even without internationalisation or 'denationalisation' of policy-making processes.

There will always be debates about whether a process is adequately democratic, not least because definitions of 'democracy' remain highly contested. It certainly involves systems enabling participation of stakeholders and citizens in the process of decision-making, so that those involved or affected can 'have their say' and so that a relatively open process of bargaining and argumentation takes place throughout the policy development and implementation process. It involves systems for majority decision-making within a political community whose members recognise some mutual relations of trust and solidarity.

For many years, the dominant approach to understanding the conditions for democracy has insisted on the need for a 'demos' – a political community with the potential for democracy – that is closely linked to the nation state. According to this approach, the internationalisation of policy-making poses fundamental challenges to democracy. The argument is that a 'demos' cannot exist at the international level, because the degree of trust and solidarity required for a 'demos' is only possible in the context of a commonly inhabited territory and a shared history that is characteristic of a 'nation' (Miller, 1995; Streek, 1998). If this assertion is true, all is not lost for democracy in a world of globalisation and transnational process. In practice, national-level parliaments and democratic institutions can at least still play a powerful role in ensuring significant accountability of national representatives in the framework of international regimes and institutions. But this understanding of the conditions for democracy would definitely imply important limits on democracy in internationalised policy processes.

However, those who challenge such traditional understandings of the limits of democratic process (Held, 1995; Linklater, 1998; Walker, 1988) have a strong case. Experiences with democratisation processes indicate that it is wrong to regard the existence of a well-developed 'demos' (of the type conceived by 'traditionalists') as a social *pre-requisite* for democratisation. If it were, progress towards democracy across much of the world in recent decades would be inexplicable. Rather, the development of political community, including trust and collective argument and solidarity, can go hand-in-hand with the development of democratic processes and institutions, so that they are mutually re-enforcing.

Rather than discount the potential of transnational democratic politics from the outset, it is more important to review the basic elements of what we mean by and want from democracy, and to explore ways of achieving these in the contemporary, 'globalising' world. Two fundamental elements of democracy are the principles that people affected by policies and decisions should be enabled at least indirectly to participate or exert influence over them, and that there should be an open process of public deliberation and argument based on rationality and public good.

To what extent do the political and social conditions exist to strengthen democratisation along these lines in internationalised policy and decision-making processes? To facilitate examination of this question, Zürn (2000) and others have aimed to unpack the notion of a 'demos', which is actually quite broad and ambiguous. In brief, this indicates that members of a polity capable of democracy should:

- Acknowledge rights of other members, including rights of liberty, respect, self-fulfilment, participation;
- Comply with legitimate obligations and decisions, and trust that others in the community will do so too;
- Have a sense of collective spirit and concern for the well-being of the collective as well as for themselves;
- Engage in public discourse, involving deliberation and argumentation as well as bargaining;
- Have significant solidarity, providing a basis for assistance and re-distribution processes.

It is easy to recognise weaknesses in each of these areas in the cosmopolitan international and transnational communities. Sceptics about the scope for a democratic polity within the EU can demonstrate real limits in each of the above dimensions amongst the nations and peoples living within the area of the European Union or North America. Such limits are even greater across the whole Euro-Atlantic area.

But it is important to recognise that most countries experience similar limitations. Modern Britain, Germany, France, Russia and the US, for example, are all struggling with the challenges of maintaining and strengthening the quality of respect for rights, trust, collective spirit, public discourse, and social solidarity in their complex, multicultural societies. There are real problems, and the conditions for good democratic process need to be continually produced and reproduced through communication, interaction, and institution-building. Although, almost by definition, these processes are stronger at the level of local communities and the 'nation-state', it is implausible to insist on a radical distinction between the level of state, region (EU, North America, and Euro-Atlantic area) and transnational developed society (e.g. OECD member states).

Across the Euro-Atlantic area and the developed industrialised countries at least, it is possible to identify shared values and understandings of rights, habits of compliance with legitimate decisions; transnational public discourses; and complex feelings of transnational public-spiritedness and solidarity. This is indeed part of the process of transnationalism and globalisation that also drives the inter-nationalisation of policy-making processes. Moreover, it is an essential context to the security policy challenges faced by countries within the Euro-Atlantic area-polities of Western Europe, North America and elsewhere do feel a sense of engagement and solidarity with people in the Balkans, Caucasus, Africa and so on that are suffering insecurity and violence, and insist that 'something must be done', including multilateral military engagements.

Thus, in principle, at least some of the key elements may exist internationally for a political community to develop democratic practices relating to peace and security issues: acknowledgement of rights, some confidence that commitments will be implemented, public spiritedness, transnational deliberation and debate, and sufficient solidarity to motivate assistance. These are more consistently present in some regions than others. Amongst NATO or OECD countries, and in certain sub-regions (such as Western Europe, the Caribbean or Southern Africa) they are probably relatively strong, and at a global (UN) level they remain fragmentary and weak. One of the advantages of unpacking what is required from a political community to engage in democratic processes is that it helps to highlight which elements are more or less present. In general, the elements that are probably weakest in internationalised security policy-making are transnational public discourses involving deliberation and real debate, and consistent feelings of solidarity. For example, transatlantic deliberations and public debates may, if anything, be becoming more disconnected after a period of relative closeness, and within the EU public debates about difficult peace and security decisions remain nationally centred. The public policy debates in 2002-2003 on whether to intervene militarily in Iraq demonstrated this. Even in this case, however, the debates and public mobilisation had important transnational structure across the NATO area and internationally, as did patterns of solidarity.

The challenges for strengthening democratic accountability and legitimacy in internationalised peace and security policy-making in the context of globalisation are thus to develop institutions for international security governance so that they (i) take advantage of the opportunities and conditions of democratic politics where they already exist, and (ii) help to strengthen wide and effective transnational policy deliberations and discourses and feelings of solidarity.

Various 'models' have been proposed for developing democratic international processes along these lines in a globalising world. McGrew (2002) organises these into three broad categories: liberal-democratic internationalism, radical communitarianism, and cosmopolitan. The liberal-democratic inter-nationalist democratic agenda aims to develop and reform pluralist international institutions in ways consistent with liberal democratic principles and to strengthen patterns of representation within them (Governance Commission, 1995). The radical communitarianist democratic agenda is broadly to build on new social movements to develop systems for self-government amongst transnational communities which are based more on mechanisms for governing according to functional or common problem areas rather than on territory or state (Walker, 1988; Dryzek, 1995). The cosmopolitan democratic agenda is to build eclectically upon the full range of democratic traditions, institutions, and public associations to complement and re-enforce national democratic processes and mechanisms (Held, 1995).

The cosmopolitan democracy approach is attractive since it can encompass practical elements of the other models within a broad agenda, taking whatever opportunities arise to reconstruct or develop governance processes to strengthen the capacity of all parts of the societies involved to have their say within international as well as national deliberative process and to influence decisions.

This is inevitably a 'multilevel' political process, in which national democratic mechanisms remain critical, but regional and international processes must also be increasingly important. For the foreseeable future, processes of information-exchange, public discourse and access and involvement of concerned stake-holders have more scope to develop at the international level than formal democratic institutions. However, there appears to be scope for developing institutions and practices that help to improve the quality of representation and engagement of all stakeholders in the process, and their capacity to ensure adequate accountability. In practice, this process has already started in many existing international security institutions and regimes, including NATO, OSCE, and the UN. But there is a strong need to develop them further to address the weaknesses of democratic accountability in internationalised security policy processes.

The EU provides special opportunities in this respect, because of the highly developed framework of EU-level institutions including the European Parliament, which offers opportunities for strengthening and developing accountability to formal institutions of representative democracy. There are interesting proposals to develop EU bodies and mechanisms that could increase opportunities for national parliamentarians and citizens to contribute and oversee EU policy processes. However, particularly in relation to foreign, defence and security policy issues, such developments are likely to remain modest for the foreseeable future. So long as the EU falls short of being a 'United States of Europe', the main challenges of developing democratic oversight and accountability in its security policy processes remain similar to those of other security institutions and regimes within the Euro-Atlantic area and beyond.

The Relevance of Parliamentary Institutions

The role of parliamentary institutions in enhancing democratic oversight and accountability in internationalised security policy must be examined in the above context. They have a critical role to play, but must be considered within a complex multilevel system of processes of consultation, engagements and open and accountable decision-making which extend beyond concerns about majority decision-making by democratically-elected legislatures. Parliamentary institutions play several distinct roles or functions in enhancing and ensuring democratic and legitimate policy processes. At the national level, these can be described as democratic legal and legislative control; democratic oversight and accountability; and representation.

The legislative function of parliaments and legislatures is clear. It includes maintenance of appropriate constitutional framework; laws and regulations governing security policy and the security sector; approving treaties; declaring war and states of emergency; approving use of armed forces or police abroad; approving government defence and security policy; approving and auditing budgets and public expenditure; regulating or approving procurement, transfers of arms and dual technologies.

In relation to oversight and accountability parliaments function through committees (such as defence, home affairs, police, intelligence services, public accounts). These committees have the power to hold inquiries, take evidence, and consider reports, for example, from the government executive, accounting offices, Ombudsman and special representatives. Committees also have the power, among other things, to receive information and reports from government and public institutions, and to determine public consultation processes.

In their representative function, parliaments represent the will of the people; provide a key representative forum for debate, consultation, argumentation, bargaining, deliberation and the development of consensus. In this context, parliaments provide a key mechanism for the release of government information to the public, and for ensuring access of citizens and stakeholders to decision-making processes, at least so that citizens and stakeholders can have their interests heard and taken into account. This representative function is critical for the democratic legitimacy of complex decision-making, where most people lack interest or expertise to directly contribute but want reassurance that decision-making takes account of people's interests and values.

All of these roles of national parliaments continue to be relevant in internationalised security policy processes. They can exert legal control over the use and engagement of national armed forces and other security sector resources in international operations. They can establish national legal frameworks determining where executive regulation and decision-making requires parliamentary approval. They continue to have legislative power in relation to budgets and public expenditure. Parliamentary Committees can hold inquiries into international security policy and programmes in which their state is involved, and can require their government officials to report, provide evidence, etc, on multilateral policies and programmes. Parliaments can be a focus for national debate about international security policies and operations. National officials, officers and agencies can be held accountable to parliament and national laws for their performance in multilateral operations.

The challenge posed to national parliaments by internationalised decision-making processes is not therefore a categorical one. Rather it consists of a challenge to:

- the quality of democratic oversight, control and accountability;
- the scope for national parliaments to insist on prior authorisation or detailed constraints; and
- the capacity and interest of national parliaments to discuss and coordinate with parliaments in other countries that participate in the internationalised policy-making processes.

Parliamentarians can lack knowledge and expertise in international security policies and programmes. Inter-governmental confidentiality rules mean that parliaments may not have access to information relevant to international operations and programmes to the same extent as they can insist upon for national programmes. International civil servants and officials, playing key roles in the implementation of international programmes, cannot usually be called to account by national parliaments, or even to give evidence. Issues of international coordination in multilateral security operations mean that parliaments are under pressure to avoid insisting on specific constraints on the use and behaviour of national armed forces (such as idiosyncratic national constraints on rules of engagement).

These are real problems. The internationalisation of a process intrinsically provides opportunities for the executive to limit access to information, hide behind international compromises, obscure lines of accountability, and so on. Moreover, it is intrinsic to international security regimes and institutions that successful multilateral coordination imposes constraints on national autonomy, including the scope for national parliaments to make specific demands on multilateral operations of international institutions.

However, it is important to recognise that national parliaments do in fact already often have real capacity to shape and influence internationalised policy processes, in defence and security matters as in other issue areas. In a detailed examination of the roles of legislatures in relation to international commitments, Martin (2000), for example, concluded that the degree of legislative influence on international cooperation exceeds usual estimates, in both presidential and parliamentary systems. The reason why the influence of legislatures is often underestimated is because it is mostly exercised through informal mechanisms such as consultative processes and in indirect ways. Excessive focus on the formal exercise of legislative rights can miss much of importance in democratic societies.

The main agendas for enhancing the role of parliamentary institutions in internationalised security policy processes are quite straightforward in principle. They must be to:

- devote more attention specifically to international policy processes and institutions;
- enhance expertise and resources to engage in these processes at a technical level;
- demand greater openness and access to information and officials, for themselves and for the wider public (at home and abroad);
- improve communication and coordination amongst parliaments of partner countries;
- develop transnational and multilateral parliamentary and representative institutions to strengthening transnational or coordinated policy discourses and standards;
- develop and identify points of leverage to strengthen their capacity to oversee and influence the intergovernmental processes;
- develop institutions and practices to enable the above.

A key problem is that most parliamentarians remain quite parochial and national in their concerns, and there are important political and organisational incentives for this that need to be addressed. Moreover, coordination and communication amongst parliaments of partner countries lags far behind coordination amongst national ministries. However, the more regularised and institutionalised multilateral security cooperation becomes, the more scope there is for parliaments to develop coordinated frameworks for access to information, collective policy discourses, and appropriate accountability. Ad-hoc coalitions amongst governments are in principle much less susceptible to regular parliamentary oversight and control than institutionalised regimes or institutions.

On security issues, as in other issue areas such as the environment or human rights where transnational democratic politics are better developed, non-governmental organisations (NGOs) play a key role in raising and pursuing transnational debates, and in ensuring that a variety of voices and policy concerns are heard throughout the policy-making and implementation processes. NGOs concerned with foreign and security policy issues remain mostly nationally based, but over the last 25 years they have increasingly developed and used transnational networks to pursue their concerns. This is very important in its own right, but also in the context of developing the roles of parliaments. NGOs and other lobby groups are a key source of information to parliamentarians on international conflict and security policy processes, and facilitate links between national deliberations and national parliaments.

A key priority in this context, in addition to encouraging the further development of these NGO roles, is to take steps to improve the representativeness of the non-governmental groups that participate and shape international security policy processes. In all issue areas, there is a problem with ensuring that the range of stakeholders engaged in internationalised policy processes is representative. Special interest NGOs and lobbyists tend to dominate civil society representation at international policy meetings. Creative thinking on ways to institutionalise mechanisms for engaging more representative social groups in internationalised policy processes is sorely needed. Proposals for EU, UN or other international citizens assemblies have been mooted, for example, but these can only be a small part of the solution. Devices to facilitate wider citizen participation in local and national decision-making are increasingly being experimented with at the national level across Europe, the Americas and elsewhere, and these need to be reviewed for potential application in transnational debates.

Overall, the interests of democratic control over multilateral security policy processes imply further institutionalisation of international security cooperation rather than less. Such institutional development needs to consistently facilitate appropriate access and participation of all stakeholders in policy-making processes. Openness and access is quite well developed in many multilateral regimes and institutions in areas such as the environment or human rights. Multilateral security institutions could adopt many of the precedents developed in these other areas.

Conclusions

The increasing internationalisation of military and security policies poses major challenges for democratic institutions and practices, and particularly parliaments, rooted as they are in national structures. International policy-making is often closed, and provides opportunities for national representatives to limit democratic oversight and accountability. There is definitely a 'democratic deficit' at this level of policy-making, in all relevant regional and international security policy processes.

However, this does not imply that such internationalisation processes are undesirable. They are essential for effective policy-making to prevent and tackle war and insecurity across the world, and are inevitable in the context of globalisation processes. The key challenge is to develop and reconstruct networks of institutions and processes that enable all concerned parliamentarians, citizens and public associations of the states concerned to follow and have their say on policy issues, to influence and shape decisions, and hold authorities and public bodies to account.

There are some bodies of opinion that it is completely unrealistic to aim to develop a transnational or international democratic politics on defence and security issues, or indeed on other public policy issues, because a polity ('demos') capable of democracy does not and cannot exist beyond the national level. We have argued in this chapter that this is unduly pessimistic. While many states struggle to develop national polities of mutual trust, solidarity and deliberative debate, there are the beginnings of international or transnational public concerns that provide a basis for strengthening democratic politics at an international level, particularly in the Euro-Atlantic area and amongst OECD countries.

The opportunities for formally establishing 'majority vote' international democratic decision-making processes for international defence and security policy-making are very limited, even in the EU. But there are many opportunities to strengthen and reconstruct institutions and mechanisms at all levels to enhance public access, participation, oversight and influence, to extend the represent-ativeness of such participation, to encourage and support wide transnational deliberative policy debates and feelings of concern and solidarity.

Parliamentary institutions have a key role to play in efforts to promote democratic influence and accountability over internationalised defence and security policy-making. National parliaments have much unexploited scope for strengthening influence, control and accountability over national representatives in international policy processes, though their national legislative, oversight and representative roles. Together with various international parliamentary assemblies and other such bodies, national parliaments can take action to promote inter-action and coordination at a regional or international level, to enable more direct and influential engagement with international policymaking. Informal and indirect mechanisms to promote participation and influence are at least as important as developing additional formal institutions. Further, parliaments can facilitate wider citizen access and participation in transnational policy processes, not insisting on greater openness and public access and information, and by working with transnational networks of NGOs and associations as well as with international and regional organisations.

There is no single formula for addressing the democratic deficit in international military and security policy making. But there are many opportunities for improving international and regional governance in these areas by adopting a 'cosmopolitan' approach to global democracy-building, and taking opportunities wherever they arise.

Chapter 3

Using Military Force under International Auspices: A Mixed System of Accountability

Charlotte Ku

Introduction

Establishing the monopoly of coercion was a crucial feature in the creation of modern states (Damrosch, 2003, pp. 39-60). Ensuring accountability to citizens for the use of military forces was a central component of the struggle to establish democratic forms of government. But since the mid-20th century, decisions about whether to use military forces can be made in international institutions far from the legislatures that democratic governments have relied on to provide such accountability. The relationship with international institutions raises concern that a country's armed forces will be involved in operations in which it has little stake or that a country's security needs will not be adequately recognised to compel an international response.

Unless there is popular support for an operation, democracies are unlikely to provide adequate resources for a sufficient length of time to carry out the decisions made by international institutions. A contemporary example can be seen in the US Congressional debate over whether to authorise the US President to wage war against Iraq (see, for example, Knowlton, 2002, p. 1 and p. 4; Allen and Vanderhei, 2002, p. A1 and p. A18). Citizens must believe that decisions have been taken in ways that accord with democratic accountability. This requires dissemination of clear information about the purposes of a proposed action, ample opportunity for debate, and procedures that make accountable the government officials who participate in decision-making on the use of force and its implementation. In this context, this chapter examines how national governments maintain accountability when their forces participate in peacekeeping and enforcement operations under the auspices of international institutions.

The first part of the chapter deals with how democratic forms of government deal with different types of peace support operations, ranging from monitoring missions to enforcement operations. The second part analyses how accountability is provided through national institutions and practices. The following part focuses on the mixed system of accountability for peace support operations, including procedures and actions on both the national and international levels. The chapter ends with some general assessments and conclusions.[1] The focus is primarily on the use of international force under the aegis of the United Nations (UN), and, to a lesser extent, under the auspices of the North Atlantic Treaty Organisation (NATO).

Democracy and Controlling the Use of Military Force

In all political systems, decisions to deploy and use military forces are among the most important that can be taken. Democratic forms of government have gone to great lengths to provide accountability in such decisions. National constitutions frequently contain special provisions specifying how and by whom these decisions are to be made. In the closing decades of the 20th century, there was a general trend 'toward subordinating war powers to constitutional control,' including 'greater parliamentary control over the decision to introduce troops into situations of actual or potential hostilities.' (Damrosch, 1996, pp. 36-40). But constitutional provisions provide only a framework for establishing democratic accountability, particularly where military forces are involved in internationally mandated operations short of full-scale war.

Each country has a political culture that grows out of its historical experience with respect to the control and use of its military forces. Although this culture may not always be reflected in formal constitutional provisions, it is certainly reflected in practice. Whatever the culture or constitutional structure, democracies share one thing in common – their citizens want to understand and to have an opportunity to approve the purposes for which *their* military forces are being used (Mueller, 1989). And, if a problem arises, they want responsible parties to be held accountable for their conduct and their decisions.[2] Given the complicated command and control structure sometimes used in internationally mandated operations, officials can engage in blame shifting if something goes wrong, making accountability difficult to maintain (see United Nations Security Council, 1999; United Nations, 1999b).

Twentieth century statesmen sought to establish an international institutional framework that would centralise decision-making about the use of force; create a system for the pacific settlement of disputes; and establish a pool of military forces available to thwart actions that violated the agreed-to international status quo. From the Covenant of the League of Nations (1919), through the Kellogg-Briand Pact (1928), and the United Nations Charter (1945), states worked to fashion an international legal and institutional system to achieve these goals.

---

1 The data presented are drawn from a recent research project, coordinated by the author. For a full overview of the background, data and research findings, see Ku and Jacobson, 2003b.

2 See, for example, CBS News Online, 2002:
http://www.cbsnews.com/track/search/stories/2003/01/02/attack/main534965.shtml [accessed 15 July 2003].

These efforts were shaped by the doctrine of collective security, intended to replace the classical balance of power's unilateral state action and *ad hoc* alliances. States would instead find security in their membership in a universal organisation. A collective security system assumes that states that have committed themselves to use military forces will do so automatically in specific situations without further domestic debate. The executive of the state will participate in the international collective decision-making process, but the basic decision will be the determination by an international institution that a state's action constituted aggression or a threat to the peace, warranting a collective response.

An inherent tension therefore exists between the expectations of collective security and the demand for democratic accountability with respect to decisions to deploy and use military forces. The tension has been evident whenever international institutions have been called upon to take action involving the military forces of member states. Different uses of military forces raise different issues of accountability. The greater the risks associated with military actions, the vaguer the immediate interests of the states providing military forces, and the greater the ambiguity of the international legal basis for action, the greater the attention that will be paid domestically to issues of accountability in democracies. In this, there is perhaps little difference whether a decision to use force is made domestically or at the international level and whether the force is used unilaterally or multilaterally.

Of the various operations undertaken by the United Nations involving military forces, there has been little controversy surrounding consensual monitoring or observation operations, as they involve minimal risk to the personnel deployed and rest on widely accepted law and practice. Since the founding of the UN, states like India, Norway, and Canada have closely identified their national interests and international role with participation in such consent-based operations. The closer the operation approaches war, as is the case with internationally-mandated enforcement and compliance actions, the more extensive the domestic debate will be in democracies. Particular scrutiny will be given to:

- the mandate or purpose of an operation;
- the nature of the participating state's contribution; and
- the likelihood of the operation's success, based on the mandate and resources provided.

Where substantial change occurs in any of these areas, new questions of accountability will arise that may require additional international and/or national decision-making. The failure to understand the changed operational demands of a mission has created failures both in meeting mission objectives and in accountability, as in Somalia in 1992 (see Chapter Six) and in Srebrenica in 1995 (see Chapter Five). Multifaceted operations make fixing responsibility difficult when there are forces from many countries operating under a command structure that relies on the UN's organisational and intelligence capacity.

Yet, the United Nations is at the apex of the international political and legal structure dealing with international security. There is no other organisation with universal membership that is also mandated to deal with issues of war and peace. Democratic states clearly prefer to have the Security Council's authorisation when they use military forces. It bestows a legitimacy that cannot be gained in any other way (Bush, 2002), which can be crucial on the international plane, but is also important legally and politically to democratic states' domestic decision-making.

The UN Charter established the framework for judging whether decisions to use force have been taken in accordance with the rule of law, one of two essential components of democratic accountability. The intent of the Charter was to centralise authority concerning the use of force in the Security Council. Under Article 39, 'the Security Council shall determine the existence of any threat to the peace, breach of the peace, or act of aggression and shall make recommendations, or decide what measures shall be taken in accordance with Articles 41 and 42, to maintain or restore international peace and security.' Under Article 42, the Security Council may authorise the use of military force. Article 43 provided for the earmarking of UN member state troops by agreement to be available to the UN Security Council 'on its call.' However, no such agreements have been completed, requiring the UN to assemble military forces *ad hoc* from UN member states whenever an operation requires them.

Table 3.1 shows the use of military forces authorised by the UN and NATO by the year of authorisation. The substantial increase in number starting in 1988 is striking. A change in Soviet policy toward using military forces under UN auspices in 1987 facilitated the authorisation of such missions by the United Nations Security Council (UNSC). Table 3.1 operations are divided into two periods: 1946-1989, and 1990-2000, a Cold War and post-Cold War breakdown.

The table places the uses of military forces under the UN and NATO into five broad categories based on: the mandate of the operation, the rules of engagement given to the military forces, whether or not they enter the territory of the state where they operate with the consent of that state, and the number and types of military personnel involved.[3] The five categories are:

- Monitoring and Observation;
- Traditional Peacekeeping;
- Peacekeeping plus State-building;
- Force to Ensure Compliance with International Mandates;
- Enforcement.

---

3   This categorisation draws heavily on the concepts developed in Evans, 1993. It is related to but different from the categorisation developed by Boutros-Ghali, 1992. More broadly, it draws on the wide literature concerning peacekeeping, including: Diehl, 1993; Durch, 1996; Thakur and Thayer, 1995; Sutterlin, 1995.

Table 3.1   Use of military forces under the auspices of the UN and NATO

Forms of Use of Military Forces	1946-1989	1990-2000
Monitoring and Observation	9 (45%)	9 (16%)
Traditional Peacekeeping	5 (25%)	2 (4%)
Peacekeeping plus State-Building	3 (15%)	23 (40%)
Force to Ensure Compliance	2 (10%)	22 (39%)
Enforcement	1 (5%)	1 (2%)
Total	20 (100%)	57 (100%)

As Table 3.1 shows, military forces were used under UN and NATO auspices much more frequently in the decade starting in 1990 and in more robust forms than in the preceding four decades. This table, however, does not capture the uses of military forces carried out unilaterally or within regional organisations such as the Organisation of American States or the Warsaw Pact. From 1946-89, the UN was called on to undertake actions where neither the USSR nor the US could hope to do more than contain each other's influence, with the exception of the Middle East, where its role emerged out of the Palestine mandate. UN-commanded operations were deployed 19 times in 1945-89, and 35 times in 1990-2000.

Table 3.1 also shows clearly that the nature of UN missions using military forces was quite different in the two periods. Monitoring and observation missions, as noted above, constituted 45% of deployments in the first period, and only 15.8% in the second. In sharp contrast to the Cold War period, when missions in the first four categories were deployed only with the consent of the host state, many operations in the 1990s did not have the consent of the host state, were more intrusive in its affairs, and were involved in intrastate conflicts.

Of the five forms of operations, the UN Security Council (UNSC) authorised all of the 19 monitoring and observation missions between 1945 and 2000, and they were conducted under UN command. The UNSC authorised 55 of the 58 uses of military forces in the other four categories. There were only three instances when the UNSC did not authorise the initial deployment of military forces. The General Assembly, acting under the Uniting for Peace resolution, recommended the First United Nations Emergency Force (UNEF I, 1956), a traditional peacekeeping operation, and the United Nations Security Force (UNSF, 1962) in West New Guinea (West Irian), a peacekeeping plus state-building operation. NATO's North Atlantic Council (NAC) authorised Operation Allied Force (1999) against Yugoslavia, a force to ensure compliance operation. Although the Security Council authorised the initial deployment of UN forces to Korea in 1950, subsequent decisions about the operation were taken by the General Assembly under the Uniting for Peace Resolution. This was also true in the case of the 1960 UN Operation in the Congo (ONUC).

The legal grounds for authorising military action have included Chapter VI of the UN Charter (pacific settlement of disputes), Chapter VII (threats to the peace), and the necessity of preventing genocide and violations of humanitarian law. Of the 74 UNSC resolutions authorising the use of force, only 29 included a reference to Chapter VII. All but one of those resolutions was voted after 1990; the one exception is UNSC Resolution 50 (1948), creating the UN Truce Supervision Organisation (UNTSO). Forty-two years later, in 1990, the Council recommended actions under Chapter VII designed to reverse Iraq's conquest of Kuwait.

These 28 references to Chapter VII constituted 50% of the 56 resolutions authorising the use of force that the Security Council adopted from 1990-2000. They included one monitoring and observation mission, one traditional peacekeeping operation, six peacekeeping-plus operations, 19 compliance actions, and the Gulf War enforcement action. The Council only authorised two compliance actions without mentioning Chapter VII, Resolution 688 (1990), concerning safe havens for Iraqi civilians, and Resolution 743 (1992), creating the United Nations Protection Force (UNPROFOR).

The central role of the Security Council in decisions regarding the use of military forces makes its decision-making processes important both for national oversight and for accountability. In this respect, the Security Council's set-up and practice can raise concerns because of the lack of transparency in its decision-making and the frequent lack of opportunity for interested states to take part in that decision-making. Article 32 of the Charter requires that parties to a dispute be represented (without vote) in the Security Council. Troop-contributing countries do not have a similar privilege.

Unless it happens to be a UNSC member, a country that contributes forces or financial resources to UN operations has no vote in deciding how to use them. This issue has been of particular concern to such troop contributors as Canada and India. In the late 1990s, almost two-thirds of the military personnel involved in operations under UN command came from countries that were not members of the Security Council. They have no say in the initial mandate and rules of engagement, nor are they present if the Council modifies the mission in the course of a military operation.

This is not a rare occurrence. In February 1961, the Security Council adopted Resolution 161, authorising ONUC to use force to prevent civil war in the Congo. This was a dramatic change from ONUC's earlier mission to provide for the orderly withdrawal of Belgian troops. The Security Council also changed the mission of UNPROFOR, created in February 1992 as a traditional peacekeeping operation. In June 1992, UNSC Resolution 761 authorised the Secretary-General to deploy UNPROFOR 'to ensure the security and functioning of the Sarajevo airport and the delivery of humanitarian assistance,' in effect transforming its mission into a compliance action. The Council later gave additional tasks to UNPROFOR, including the disastrous requirement to protect Srebrenica, Tuzla, Zepa, Goradze, and Bihac as 'safe areas'.

Another example of a change of mission after deployment with far-reaching consequences took place in Somalia. The UN operation began in early 1992 when UNSC Resolution 751 created the United Nations Operation in Somalia I

(UNOSOM I), a peacekeeping-plus-state-building mission with a mandate to deliver humanitarian aid. The violent conflict among Somali factions made the execution of this mission impossible. The Security Council then accepted the offer of the United States to use its military forces to establish a secure environment, and created, in Resolution 794 (1992), Unified Task Force (UNITAF). After this US-led force established a secure environment, UNSC Resolution 814 (1993) established United Nations Operation in Somalia II (UNOSOM II) to take over UNITAF's force protection role and continue the humanitarian mission of UNOSOM I. But when this proved impossible because of a continuing hostile environment, the Security Council adopted Resolution 837 (1993), authorising all necessary measures to arrest, detain, prosecute and punish those who incited attacks against UN peacekeepers. The muddle of 'mission creep' in Somalia left many member states skeptical about contributing to future UN peace operations.

The Security Council's proceedings are frequently not transparent. Those who do not participate in its deliberations cannot be certain about the grounds for decisions that are or are not taken. This was particularly a problem with respect to the transformation of the mandates of UNPROFOR and UNOSOM II. It was also a problem with respect to the United Nations Observer Mission in Uganda-Rwanda (UNOMUR), when in the face of increased killing, the Security Council refused to expand the mission and instead reduced its size. Lack of transparency confounds democratic accountability by limiting possibilities for understanding the bases and purposes of UN-authorised military operations. This precludes the informed debate and opportunity for oversight that are important for democracies.

The issue of transparency also arises in another way. In 22 of the cases in which the Security Council authorised the use of military forces, it simply authorised individual states or groups of states to take action. The UN did not command these operations, which included most of the more robust uses of military forces. The Council asked states conducting the operations to report on their actions, but the frequency of such reports and the extent of detail included in them have varied greatly. In most cases, the reports have been perfunctory, leaving much to the discretion of the states carrying out the operations (Sarooshi, 1999).

Providing Accountability through National Institutions and Practices

Democratic governments have established procedures for authorising the use of military forces. There are differences between presidential and parliamentary systems, but in both, popular support is crucial if a government is to persevere in a military operation over time. An elected government must periodically face voters, in the ultimate test of democratic accountability.

Moreover, democratically-elected legislatures are increasingly unwilling to leave use-of-force decisions to the executive alone. There is thus a tension between commitments the executive has made to international institutions and its own domestic accountability procedures. As military forces have increasingly been used under the auspices of international institutions, democratic governments have struggled to adapt established procedures to new situations.

The concept involved in Article 43 of the United Nations Charter was that military forces made available to the UN under these agreements 'for the purpose of maintaining international peace and security' would be committed to UN operations without further national authorisation. However, Article 43 agreements were never put into place. The armed forces of the NATO countries are, by definition, wholly or in large part stationed in the territory covered by Article 5 of the North Atlantic Treaty, but until September 2001, there had never been an Article 5 attack on the North Atlantic area. National decisions have therefore been required every time that the UN or NATO has decided that military forces should be used. Because of this, maintaining democratic accountability involves procedures at both the international and national level. Democratic accountability depends on how well these procedures work and how well they fit together.

In the experience of nine countries examined,[4] the debate at the national level has been deeper and more extensive the larger and riskier the military operation and the murkier the international legal basis for action. Some of the nine have developed explicit formal guidelines. Norway and Japan have enacted laws that govern their participation in military operations conducted under UN auspices. The United States has enunciated policies in executive documents like PDD-25. While the others have not done this, their actions have followed implicit guidelines. The extent to which the legislature has been involved in decisions to contribute military forces to international operations varies by country and by type of operation.

Monitoring and observation missions have been handled relatively simply, except in Japan and Germany. The executive acting on its own authority has routinely assigned military personnel to such missions. Frequently, however, governments have only felt free to assign those personnel that volunteered for these missions. Until the passage of the peacekeeping law in 1992, Japan's government felt that it could not assign Japanese Self-Defence Forces (JSDF) personnel outside Japan. The same was true for Germany, until the question of deploying Bundeswehr personnel outside the NATO area was resolved by a 1994 constitutional court ruling (see Kress, 1995).

Traditional peacekeeping has also been relatively unproblematic. The number of personnel required in traditional peacekeeping has generally been modest. In Norway, the legislature gave the executive authority to assign up to a certain number of military personnel to traditional UN peacekeeping operations, though this was limited to volunteers. In Canada and India, the executive branch routinely assigned personnel to traditional peacekeeping missions without parliamentary involvement. The United States regularly provided transport and logistics support to traditional peacekeeping missions, and the president felt no need to request congressional authorisation. UK practice has been similar to that of the US. Since all five traditional peacekeeping missions predated their decision to take part in international military operations, neither Germany nor Japan participated in them.

---

4   Canada, France, Germany, India, Japan, Norway, Russian Federation, United Kingdom, and the United States.

The other three types of operations (peacekeeping plus state-building, force to ensure compliance with international mandates, and enforcement), where the costs and potential risks are greater, have been more complicated. Because they are closest to the classical use of military forces, it is useful to start with enforcement operations. Almost a million military personnel were involved in the Korean War coalition, and more than 800,000 in the Gulf War, vastly greater numbers than in any of the other military operations conducted under the UN or NATO. As a result, especially in the US and the UK, there was extensive oversight of the government's political and military decisions.

In 1950, President Truman believed that he had the authority to commit US forces in Korea without formal congressional authorisation (US Senate, 1950, pp. 3373-81)[5] although he did consult with congressional leadership. Since the Korean War, the ability of the executive to act without formal congressional authorisation has become problematic, politically if not legally. Congress insisted that it had to authorise the use of US forces in the Gulf, although all presidents since 1973 have disputed the constitutionality of the War Powers Resolution. The British Parliament, the French Assemblée Nationale, and the Canadian Parliament, like their US counterpart, all adopted resolutions authorising or approving the executive's decision to deploy national military forces to liberate Kuwait, in accordance with Security Council Resolution 678 (29 November 1990).

The 'struggle' between the legislature and the executive is present in all democracies. In parliamentary systems, the debates and the legislative history have been less complex, since by definition the government has a legislative majority. But in all examined countries, there have been parliamentary discussions about the use of military forces under the auspices of international institutions. Often these discussions have ended with a resolution taking note of or approving government policy.

In Canada, India and Norway there was historically a strong national consensus in favor of participating in UN-sponsored or mandated military operations that tended to limit parliamentary debate and dissent. But this consensus began to change as international military operations became more robust and departed from the culture of peacekeeping, shaped by such factors as political culture (Norway) and leadership (Pearson in Canada, Nehru in India). Media and public reaction to international military operations have played an important role in questioning a country's extended involvement in operations that lack clear national purposes or mission objectives. This was evident in the debates in Canada and Norway on their participation in Operation Allied Force (Nustad and Thune, 2003, pp.154-175; Hansard, HC, 7 October 1998, as cited in Hampson, 2003, p. 141).

Policy changes adopted in the 1990s allowed Japan, Germany and Russia to participate in UN military operations, but legislative approval is required in all three countries for the deployment of troops.[6] The German Constitutional Court

---

5   Whether this case constituted a precedent for future authorisations to deploy US military forces has been debated at length. See, for instance: Fischer, 1995, p. 21-39.

6   Law Concerning Cooperation in UN Peacekeeping and Other Operations, Japan, 1993; Federal Constitutional Court of the Federal Republic of Germany, 1993.

concluded that deployments outside the NATO area are permissible as long as there is 'constitutive approval' from the Bundestag for each deployment. This enabled all political parties in Germany to accept the concept of overseas deployment by assuring that they would all have a voice in the decision to deploy before any commitment is made.

While enhancing domestic democratic accountability, practices and legislation in many countries have hollowed out the automatic commitment to use military forces for collective action envisaged in the doctrine of collective security. Nevertheless, in legislative debates in the US, the UK, France, Canada and Norway, the question of whether the UN had authorised a military operation remained an important one. For many legislators, UN authorisation was essential for them to consent to the use of national military forces.

Some states have specified conditions under which they will commit their military forces to an international operation. The Japanese peacekeeping law establishes the most stringent conditions. The Japanese Self-Defence Force (JSDF) may only be deployed if a ceasefire has been established and if the host country gives its consent. In addition, JSDF rules of engagement permit the use of deadly force only in response to direct attacks upon Japanese peacekeepers. They may not use deadly force to defend the forces of another country. In effect, the Japanese peacekeeping law precludes the deployment of the JSDF in enforcement and compliance operations.

Table 3.2 shows conditions under which the nine countries examined will allow their military forces to be deployed in international operations.

Table 3.2   Conditions under which countries are willing to allow their military forces to be deployed in international operations

State	Conditions			
	Ceasefire in Place	Host Country Approval Granted	Other	Rules of Engagement Limited to Self Defence
Canada	No	No	No	No
France	No	No	No	No
Germany	No	Yes	No	No
India	No	Yes	No	No
Japan	Yes	Yes	No	Yes
Norway	No	No	No	No
Russian Federation	No	No	No	No
United Kingdom	No	No	No	No
United States	No	No	Yes	No

Five of the nine countries, France, India, Russia, the UK and the US, have used their military forces unilaterally since World War Two. In terms of democratic accountability, in the long-standing democracies, decisions to deploy military forces unilaterally or collectively have been taken by roughly the same procedures. For France, the UK and the US, two crucial tests of democratic accountability were the Gulf War and Kosovo. The nearly six months between the Desert Shield deployment and the start of Operation Desert Storm, in the one case, and the NATO Activation Order and the first airstrikes in the other, allowed ample time for public debate to create an 'enlightened public understanding' (Dahl, 1998, pp. 37-8).

UNPROFOR (Bosnia), UNOSOM II (Somalia), and UNOMUR (United Nations Observer Mission to Uganda-Rwanda) were different. There was very little public awareness and debate with respect to these operations. In part, this was due to the lack of transparency of Security Council proceedings. In February 1994, the Council rebuffed and quietly buried Belgium's request to strengthen UNOMUR (Kuperman, 2001, p. 110; United Nations, 1999a). In these cases, national and international procedures did not fit together in ways that facilitated democratic accountability and an effective international response.

Participation in enforcement or compliance operations is unlikely to be as automatic as the doctrine of collective security envisioned. Their risk means that individual states or coalitions of the willing want to retain control of them, as they did in 23 of the peacekeeping-plus-state-building and force-to-ensure-compliance cases examined. The Security Council authorised 22 of them; the North Atlantic Council authorised one, Operation Allied Force. Both enforcement actions, in Korea and the Gulf, and 19 of 22 (86%) compliance operations were carried out by coalitions of the willing. Several of the missions in the former Yugoslavia and the UN-authorised Multinational Force in East Timor were organised on a regional, rather than a universal basis. When more robust military action is required, states have generally been unwilling to put their military forces under UN command.

Four compliance operations were under UN command: ONUC, UNPROFOR, UNOSOM II, and UNTAET (United Nations Transitional Administration in East Timor). The first three became controversial because the nature of the mission was changed by the Security Council without public or national legislative debate. France and the Soviet Union refused to pay the amount that they had been assessed to fund ONUC operations. This created a financial crisis for the UN and led to an Advisory Opinion on Certain Expenses of the United Nations from the International Court of Justice (Certain Expenses of the United Nations Case, 1962).

This may have been a factor leading the UN to delegate the conduct and funding of more robust military operations to individual states or coalitions of states. The Panel on United Nations Peace Operations put it succinctly in its report:

> The Panel recognises that the United Nations does not wage war. When enforcement action is required, it has consistently been entrusted to coalitions of willing States, with the authorisation of the Security Council acting under Chapter VII of the Charter (United Nations, 2000, p. 10, para. 53).

While this provides for a measure of domestic oversight of military operations, it can leave a considerable amount to interpretation by the strongest power in any coalition.

A Mixed System of Accountability

What this analysis provides is a picture of a mixed system of accountability involving procedures and actions at both the international and national levels (see also Chapter Four). It involves formal constitutional and legislative provisions as well as informal factors such as the media and public opinion. Some practices are well established while others are still in formation. In some areas, practices are more in accord with the tenets of democracy – participation in decision-making and the rule of law – than in others. Informal factors also play a role in providing accountability. These factors can be grouped into three broad categories:

- Political culture;
- Political relationships (leaders, contending political elites, budgetary commitments);
- Societal factors (the military, the media, public opinion).

Table 3.3 shows the number and importance of informal factors increasing with the level of violence and risk of an operation. Table 3.4 summarises the ways in which the international community and the nine countries studied have attempted to deal with questions of democratic accountability when using military forces under the auspices of international institutions.

The first and second columns show how issues of international and national authorisation have been dealt with in the 77 (76 UN authorised and one NATO authorised) uses of forces from 1946 through 2000. During the second half of the 20th century, international authorisation gained growing acceptance as a condition for using military forces for democracies. Judith A. Miller, former General Counsel of the U.S. Department of Defence reflected on this:

> From daily experience, I learned how helpful it is to have a UNSC resolution authorising the use of force: it gives a unifying legal basis for action and analysis that we did not have in [NATO authorised] Kosovo, where each participating nation took its own path to concluding that action there was consistent with international law. The varying paths to that conclusion sometimes led to very real disagreements about whether certain actions or targets in prosecuting the campaign were proper. More pragmatically, I saw every day how our ability to fight or even to preposition supplies is necessarily dependent on other countries who willingly permit overflights; allow us basing privileges; or share resupplies, intelligence, and a host of other facilitators that make it possible for our men and women in uniform to operate effectively (Miller, 2002, p. 227).

Table 3.3 Domestic factors that matter by form of use of military forces

Forms of Use of Military Forces	Political Culture	Political Relationships				Societal Factors	
		Top Leaders	Contending Political Elites	Budgetary Commitments	Military	Media	Public Opinion
Monitoring and Observation	++	-	-	-	-	-	-
Traditional Peacekeeping	++	++	+	+	+	-	-
Peacekeeping plus State-Building	+	++	+	+	+	+	+
Force to Ensure Compliance	-	++	+	+	++	+	+
Enforcement	-	++	+	++	++	++	++

Key:

++ Most Important

+ Important

- Less Important

Source: Mingst 2003, pp. 61-80.

Table 3.4   Uses of military forces and a mixed system of accountability

Forms of Uses of Military Forces	Forms of Authorisation and Responsibility				
	International Authorisation	National Authorisation	Civilian Control	Civilian Responsibility to Military	Responsibility to Comply with Norms
Monitoring and Observation	UN Security Council	Executive (and legislature: Germany, Japan and Russia)	Mixed International and National	National	Mixed International and National
Traditional Peacekeeping	UN Security Council and General Assembly (France and Russia: UNSC only)	Executive (and legislature: Germany, Japan and Russia)	Mixed International and National	National	Mixed International and National
Peacekeeping plus State-Building	UN Security Council and General Assembly (France and Russia, UNSC only)	Executive (and legislature: Germany, Japan and Russia)	Mixed International and National	National	Mixed International and National
Force to Ensure Compliance	UN Security Council and NATO Council (India and Russia: UNSC only)	Executive (and legislature: Germany, Japan, and Russia) and public opinion	Mixed International and National	National	Mixed International and National
Enforcement	UN Security Council	Executive, Legislature, and public opinion	Primarily National	National	Mixed International and National

Source: Ku and Jacobson, 2003a, pp. 349-383.

The nine countries studied differed on whether the United Nations Security Council was the only body that could legitimately give this authorisation. International authorisation, in any case, was never sufficient alone; national authorisation was also always required. The result has been that member states decide on a case-by-case basis whether to contribute their military forces to particular operations and what forces to contribute (Lobel and Ratner, 1999, pp. 124-54).

The remaining three columns of Table 3.4 show whether issues of civilian control, civilian responsibility, and military responsibility to comply with norms are dealt with at a national or international level or through a combination of the two. It is striking that only civilian responsibility remains exclusively national. Direct international mechanisms to deal with military responsibility to comply with norms in UN operations were introduced only in the 1990s (United Nations, 1999b).

What Table 3.4 shows is that the closer internationally-mandated operations move towards war, the greater the degree of national supervision and regulation. This should not be surprising since the UN relies on troops from member states, has only rarely commanded operations that involve a high level of risk to soldiers, and has delegated enforcement actions to capable and willing states.

Techniques that specifically enhance national parliamentary oversight in this mixed system can be grouped into three categories:

- Legislative authorisation;
- Inquiry including parliamentary question periods;
- Political consensus.

Legislative authorisation Of the nine countries examined, legislative authorisation is required for the deployment of troops in international operations by Japan, Germany and Russia. Japan's peacekeeping law requires Diet approval for the dispatch of JSDF units to UN operations under highly restrictive conditions.[7] German military deployments outside the NATO area require 'constitutive approval' from the Bundestag for each deployment.[8] A decision to deploy Russian troops outside of Russia is made by the President through a request to the Federation Council (Tuzmukhamedov, 2003, pp. 257-279).

It may be too early to determine whether there is a growing trend towards legislative involvement, but it is interesting to note that when permission for overflight rights was sought by the US during the Kosovo conflict, Hungary, Bulgaria and Romania all took the matter to their respective parliaments (Damrosch, 2003, pp. 39-60).

In the US, the constitutionality of the War Powers Resolution remains an open question. Enacted in 1973 as American forces withdrew from South Vietnam,

---

7 See the Law Concerning Cooperation for the United Nations Peacekeeping Operations and Other Operations, 19 June 1992, as discussed in Shibata, 2003, pp. 207-230.

8 For a full discussion of the German legislative requirement, see Nolte, 2003, pp. 231-256.

the Resolution imposes a 60-day limit on the engagement of US armed forces in hostilities without congressional authorisation. Presidents have resisted complying with the resolution, but US courts have never ruled on its constitutionality. The most recent effort to secure a court ruling took place in 1999 in connection with the US participation in air strikes against Yugoslavia. Like other such efforts, this one was also dismissed by the courts as 'non-justiciable.' (Glennon, 2003, pp. 323-348).

Inquiry   Although often *post hoc*, parliamentary inquiries are nevertheless available to examine breaches of responsibility and maintain accountability. On a more routine basis, parliamentary question periods are available to seek information about and clarification of military operations. Examples of such inquiries and legislative oversight include:

- The Canadian Commission of Inquiry into the Deployment of Canadian Forces in Somalia to study the conduct of eight Canadian soldiers charged with the death of a local Somali in 1992 (see Chapter Six).
- UN and Dutch official inquiries into the conduct of the Dutch battalion that failed to protect the Bosnian Moslem population entrusted to its care in the 'safe area' of Srebrenica in 1995 (see Chapter Five).
- The French National Assembly Information Commission to examine the decision to intervene in Rwanda in 1994 (Boyer et al., 2003, pp. 280-299).
- The UK House of Commons Foreign Affairs Committee Report on the international legality of Operation Allied Force in June 2000.[9]

Political Consensus   Of the three techniques for maintaining parliamentary oversight over executive actions, perhaps the least satisfactory is that of political consensus. With regard to UN operations in particular, political consensus that participation was in the national interest and central to a country's foreign policy led to practiced and stream-lined decision-making processes in India, to Canada's proud record of taking part in every peacekeeping mission until the 1990s, and to Norway's participation in peacekeeping. These consensus approaches have now lasted for more than 50 years, but could break down if basic assumptions supporting the consensus vanish. Indeed, for some Norwegians, the consensus itself is beginning to be seen as anti-democratic as views outside of the consensus are dismissed.

Conclusions

As we assess the experiences of these nine countries, it appears that accountability is not a problem at the lower end of military operations – where the level of force

---

9   For example the United Kingdom H.C. Foreign Affairs Select Committee Fourth Report, 2000, quoted in White, 2003, p. 322.

used is limited, the number of troops is small and they operate with the consent of the parties concerned. Where there is greater risk, where operations are undertaken without the consent of the conflicting parties, and where the international political and legal bases for operation are in doubt, accountability concerns arise.

Parliaments and legislatures are key to democratic accountability within national systems. Yet, executives often have broad authority to commit a country's armed forces and timely parliamentary participation in the decision to commit troops can be difficult in times of crisis. At the same time, complex deployments require months of planning and preparation before they are staged and usually provide time for consultation and debate. Once troops are committed, parliaments often feel constrained from taking any action that might be regarded as jeopardising the safety of or support for their troops in the field.

National sources of accountability are important in providing oversight to international operations because of the relatively underdeveloped system of international accountability that currently exists. Recognition of this led the UN Secretary-General to appoint a Panel on Peace Operations that recommended institutionalising processes to tie more closely international and national responsibility. For example, that troop-contributing states should receive the same information the Security Council does 'pertaining to crises that affect the safety and security of mission personnel or to a change or reinterpretation of the mandate requiring the use of force' (United Nations, 2000).

There is a need for flexible and sustainable national and international methods to provide oversight and accountability. Developing the tools for effective use will be a matter of practice and experience. There is evidence that with time, systems of international decision-making and national accountability can work together to ensure appropriate legislative oversight in democracies that take part in international operations. But those systems are still evolving, particularly at the more robust end of the use of force spectrum. As a legal system that relies heavily on practice to determine both its form and content, international law depends on national debate and action to fill in areas where gaps exist or where practice remains unsettled. The debates over the legality of 'humanitarian intervention' that occurred in the immediate aftermath of NATO's actions in Kosovo allowed parliaments and legislatures the opportunity not only to debate a current situation, but to shape international legal obligations for the future.[10]

Concerns for domestic accountability and national oversight in the use of military forces need not be and have not been subordinated to the need for internationally-mandated military operations. On the contrary, effective international operations in today's security system rely on effective ties to those who must contribute to these operations. This means accountability not only to the troop-contributing countries, but also to the troops themselves and ultimately to the people these operations are called on to assist.

We may conclude that international authorisation of the use of force alone is insufficient to provide legitimisation and to uphold democratic accountability.

---

10 See for example, Roberts, 1999; House of Commons, 2000; AJIL, 1999.

National authorisation mechanisms need to be added in order to enhance the legitimacy and democratic accountability of the use of force.

As we have seen, parliamentary oversight is one of the most important elements on the national level enhancing legitimisation and democratic accountability. Parliamentary oversight consists of the three different elements, parliamentary authorisation of the use of force, parliamentary inquiries, as well as political consensus. If applied efficiently, all these elements taken together will increase the legitimisation and the democratic accountability of the use of force under international auspices.

In spite of the interdependence between national and international processes to date, international and national legitimisation and accountability mechanism are poorly adjusted. An important ongoing challenge will be to coordinate the international and national systems of legitimisation and accountability concerning the use of force under international auspices.

PART III

THE UN CONTEXT

Chapter 4

Parliamentary Accountability of Multinational Peace Support Operations: A Comparative Perspective

Hans Born and Marlene Urscheler

Introduction

During the Cold War, peace support operations (PSOs) were very limited in both numbers and scope, mostly because decision-making at the UN Security Council (UNSC) was severely constrained due to superpower rivalry. PSOs primarily consisted of the interposition of lightly-armed forces between parties to a conflict. Their limitation in scope was due to very restrictive rules of engagement, based on the peacekeeping principles of impartiality, neutrality and non-use of force. PSOs became more frequent after the end of the Cold War and the number of instances of UN involvement in conflicts increased substantially. Since 1945, there have been 54 multinational PSOs under UN mandate, with no less than 35 of these having been authorised by the Security Council between 1990 and 2000.[1] The UN is currently undertaking some 15 PSOs, involving 45,145 military personnel and civilian police (plus international staff and local personnel), 87 contributing countries and a budget of 2.77 billion dollars (United Nations, 2002).

Not only have the numbers become more impressive, but PSOs have become much broader in terms of both mandate and scope. Nowadays, PSOs take place in complex emergencies, and in some cases transitional administrations have even been created with a wide range of tasks (e.g. East Timor). The aforementioned three basic principles have at times been overridden. Nowadays, the mandates of many PSOs include the right to use force for protecting the operation or the goals of the operation, meaning the use of force beyond the self-defence of troops.

For as long as PSOs have existed, and especially in the 1990s, they have been evaluated and researched. These studies concentrate on the effectiveness of PSOs, 'lessons learned', the military decision-making process, the well-being of soldiers, the cooperation between NGOs and military units, cooperation between

---

1 See http://www.un.org/Depts/dpko/dpko/ques.htm [accessed 9 May 2003].

different countries, etc.[2] Paul Diehl (2001, pp. 202-226) analyses the different factors leading to the success or failure of a PSO in great depth, considering issues such as the impact of the organising agency, timing, consent accorded by the host state and other factors. Additionally, literature on parliaments rarely pays any attention to the parliamentary oversight of the military in general and PSOs in particular, since most scholars studying 'legislative affairs' focus on the general trends and powers of parliaments (e.g. Von Beyme, 2000; Olson, 1994; Norton, 1998). Despite some exceptions (Born, 2003a; Damrosch, 2003; Assembly of the WEU, 2001a; Wulf, 2003), less attention has been given to the crucial aspect of the democratic accountability and parliamentary oversight of PSOs. In spite of this rather modest interest shown by scholars, it is an important topic for at least four significant reasons.

Firstly, from a democratic governance point of view, no area or institution of the government can be exempted from parliamentary oversight, and this includes the government's foreign and security policy. Nowadays, it is important to apply this principle to PSOs, because they have evolved from marginal phenomena to an important tool for the maintenance or creation of international peace and stability and entered the mainstream as an instrument of national policy. PSOs are currently the prime activity of armed forces in most democratic societies (Haltiner and Klein, 2002).

Secondly, the argument that decisions on PSOs should only be taken by government and military officials and not by parliamentarians is flawed because many aspects of PSOs, such as the mandate and the rules of engagement, may have major political consequences. Therefore, the decision to commit troops to a PSO should most definitely involve the parliament.

Thirdly, some authors argue that PSOs are not carried out solely in pursuit of international peace and stability, but rather that they can be subject to political misuse and selective application. The absence of an impartial worldwide mechanism for deciding when, how and in which areas PSOs take place (Franck and Rodley, 1973), turns democratic accountability and, especially, parliamentary oversight into crucial elements of an appropriate system of checks and balances. Parliamentary oversight of governmental decisions and actions decreases the risk of any political misuse of PSOs.

Fourthly, PSOs are certain to fail if they are only backed by good intentions and lack sustained public political support in the contributing states (United Nations, 2000). The contributors' governments need public support for carrying out PSOs as troops and public funds are involved. By debating and authorising PSOs, parliaments are crucial for securing (or withholding) public support of PSOs (Lunn, 2000). Parliaments are an important link between the society, the government and the armed forces. For this reason, it is in the interests of the government to engage parliament in the process of sending troops abroad as much as possible, given that parliamentary debate and vote largely enhance democratic legitimacy and public support. As Chapter Three points out, parliamentary

---

2   For an example, see: Armed Forces and Society, 1997; Jett, 2000, Conaughton, 2001; Diehl, 2001; Pfaff, 2000; Thakur and Schnabel, 2001.

legitimacy is especially needed if the PSO involves the active use of force, high risks for the UN troops or if the belligerent parties do not give their full consent for the intervention.

The basic question that is addressed in this chapter concerns the extent to which parliaments are able to exercise oversight on PSOs. The actual focus of the research is limited in two ways. Firstly, the focus is on parliaments because only parliaments are able to provide democratic oversight that is embedded in the broad range of control mechanisms and institutions which normally exist in democracies, such as: executive control; judicial oversight; oversight by independent audit offices; NGOs and think-tanks in civil society (Norton, 2002; Born, 2003a). Secondly, the focus is not placed on military interventions in general, but on multinational PSOs with a UN mandate in particular. Therefore, wars of aggression as well as purely national PSOs or PSOs without a UN mandate are not taken into account. PSO is used as a generic term, encompassing a variety of interventions, based on the UN Charter, Chapter VI ('The Pacific Settlement of Disputes') and Chapter VII ('Action with respect to Threats to the Peace, Breaches of the Peace, and Acts of Aggression').[3] Using Charlotte Ku's categorisation, multinational PSOs may range from Monitoring and Observation Missions, Traditional Peacekeeping, Peacekeeping plus State-building, Force to Ensure Compliance to Enforcement Operations. All these PSOs are regarded as operations for which troops are deployed abroad under the aegis of the UN. Though these operations differ in terms of the use of force and consent of belligerent operations, for the purpose of this analysis no distinction is made between these operations (see Chapter Three). The third limitation in scope is that only parliaments of the troop contributing state are under study. The accountability to the parliaments of the states that are to receive the troops is significant as well, but falls outside the scope of this research.

For the purpose of addressing the research question, the chapter is based on a comparative analysis of the powers and resources of national parliaments and their parliamentary defence committees in Belgium, Canada, the Czech Republic, Denmark, France, Germany, Hungary, Italy, the Netherlands, Norway, Poland, Portugal, Spain, Sweden, the United States and the United Kingdom. These countries have been selected because they share certain basic characteristics that are crucial for the topic under consideration. On the one hand, they are all democracies in the Euro-Atlantic area, where parliaments normally play a significant role in political processes and all of them are characterised as 'free countries' according to the Freedom House Survey, i.e. countries in which political rights and civil liberties are fully respected (Freedom House, 2003). Additionally, the countries examined share a long-standing experience of participating in PSOs. On the other hand, the selection includes some countries with different political

---

3 According to former UN Secretary General Dag Hammarskjold, traditional peacekeeping is considered to be a Chapter 'Six and a Half' operation as it does not include the use of active force but goes beyond purely diplomatic means. For a more detailed discussion on the relation between the UN Charter and PSOs, see, for example, Hillen, 1998, pp. 1-33.

systems (presidential and parliamentary democracies), allied and neutral states (NATO and one non-NATO member), as well as varied historical factors (consolidating and established democracies).[4] The research was based on a questionnaire consisting of 57 items, ranging from the resources of the parliamentary defence committee, general parliamentary oversight powers, defence budget control, defence planning, procurement to military personnel management and PSOs.[5] The use of a questionnaire was necessary as some elements of parliamentary oversight in general and of PSOs in particular are not designed by law but by customary practice. The questionnaires were filled out by members of the parliamentary committee on defence or security policy, who play an important role in the oversight of defence issues and of PSOs in particular.[6] The results of the research are not so much a reflection of an 'objective reality' of parliament's powers, practices and resources, as a perception of this reality according to those parliamentarians. The data obtained was compared with information retrieved from open sources (e.g. parliaments' websites and the national constitutions). After the data was processed, the results were sent back to the parliaments, thus enabling them to clarify any possible ambiguities and for a last check on the accuracy of the data.

The chapter is structured as follows. Firstly, attention is paid to the relevant aspects of political decision-making on PSOs, especially within the context of the UN. Next, the focus is on the specific role of national parliaments in the oversight of PSOs. Then the main findings of the research concerning parliamentary oversight of PSOs in 16 countries are presented and analysed. The chapter concludes that there are great variations amongst the parliaments in the selected countries, varying from parliaments with a marginal influence on government's PSOs to parliaments with a substantial (co-)policy-making role. In the end, the parliamentary oversight of PSOs not only depends on oversight powers, but also on the resources of parliamentary committees and the willingness of parliamentarians to hold the executive accountable.

---

4   Poland, the Czech Republic and Hungary are regarded as full parliamentary or presidential democracies (Freedom House, 2003), beyond the initial phase of transition towards democracy.

5   In this chapter, the focus is on those items of the questionnaire which are related to powers and resources of parliamentary oversight of PSOs. For a complete overview of the research results, including parliamentary oversight of procurement, military personnel and defence planning, see Van Eekelen, 2002.

6   The research was carried out in cooperation with the International Secretariat of the NATO Parliamentary Assembly and the parliamentary defence committees (or their equivalent) of the 16 selected countries, to whom the authors are grateful for their assistance. The research was carried out in 2002.

Political Decision-Making on PSOs

As mentioned in the introduction, PSOs became a mainstream instrument of national security policy and various types of PSOs have appeared since the end of the Cold War, some of which either completely abandon or only partially respect the basic principles of classical peacekeeping. In analysing the most relevant literature relating to PSOs, one can conclude that the mandate, rules of engagement, risk assessment, chain of command, duration of the mission and the financial consequences are the most important aspects of political decision-making.[7]

The mandate defines the aims of the mission, which may be grouped into different types of missions, ranging from low use of force to high use of force: monitoring and observation missions; traditional peacekeeping missions, force exerted to ensure compliance with international mandates and enforcement (see Chapter Three; Diehl, 2001, p. 218). The need for democratic accountability and parliamentary oversight is greater when a higher level of force is used, as this implies higher risks both for the local population and the troops (see Chapter Three).

The rules of engagement, which are often included in the mandate, are crucial in political terms as they define the level of force which the troops may use and under what circumstances. Depending on the mandate, the rules of engagement may permit the use of force for self-defence alone (minimum-level) up to the use of all necessary force required to safeguard the objectives of the mission (i.e. the maximum-level) (Born, 2003a).

Another elementary aspect of policy-making is the assessment of the risks for the troops in PSOs. Political leaders have to define what level of risks for the troops involved is deemed to be acceptable. The so-called 'body bag' hypothesis is relevant for this aspect of decision-making on PSOs. This hypothesis refers to the general belief that, in democracies, public opinion cannot accept casualties when troops are dispatched abroad on PSOs and that public support for PSOs will erode as soon as casualties occur (Everts, 2002). Based on this belief, political leaders of democracies plan PSOs in such a manner that the risk of casualties is virtually nil. However, in spite of this widespread belief, public opinion seems to support PSOs and accept casualties, providing that in their eyes, the PSO is effective and meaningful (Burk, 1995). Parliamentary debates and votes on deploying troops abroad could bolster public opinion in favour of PSOs.

In terms of political accountability, a precise definition of the chain of command is crucial for clarifying to whom the military commanders are accountable. In case of multinational PSOs, National Contingent Commanders report to the Force Commander, who in turn reports to the UN Secretary-General (UNSG). Experiences with previous PSOs show that a vague or contradictory chain of command can endanger the entire PSO, as was the case, for example, with UNPROFOR in Bosnia (United Nations 1999b). The duration of a PSO is often

---

7   See literature mentioned in footnote 2.

also partly influenced by political decision-making. In this regard, a distinction has to be made between the duration of the PSO and the duration of the contribution of troops from a particular country. Parliaments can require a government to withdraw its troops if the PSO's objectives are not met or if intolerable levels of casualties occur. Last but not least, as peace missions are rather costly, the budget available is the last point of political decision-making.[8] Many multinational PSOs under UN mandate were hampered by financial problems (Diehl, 1993, pp. 75-77), and, therefore, the UN is dependant on voluntary contributions and expects that the 'wealthy' states in particular finance their own military contribution to a PSO (see, for example, United Nations Association – UK, 2003).

The mandate, rules of engagement and chain of command are decided upon at the international level (UN) and can only be altered very slightly by individual contributing countries. On the basis of the decisions taken at the international level, the national governments (and the parliaments overseeing them) take the decision to participate or not in a PSO. The duration and budget of deployed troops, however, are subject to national decision-making. States can decide to commit a budget and troops for a limited period of time or to withdraw or threaten to withdraw the troops. For example, the US threatened to block an extension of the UN presence in Bosnia because the US disagreed with the UN policy towards the International Criminal Court in The Hague (BBC News, 2002).

In the multi-layered decision-making process regarding PSOs at the United Nations, we have to distinguish between different decision-making levels (Simmo, 1995, p. 534): the UN Security Council, the Secretary-General, the Forces Commander, National Contingent Commander, the UN Department of Peacekeeping Operations and the UN General Assembly. The initiating body for almost all PSOs is the Security Council, as this body is responsible for maintaining peace according to Article 24 of the UN Charter (Charter of the United Nations, 1945). The Security Council needs to adopt a resolution in order to create a PSO and this requires nine votes in favour, including the concurring votes of the five permanent members (Charter of the United Nations, 1945, Article 27). However, almost two-thirds of the national military contingents come from countries which are not members of the Security Council (see Chapter Three). These countries are not able to take part in the formal decision-making on the initial mandate and the rules of engagement of the PSO, nor are they present if the Security Council changes the initial mandate. Therefore countries which are not represented in the Security Council may find themselves committed to PSOs which are not (or are no longer) in line with national interests or public opinion. This may cause a rift between the electorate and its representatives on the one hand and the government on the other hand, which is obliged to follow its international commitments (Assembly of the WEU, 2001a). In order to alleviate this disadvantageous situation, in 2001 the Security Council adopted a resolution in order to strengthen cooperation between troop-contributing countries, the UN Security Council and the UN Secretariat. Among other things, the Security Council obliged itself to conduct

---

8   All UN peace support operations together cost approximately 2.6 billion dollars a year. See http://www.un.org/Depts/dpko/dpko/ques.htm#uniforms [accessed 25 June 2003].

public and private consultations, hearings and meetings with troop-contributing states.[9]

After the Security Council adopts a resolution on a PSO, it normally tasks the Secretary-General with formulating the precise mandate of deployed troops as well as the details of its functioning (Simma, 1995). The UN Department of Peacekeeping Operations is responsible for the day-to-day management of PSOs. The General Assembly normally only plays a very limited role in respect to PSOs, but it has the right to call for a PSO as it did in its 'Uniting for Peace' Resolution in the Korean War.[10] The General Assembly has to adopt the entire budget of the UN, including the budget for PSOs. It is often the case that the General Assembly adopts the budget for PSOs before the member states, with respect to their own budget laws, are in a position to react. As previously mentioned, the Secretary-General appoints the Forces Commander to whom the National Contingent Commander reports.

Due to the inter-governmental nature of the UN and the absence of a controlling parliamentary body, some scholars hold the opinion that UN decision-making suffers a great democratic deficit (Scholte, 1997, pp. 27-28). The democratic deficit at the international level is characterised by the complete lack of elections of representatives by the people and lack of democratic oversight of institutions as well as the existence of a large expert-staff, which, exempted from democratic scrutiny, prepares decisions. As concerns PSOs, the decisions taken by the Security Council, whose members consist of appointed officials and not of directly-elected representatives, are not subject to the control of any other institution than their national governments. The decision-making process of the Security Council often takes place *in camera*, which does not facilitate oversight by the general public, national parliaments, or governments that are not represented on the Security Council.

International organisations, such as the UN, are increasingly assuming new responsibilities and what were formerly national competencies. However, at the international level, no internationally-elected parliament exists that is able to oversee the newly-assumed powers. Though the UN has an Assembly, it does not consist of representatives who are elected directly by the people and it plays a marginal role in PSOs decision-making. Therefore PSO decision-making powers are delegated to the UN level without the necessary instruments of democratic oversight. To date, it remains the task of national parliaments to exercise democratic oversight of the government's representation at the international level with regards to PSOs, which is the topic of the next two sections, that is, the research findings on parliamentary oversight of PSOs in 16 selected states.

---

9   UN Security Council Resolution 1353 (2001), available from:
    http://www.un.org/News/Press/docs/2001/sc7070.doc.htm [accessed 2 July 2003].
10 Resolution 377 (V) 'Uniting for Peace', available from:
    http://www.un.org/Depts/dhl/landmark/pdf/ares377e.pdf [accessed 2 July 2003].

Parliamentary Oversight of PSOs: Powers, Resources and Willingness

Since the end of the 17th Century, political systems have gradually become 'parliamentarised', meaning that parliaments have acquired more and more powers to hold the executive to account.[11] The importance of the role of parliaments in issues of national defence and the military has increased markedly, despite these traditionally being regarded as a prerogative of the King and the executive. Among other things, and after long struggles, parliaments were able to oversee the use of force via controlling the manning and financing of the armed forces. Additionally, a practice has been established whereby international agreements leading to military obligations are subject to parliamentary debate. More recently, constitutions increasingly include provisions on participation in international organisations (Damrosch, 2003, p. 43).

The role of parliaments in PSOs takes place within the wider context of political systems. In addition to the representative, legislative and elective functions,[12] exercising oversight of the government's policy is one of the four main parliamentary functions in any political system (Chapter One; Olson, 1994, pp. 6-7; Von Beyme, 2000, pp. 72-107). All four functions are to some extent related to the oversight of PSOs. The representative function, i.e. the representation and articulation of interests (Von Beyme, 2000, pp. 72-73), greatly influences parliament's point of view on sending troops abroad. More important, the representative function gives legitimacy to parliament's approval or rejection of the use of force. In turn, if a parliament stands behind the government, it might favourably influence public opinion for deploying troops. Therefore most political leaders in democracies seek parliamentary debate and consent before sending troops abroad, even when they are not constitutionally obliged to do so. The legislative function is relevant as it shapes the constitutional and legal framework, which gives parliament powers to oversee PSOs. Since the elective function refers to parliament's ability to elect and to dismiss the government, especially in parliamentary democracies, parliament can use this power to threaten governments wanting to embark on particular PSO without parliamentary consent.

A complete parliamentary oversight of PSOs should include all major aspects of political decision-making on PSOs, which are, as previously mentioned, the prior authorisation for the PSO, debating and deciding on the mandate, operational aspects as well as the budget and duration of the PSO. The more these political decision-making aspects of PSOs are part of parliamentary oversight; the more international use of force is 'parliamentarised'. Parliament's ability to oversee PSOs depends on three elements: (1) constitutional and legal powers, (2) resources and (3) the willingness of parliamentarians to hold the executive to account (see, for example, George and Morgan, 1999, p. 2; Van Eekelen, 2002).

---

11 For a further analysis on the rise of parliamentary democracy, see Von Beyme, 2000.
12 The elective function refers to recruiting and selecting members of the cabinet.

Table 4.1   Elements of parliamentary oversight of peace support operations

Elements of parliamentary oversight of PSOs	Description
(1) Legal Powers to exercise oversight on PSOs.	• Power to acquire information about peace support operations (inquiries, visiting troops abroad, questioning the responsible minister). • Power to approve or reject peace support operations (as well as the power to discuss and approve the mandate, operational aspects of the PSO and the duration of the mission). • Power to control the budget of peace support operations and supplementary budget requests.
(2) Resources to understand and evaluate PSOs.	• Specialised parliamentary defence committee. • Parliamentary Staff attached to defence committee. • Budget of the parliamentary defence committee. • Consultations with experts in civil society.
(3) Willingness to support governments' policy on PSOs.	• Public opinion and media pressure. • Pressure from government through party discipline. • Intricacies of the particular PSO under scrutiny.

Parliamentary Oversight Powers

In combining the general literature on parliamentary oversight powers with the aspects of political decision-making on PSOs as described earlier, three parliamentary powers to oversee peace support operations can be distinguished.[13] The first power of parliamentary oversight is concerned with getting sufficient and accurate information. PSOs are subject to international decision-making at the UN level, involving requirements of confidentiality and often have to be decided upon within a short timeframe, not to mention the technicality of the subject-matter (Assembly of the WEU, 2001a, p. 4). Therefore PSOs are difficult to oversee for national parliamentarians, who often rely on information from the government and global mass media. It is important that parliaments have and make use of their constitutional and legal powers to force the government to provide parliament with all relevant information on PSOs. These powers include the right to question the relevant members of the executive, the right to have them testify under oath, the power to hold an inquiry and hearings, the right to obtain any document belonging to the executive as well as the right to visit the troops abroad. The second group of powers relates to the constitutional or legal powers of parliament to approve or reject PSOs in advance. Such a legal provision furnishes the parliament with a very powerful tool and guarantees that the parliament is informed about the involvement

---

13 For literature on parliamentary powers, see for example Von Beyme, 2002; Norton, 1998 or Olson, 1994.

of troops deployed abroad in an accurate and timely manner. In addition, a parliament may have the right to debate and assess the most important political issues of peace support operations, being the mandate, risks involved for troops, rules of engagement, the chain of command as well as the duration of the peace support operation (see previous section). Though parliaments may not have the ability to decide upon the mandate, rules of engagement and chain of command (as to a large extent, they are decided upon at UN level), parliaments can take these elements into account when debating and voting on PSOs. The third power of parliamentary oversight is the control of the PSO's budget. The power of the purse is generally regarded as one of the oldest and decisive powers of parliament. The power of the purse applies to both the regular yearly defence budget, including PSOs and the power to approve or to reject supplementary defence budgets for PSOs. Supplementary budget approvals are important because PSOs often occur unexpectedly. Even if a parliament lacks the right to approve or reject the government's decision to deploy troops abroad, it can obstruct government policy by rejecting supplementary budget requests. A vote on a supplementary budget request for peace support operations can be regarded as an implicit vote on the government's decision to deploy troops abroad in peace support operations.

In the remainder of this section the focus is on the research findings related to these three powers of parliaments to oversee PSOs in the 16 selected countries. As is apparent from the comparative research, all parliaments possess the necessary constitutional and legal powers to retrieve information from the executive, including the right to question the minister, to summon military and civil servants as well as to organise hearings. However, as brought to the forefront by the comparative research, the Italian and Polish Parliaments do not have the power to start an independent parliamentary inquiry into defence issues including, among others, PSOs. These two parliaments lack an important instrument to learn lessons from (failed) PSOs independently from the government. As Chapters Five and Six of this volume show, parliamentary inquiries are an important tool for evaluating PSOs and can be considered an outlet for tensions and emotions in society if PSOs fail or if major scandals occur. Additionally, the Portuguese Parliament does not have the power to visit Portuguese troops which are deployed on PSOs abroad.

A wide variation exists between countries as far as the constitutional and legal powers of the parliament to oversee PSOs are concerned (see Table 4.2). The parliaments of Belgium, Canada, France, Poland, Portugal, Spain, USA and the UK do not have the power of prior authorisation. The majority of these countries are either presidential-parliamentary democracies or parliamentary Westminster-type democracies. The presidential-parliamentary democracies are Poland, US, France and Portugal (Karatnycky and Piano, 2002, pp. 736-737), where the President is the Commander-in-Chief and has special prerogatives concerning foreign and security policy.

Table 4.2 Parliamentary oversight powers concerning PSOs as indicated by the spokesmen of parliamentary defence committees (2002)

Parliamentary powers and PSOs	Approval of sending troops abroad *a priori*	Approval of a mission's mandate	Approval of operational issues (rules of engagement, command/control and risk assessment)	Right to visit troops abroad	Decision on the duration of the mission
Belgium	No	No	No	Yes	No
Canada	No	No	No	Yes	No
Czech Rep.	Yes	Yes	No	Yes	Yes
Denmark	Yes	Yes	Yes	Yes	Yes
France	No	No	No	Yes	No
Germany	Yes	Yes	Yes	Yes	Yes
Hungary	Yes	n/a	n/a	n/a	n/a
Italy	Yes	n/a	n/a	Yes	n/a
Netherlands	Yes	Yes	Yes	Yes	Yes
Norway	Yes	No	No	Yes	No
Poland	Yes	No	No	n/a	No
Portugal	No	No	No	No	No
Spain	No	No	No	Yes	No
Sweden	Yes	Yes	No	Yes	Yes
UK	No	Yes	No	Yes	No
USA	No[14]	No	No	Yes	Yes

Yes: the parliament possesses the power.
No: the parliament does not possess the power.
n/a: not available or not applicable.

As far as the US is concerned, the division of powers between the President and the Congress is unclear and continues to produce tensions (see Chapter Eight). On the one hand, the US Congress has the power 'to declare war',[15] but deploying troops abroad in the context of PSOs is not the same thing as waging war. In this context, in 1973, after the Vietnam War (an 'undeclared' war), the US Congress passed the War Powers Resolution requiring the President to consult with Congress whenever military action is contemplated and to report to Congress whenever armed forces are involved in hostilities abroad. Moreover, the Resolution bars any continued

---

14 *A posteriori,* according to US Congress War Powers Resolution, available at: http://www.yale.edu/lawweb/avalon/warpower.htm [accessed 29 July 2003].
15 US Constitution, Article I, Section 8, Clause 11.

deployment of troops unless the Congress gives its consent. If Congress does not consent within 60 days, the President must withdraw the troops within 30 days.[16] On the other hand, the President is 'Commander in Chief of the Army and Navy of the United States' (US Constitution, Article II, Section 2). Various Presidents continue to dispute the Congressional point of view that the Congress is empowered to approve troops being dispatched abroad in advance. Damrosch (2003, pp. 48-51) shows that in various deployment of troops abroad, the President sometimes asks the consent of Congress (e.g. First Gulf War and Bosnia) and on other occasions he does not seek Congressional support (e.g. Somalia, Haiti), implying that it is up to the President whether prior Congressional authorisation for a PSO is sought or not.

The French Constitution of 1958 provides no procedure for prior parliamentary authorisation concerning forces outside of France (Lamy, 2000). Nevertheless, international agreements, among them those involving the deployment of troops abroad, have to be submitted to the parliament.[17] According to a report by the French Parliamentary Defence Committee (Lamy, 2000), during the 1990s, with the exception of the First Gulf War in 1991, the French President did not seek prior parliamentary authorisation for the deployment of troops in Yugoslavia (UNPROFOR, IFOR, and SFOR), in Albania (Operation Alba in 1997) as well as in Kosovo (Allied Force and KFOR since 1999) which were all undertaken by the executive without parliament having any say in the decisions (Lamy, 2000).

In Poland, the President is the Supreme Commander of the Polish Armed Forces (Constitution of the Republic of Poland, 1997, Article 134.1) and during peacetime he exercises the command of the armed forces through the Minister of Defence (Constitution of the Republic of Poland, 1997, Article 134.2).[18] The Portuguese Constitution of 1997 mentions that the President is the Commander-in-Chief of the armed forces (ex officio).[19]

In addition to these presidential-parliamentary democracies, neither the Canadian nor the British parliaments have the power of prior authorisation for PSOs. These parliaments are so-called 'Westminster-style' parliaments, in which the powers between parliament and government are fused and in which the government dominates the parliamentary agenda (Norton, 1998, pp. 2-3; Lijphart, 1999, pp. 10-30). Winslow refers to the Canadian political system as an 'elected dictatorship' (see Chapter Six). The parliaments of the other two selected countries who remain without prior authorisation power are Belgium and Spain. It is unclear why this is the case, perhaps because they are monarchies or because they are

---

16 50 U.S. Congress par. 1542-1544, available at:
   http://www.yale.edu/lawweb/avalon/warpower.htm [accessed 29 July 2003].
17 French Constitution, 1958, Article 53, as mentioned in Assembly of the WEU, 2001a, p. 11
18 An English version of the Polish Constitution is available from:
   http://www.oefre.unibe.ch/law/icl/pl00000_.html [accessed 29 July 2003].
19 Available in English on the website of the Portuguese Parliament:
   http://www.parlamento.pt/ingles/cons_leg/crp_ing [accessed 29 July 2003].

former colonial powers, in which political systems, according to the Assembly of the WEU (2001a, p. 6), the executive often has special prerogatives for deploying troops abroad. Further research is needed into this issue.

The parliaments of the Czech Republic, Denmark, Germany, Hungary, Italy, Norway, the Netherlands and Sweden have the power to approve or reject PSOs in advance. All these states are parliamentary democracies (Karatnycky and Piano, 2002, pp. 736-737); some of them are either monarchies (Denmark, Norway, Sweden, and Netherlands) or former colonial powers (Germany, the Netherlands, and Italy). The Danish Constitution obliges the government to seek consent from parliament in case of deployments 'against a foreign state' (Constitution of the Kingdom of Denmark, 1992, Art 19.2).[20] Though formally speaking this provision applies to use of force against a state, as a matter of established practice, the government has to get approval from the Danish Parliament before making any commitments concerning PSOs (Assembly of the WEU, 2001a, pp. 8-9). In Sweden, in order to comply with the regulations of the Constitution, the armed forces can only be sent abroad in accordance with a (special) law that sets out the grounds for such action and with international treaties and commitments (Constitution of the Kingdom of Sweden, 1975, Chapter 10, Art 9, paras. 1-3).[21] Hungary is an interesting point in case because the Constitution requires a majority of two-thirds of the votes of the members of parliament (Constitution of the Republic of Hungary, 1949, Article 19 [3] and [6]). Sending troops abroad is one of the few decisions that needs to be based on a qualified majority in parliament. It is also one of the few cases in which the parliamentary opposition has the opportunity to influence government policy, as its cooperation is necessary for reaching the two-thirds majority. Therefore, in the past, domestic issues played an important role and not so much the specific deployment of troops abroad. NATO put Hungary under pressure to change this procedure as it is seemingly not very instrumental if NATO needs Hungary's cooperation in out-of-area operations.[22] However, this will require a change in the constitution, which is a long and complex process, to be approved by a qualified majority in parliament.

In Italy and the Netherlands, the constitution does not explicitly mention that the government has to acquire *a priori* approval for deploying troops abroad, but it is regarded as a matter of customary practice (see Chapter Five; Assembly of the WEU, 2001a, p. 13). Not all of these parliaments which have the power of prior authorisation of PSOs, have the same subsequent powers, that is the power to discuss and approve the mandate, operational issues as well as the budget and duration of the mission. Only the parliaments of the Netherlands, Germany and Denmark as well as, to a lesser extent, Sweden and the Czech Republic are in a

---

20 Available in English at http://www.oefre.unibe.ch/law/icl/da00000_.html [accessed 9 June 2003].
21 http://www.riksdagen.se/english/work/fundamental/government/index.htm [accessed 9 June 2003].
22 According to interview with Hungarian Expert on Security and Defence Issues (June 2003).

position to exercise more detailed oversight (see Table 4.2). The parliaments of Norway and Italy, however, do not have these detailed oversight powers. They have the power of prior authorisation for deploying troops abroad, but no additional powers. One might state that those parliaments which lack these additional powers, give the government a 'blank cheque', after debating and voting on the decision to deploy troops abroad.

However, even in the case where the parliament does not have the constitutional or legal powers to oversee PSOs, they may exercise oversight via controlling the budget of PSOs. The following table provides information on the financial oversight powers of the parliament.

Table 4.3   Parliamentary power to control the budget of peace support operations as indicated by the spokesmen of parliamentary defence committees (2002)

Parliamentary powers and budget	Approval of the budget of the peace support operation	Approval of supplementary budget requests
Belgium	n/a	Yes
Canada	No	Yes
Czech Rep.	Yes	Yes
Denmark	Yes	Yes
France	No, only *a posteriori*	Yes
Germany	Yes	Yes
Hungary	Yes	Yes
Italy	Yes	Yes
Netherlands	Yes	Yes
Norway	Yes	Yes
Poland	No	n/a
Portugal	No	Yes
Spain	Yes	Yes
Sweden	Yes	Yes
UK	Yes	Yes
USA	Yes	Yes

Yes: parliament possesses the power.
No: parliament does not possess the power.
n/a: not available or non-applicable.

As previously mentioned, parliaments may have two opportunities to discuss the budget of PSOs. In some countries, a separate budget is presented to the parliament, in other countries the PSO budget is part of the yearly defence budget.

Furthermore, in some countries, the parliament may approve additional budgetary requests. Most parliaments, except for those of France, Poland, Canada and Portugal, are in a position to discuss, approve or reject the budget for PSOs and are therefore able to block their governments' decision to deploy troops abroad by withholding funds. This happened, for example, to the US military contingent during the UN PSO in Somalia. After the first casualties were incurred in 1993, the US Congress stopped the funding for the US troops in the PSO, after which the troops were withdrawn in 1994 (Damrosch, 2003, p. 49). Otherwise, all parliaments (no data is available for Poland) are in a position to approve or reject supplementary budget requests, and, in doing so, are able to discontinue a PSO. Therefore, even if the parliament lacks the constitutional or legal powers to exercise detailed oversight of PSOs, via the power of the purse they may influence government policy on PSOs. This is one of the reasons why the US Senate is very powerful as both the Senate and House have far-reaching control over the budget. Both the Plenary and the Committee on Armed Services of the US Senate 'can exercise the power of the purse to prevent, condition or stop participation in missions'.[23] However, generally speaking, the power of the purse does not entirely compensate for the lack of a constitutional power of prior authorisation. After the troops are sent abroad on a PSO, pulling them out at an early stage of the mission is problematic. Such an act might endanger the PSO or damage the international reputation of a country contributing troops as well as fomenting disaster for other perhaps much weaker contributory nations.

Resources of Parliamentary Defence Committees

Parliamentary oversight is not only dependent on the legal power to oversee PSOs. Indeed, the parliaments' resources are equally important. Effective parliamentary oversight of the security sector requires expertise and resources within and outside the parliament. Therefore a second factor plays an important role in parliamentary oversight, and that is the resources provided to the parliament, including: the existence of a specialised defence committee; appropriate parliamentary staff; a budget for the defence committee; and the support provided by outside expertise. Without these resources, the parliament is unable to analyse and criticise the information provided by the executive. Given the complexity of PSOs, a well-developed committee structure and access to resources is essential for exerting substantive oversight of the government's policy. As a matter of fact, 'the committee stage' has become a central element of parliaments throughout the world (Mattson and Stroem, 1996). The main research findings on parliamentary resources are summarised in Table 4.4.

---

23 According to a staff member of the US Senate Armed Services Committee (2002).

Table 4.4 **Resources of national parliamentary defence committees as indicated by the spokesmen of parliamentary defence committees (2002)**

	Members of Parliamentary Defence Committee	Parliamentary Defence Committee Staff	Budget Defence Committee (Euro)	Making use of outside expertise
Belgium	17	1	*	Yes
Canada	16	3	n/a	Yes
Czech Rep.	19	4	*	Yes
Denmark	17	3	33,333	Yes
France	72	11	130,000	Yes
Germany	38	8	n/a	Yes
Hungary	15	2	4,000	Yes
Italy	43	4	*	Yes
Netherlands	27	5	25,000	Yes
Norway	10	1	n/a	Yes
Poland	19	4	*	Yes
Portugal	26	3	n/a	Yes
Spain	40	4	*	Yes
Sweden	19	5	500,000	Yes
USA	25	50	5,800,000	Yes
UK	11	7	n/a	Yes

*) These Parliamentary Defence Committees lack their own budget, but make use of their parliaments' general budget;
n/a: not available or non-applicable;
Yes: parliament has the possibility of making use of outside expertise.

The data on resources is related to the parliamentary defence committee of the selected countries, which is the committee dealing with the various aspects of PSOs.[24] All selected countries possess a defence committee: a prerequisite for exercising effective oversight in that policy field and whose existence signifies an institutionalised way of dealing with parliamentary oversight (Norton, 1998, p. 1996). The other common feature is that all defence committees make use of external expertise, such as expert consultants at universities, research institutes or NGOs. The selected parliaments differ in terms of numbers of members and staff

---

24 In addition some other parliamentary committees deal with a particular aspect of PSOs, such as the foreign affairs committee and the budget committee which deal with foreign policy aspects and financial aspects of PSO, respectively.

as well as the available committee budget. The smallest committee on defence is found in Norway (10 members) and the largest committee is that of France (72 members).

The size of the committee does not have a linear impact on the effectiveness of parliamentary oversight on defence and PSOs. Too many members on a committee may transform the committee into a debating club instead of a working committee. On the other hand, too few members would impede the necessary task specialisation that is inherent to covering the security sector. Additionally, party rivalry inside the committee may detract from a constructive working climate (Von Beyme, 2000, p. 60). Therefore, it is not possible to draw unequivocal conclusions from this data.

As regards the committee staff, their size varies from one staff member for the Norwegian parliamentary defence committee to 50 staff members working for the US Senate Committee on Armed Services. Staff members usually prepare and organise committee meetings, maintain contacts with government and defence officials, collect information and help interpret government information. Therefore, they are vital for effective committee work and one can assume that more staff generates more support and therefore more effective oversight of defence issues, including PSOs. The same relationship may be assumed between the budget of the defence committee and effective oversight. The greater the budget, the more possibilities are available for undertaking parliamentary inquiries, to organise hearings, and to hire both staff and outside expertise. The US Senate has access the largest financial resources (5.8 million Euros) whereas the Hungarian parliamentary defence committee has a budget of just 4,000 Euros. Remarkably, the French Defence Committee has a lower budget than the Swedish Parliamentary Defence Committee, though one might expect the French Committee to oversee a larger military. However, out of all parliaments studied, the US Senate Committee for Armed Services seems to be the best resourced committee in terms of committee staff and budget.[25]

Willingness to Hold the Executive to Account

That said, even if the legal basis for parliamentary oversight is impeccable and the parliament has sufficient resources and expertise to deal with PSOs, effective parliamentary oversight of the peace support operations cannot be taken for granted. The last element, the political willingness of the parliamentarians to use the tools and mechanisms at their disposal, is a crucial condition for the effective parliamentary scrutiny of the security sector. The political willingness to endorse a PSO is dependent on the issue itself as well as on outside pressures i.e. parliamentarians are often influenced by public opinion and the media 'to do something' when civil wars occur. As shown elsewhere in this volume, Dutch

---

25 The data presented on the US case does not taken into account that the US Senate Armed Services Committee can avail itself of the Congressional Research Service which employs approximately 800 staff members as well as the Library of Congress staff and resources.

parliamentarians and government leaders were under heavy pressure from public opinion and the media to restore peace and order in Bosnia (see Chapter Five). Furthermore, the political willingness of parliamentarians is influenced by pressures exerted by the government. By imposing party discipline, governments try to limit the freedom of individual parliamentarians of the parliamentary majority to vote against government's intention to deploy troops in PSOs (see Chapters Five and Nine). In this regard, a public vote on PSOs is not only about the PSO itself, but also a home affairs test of whether the government still enjoys broad support in parliament.

In addition to these outside pressures, the subject matter of the PSO is also relevant. Generally speaking, since the end of the Cold War a 'new debate' has taken place on PSOs, in which a centre-left wing consensus arose on the utility of the use of force for PSO purposes (Everts, 2002, p. 7). More centre-right wing politicians tend to favour PSOs if it serves national interests. However, after the initial enthusiasm for PSOs at the beginning of the 1990s, the willingness to embark on a PSO is no longer only driven by the impulse 'to do something', but also by realism and the feasibility of PSOs as a vehicle for intervention when intervening in civil wars and failed states (Jett, 2000). Additionally, we might expect the type of PSO to influence the willingness of parliamentarians to agree with despatching troops abroad. As Chapter Three points out, the larger and riskier the operation, the deeper and more intense the debate will be on the national level. Parliamentarians are more careful and perhaps even reluctant to approve enforcement operations because of the great risks for the troops and because the absence of the belligerent's agreement to the intervention.

As research into the willingness of parliaments requires in-depth and qualitative research on political processes leading to PSOs in each country, it falls beyond the scope of this quantitative research on parliament's role in PSOs. To date, no comparative data is available on parliamentarians' willingness concerning PSOs. Therefore, the working assumption has been made that there is a certain degree of willingness among parliamentarians to support PSOs, and that the level of willingness is influenced by pressures from the government, media, and public opinion as well as the particular intricacies related to each PSO.

Conclusions

As mentioned in the introduction, in current scholarly literature little or no attention is given to the parliamentary oversight of PSOs. The comparative research presented in this chapter aimed to contribute to filling this gap by comparing the role of parliament in PSOs in 16 selected democracies in the Euro-Atlantic area. The starting point of the research is that parliaments should play a role in PSOs as these are an important aspect of security policy. Additionally, as shown in this chapter and also in Chapter Three, the UN is not a democratic organisation due to its inter-governmental nature and the absence of an international parliamentary controlling body. Therefore, only national parliaments are entrusted with the responsibility of exercising democratic oversight of multinational PSOs. This raises concerns as the military and security policy are increasingly 'internationalising' (see Chapter Two). The research findings show that some parliaments are only marginally involved in decision-making on deploying troops abroad at the national level (see below), let alone at the level of the United Nations. Other parliaments, which have the full ability to hold their national government to account for deploying troops abroad, may face difficulties in keeping track of the complex decision-making at the international level, which has often taken place behind closed doors.

Regarding the quality of the data, it is important to underline that this was provided by the members of parliament or staff members of the parliaments in the 16 countries in question. As previously stated, the results are not so much 'hard objective data' but rather are the parliamentarians and staff members' perceptions of their own resources and powers for exercising parliamentary oversight. The research has its limitations. Firstly, neither countries lying outside the Euro-Atlantic area nor transition states were taken into account. Secondly, more qualitative aspects of parliamentary oversight, such as the willingness of parliamentarians to hold the executive to account, are beyond the scope of this research. These two issues, i.e. expanding the scope of countries as well as an in-depth review of each country, indicate possible directions for future research.

Having said that, the findings demonstrate substantial differences in the nature and functioning of the parliaments of the countries studied. With regards to the powers to oversee PSOs, the first interesting result to come out of the research is that three groups of parliaments can be identified. Firstly, parliaments without the power of prior authorisation of PSOs. The parliaments of Belgium, Canada, France, Portugal, Spain, US and the UK belong to this group. Most of these countries are either presidential-parliamentary democracies or 'Westminster-style' parliamentary democracies, in which the executive has far-reaching powers on foreign and security policy. In the terminology of Polsby (1975), these parliaments can, at best, be considered as 'arena'-parliaments. They lack the power to restrain the government from sending troops abroad; nevertheless they are capable of organising public parliamentary debates in the plenary on pending PSOs. Though such a debate is not concluded with a vote, it can contribute to the public support and democratic legitimacy of a PSO, which is particularly important in cases where casualties occur on the mission. Therefore, many governments in these and other democracies seek parliamentary consent for deploying troops abroad, even if legally they are not obliged to do so. Additionally, most of these 'powerless' parliaments possess the power of the purse and are able to vote on the budget for PSOs. The disadvantage of the power of the purse is that the troops may have already have been sent abroad. Once that happens, it is difficult to withdraw them as to do so could endanger the PSO and damages the international reputation of the country that is contributing troops.

A second group of countries consists of parliaments that possess the power to approve or reject participation in PSOs in advance, but only in a general way, and without overseeing important aspects of political decision-making of PSOs, such as the mandate, operational aspects and especially the duration of the mission. The parliaments of Norway and Italy belong to this category. These parliaments give the government a 'blank cheque' to go ahead with the PSO after giving their initial approval. The third group of parliaments oversee all the aspects of PSOs, including prior authorisation, the mandate, operational aspects and the duration of the mission. This group of countries includes Germany, Denmark, the Netherlands and to a lesser degree the Czech Republic and Sweden (who do not deal with more operational issues).The third group have far-reaching powers to restrain executive power.

Although we live in the 'age of parliaments' (Patterson and Copeland, 1994, p. 1), the research findings show that the 'parliamentarisation' of PSOs has not completely taken place in all states. In seven of the 16 selected states, the parliament plays a marginal role in PSOs. But is this undesirable? Or to put it in other terms: is the best parliament a parliament with the greatest powers of oversight on PSOs? This is a normative question which is difficult to answer outside of the political context. As the findings show, parliaments in a presidential or Westminster parliamentary system tend to have less powers of oversight. It is difficult to assert that one political system is less democratic than another system. However, if one was to take it that in a democracy all essential matters of society should be subject to decision-making by the people or their representatives as a starting point, parliaments should play a role in PSOs since they fulfil a key function in the contemporary foreign and security policy of most countries. It is essential that the authority for using the state's monopoly of force is not only in the hands of the executive, but spread out over the executive, legislative and judicial branches of the state. Each branch has its own function and helps to keep the political system in balance.

Because PSOs are subject to international decision-making in the UN (often behind closed doors) confidentiality measures and because PSOs may take place abroad in conflict zones, parliamentarians face great difficulty in overseeing them. Therefore, in addition to oversight powers, the resources and expertise of the parliamentary defence committee are also essential. Without a parliamentary staff, an adequate budget and access to external expertise, it is difficult for a parliament to acquire the necessary expertise and second opinions to validate and assess the government's information on PSOs. The research shows that parliaments vary greatly with regards to the availability of financial resources (from 4,000 Euros to 5.8 million Euros) and staff expertise (from one to 50 staff members).

In spite of a cross-party and, for the most part, post-Cold War political consensus (especially by the Western European Centre-Left) on the utility of PSOs, the willingness of parliamentarians to oversee and criticise PSOs in their various forms cannot be taken for granted. Parliamentarians are exposed to pressures from the government, their political parties, the media and public opinion, and, perhaps, their own conscience plays a role too. Future research could be conducted on the willingness of parliament to oversee PSOs in an independent and serious manner: such research would be invaluable for further dissecting the role of the parliamentarian not only in this important and pressing area of security sector oversight, but in others as well.

Chapter 5

Srebrenica, Dutchbat and the Role of the Netherlands' Parliament

Jan Hoekema

Introduction

This chapter focuses on the way the government and parliament of the Netherlands dealt with the democratic deficit in a specific area of security policy and parliamentary accountability, i.e. peacekeeping and more specifically, the participation of the Netherlands in the United Nations Protection Force (UNPROFOR) in the former Yugoslavia between 1992 and 1995. As part of UNPROFOR, the Dutch Battalion (Dutchbat) was responsible for protecting the UN Safe Haven of Srebrenica, but was unable to stop the invading Serbs, resulting in the death of approximately 7,000 civilians (NIOD, 2002).[1] This chapter sets out in some detail the background of a definite trend of growing parliamentary involvement in decision-making processes on the deployment of Dutch troops to peacekeeping missions, starting as early as the late 1970s, and describes the various ways and means of implementing the acquired right of parliaments' near formal consent before such a deployment. The chapter illustrates the difference between NATO operations as originally envisaged in the North Atlantic Treaty where no formal consent is required and peacekeeping and peace-enforcing missions, both inside and outside NATO, where such consent is required before the Netherlands can participate in a mission. Finally, the chapter refers to changes in the Dutch Constitution, codifying this trend of growing parliamentary involvement. In short, UNPROFOR is used as a case study for the general issue of parliamentary oversight, though it should be stressed that both the measure of involvement and the nature of the operation – and specifically for the Netherlands – the dramatic end of UNPROFOR in Srebrenica are worth considering at length as a most interesting case with strong implications for the present day. The chapter covers a time span of some 20 years in all, but concentrates on the period 1992–1995.

---

1 Nederlands Instituut voor Oorlogs Documentatie (NIOD, Netherlands' Institute for War Research) was tasked by the government to carry out an independent official inquiry into the Srebrenica tragedy and the role of Dutchbat/UNPROFOR. The official NIOD research report on UNPROFOR and Srebrenica is available from http://194.134.65.21/srebrenica [accessed 18 June 2003].

Parliament and Peacekeeping

In the Netherlands, a long-standing tradition already existed on the involvement of parliament in matters of peacekeeping, focused for obvious reasons on the actual deployment of Dutch troops abroad. In 1979 the spokesman for the then opposition Liberal-Democrat Party (D66) successfully tabled a parliamentary motion in which he asked the government to consult with parliament on decisions to send out troops on UN missions (NIOD, 2002, p. 502). The reason, at the time, was partly practical, as conscripts were to be sent out involuntarily for the pending United Nations Interim Force in Lebanon (UNIFIL) and this caused uproar within Dutch society. Moreover, the Dutch parliament was completely surprised when the then Dutch government decided to take part in the United Nations Interim Force in Lebanon (UNIFIL) with an armoured infantry battalion. Therefore parliament required that it was at least consulted before such decisions were taken (NIOD, 2002, p. 502). In 1987, the parliament adopted a motion to stipulate the right of the parliament to be consulted in a 'timely' manner prior to any deployment, if conscripts were to be deployed involuntarily. Some years later, at the end of 1994, the parliament tabled an important parliamentary motion which demanded the right of parliament not only to be involved and consulted, but also asked for consent in any (major) decision on the deployment of troops in peacekeeping missions, and significant changes in the mandate and/or location of the mission in question. The motion was supported by all parties in the parliament, with the notable exception of the Market Liberal Party (VVD), to which the then Minister of Defence belonged. Previous governments were always reluctant to acknowledge and codify the right of parliamentary approval, using the argument that customary law was already sufficient in itself: the parliament would always have the right to 'send a government home' when it disagreed with a decision to deploy troops in an operation. The government would then simply lack any political trust from parliament.

As is often the case, any trauma that is experienced may be exacerbated by psychological-emotional processes. The trauma experienced by Dutch society after the Srebrenica tragedy was overcome in a similar way, by what could be called 'political instrumentalisation'. Questions like 'what are the lessons learned?', or 'what should we do differently next time?' dominated the Dutch discussion on what conclusions could be drawn from the failure of UNPROFOR in general and the safe areas in particular for future peacekeeping missions. In December 1994, the government refused to accept parliamentary approval rights. Instead it produced a White Paper on Framework for Review (known in Dutch as 'Toetsingskader', 1995) which provided a framework for governmental and parliamentary decision-making on peacekeeping and peace-enforcing operations. This White Paper listed no fewer than 14 points of attention which the parliament should use as a checklist for taking a decision to approve the deployment of troops abroad. The main elements of the parliamentary Framework for Review are: (1) Dutch national interest, (2) international law, (3) the mandate of the UN or another international organisation with mandating authority like the OSCE or NATO, (4) solidarity both with allies and with countries afflicted by conflict, (5) credibility of the Netherlands abroad, (6) the distribution of responsibilities with other participants, (7) military risks and burdens, (8) the exit strategy and the actual possibilities for the armed forces to deliver the required goods and servicemen. (Toetsingskader, 1995; NIOD, 2002, p. 1699).

One element of the Framework of Review is worth closer attention, being the issue of credibility. This refers to the fact that, traditionally, large segments of the Dutch armed forces were made permanently available to the UN in a standard package offer for peacekeeping services. If the Netherlands were to not deliver on this promise, a credibility problem could arise. The UN itself and, even more importantly, UN member states would view the Netherlands as not being entirely credible and trustworthy, which could damage the country's international position. All these points of attention were thoroughly reviewed and discussed in long and heated debates. In November 1995, the parliament accepted the White Paper.

In the late 1990s, the government finally decided to yield to the parliament and agree to codify the principle of parliamentary approval in the Dutch Constitution. In 2000, after a long and complex procedure, the Constitution was finally changed accordingly. The most relevant new Article of the Constitution i.e. Article 100.1, reads as follows:

> The Government provides the Parliament prior information about the deployment or the availability of the armed forces to maintain and promote the international legal order (Constitution of the Kingdom of the Netherlands, 2002, Article 100.1).

Another part of Article 100 refers to the role of the armed forces in humanitarian relief in the event of an armed conflict. The Constitution is supposed to cover this type of use of the armed forces as well. The second subtitle of this Article creates an exception to the rule of prior consultation, stating that 'urgent reasons might prevent prior information', in which case information is provided as soon as possible thereafter. Clearly, this is an escape clause, which any government might utilise in an emergency situation of a practical nature. The crux of Article 100 is the element of maintenance and promotion of the international legal order. NATO operations of a 'classical' nature as envisaged in the Cold War period (an attack on a NATO member state or NATO territory) are exempted and covered by a separate article which states that the government has supreme authority over the armed forces. This Article (97) does not mention parliament, although the parliament does have the right to approve or reject a formal declaration of war (Article 96). This is clearly an extremely remote possibility in present-day international politics, although some discussion emerged in the Kosovo campaign in 1999 as to whether or not NATO countries were to be considered to be 'at war' with the former Federal Republic of Yugoslavia.

Most political parties in parliament had two reasons for codifying the parliamentary approval of deploying troops abroad in the Constitution. First of all, participation in peacekeeping operations represents an important foreign policy and defence issue, the modern variety of the older war or peace situation, and simply by virtue of that, too important to be left to the government alone. Even more importantly, peacekeeping involves the deployment of Dutch servicemen in potentially risky operations. Parliamentarians could and would be asked questions by the public on the rationale for the mission, the assessment of risks, the goals and terms of the mandate, etc. Therefore parliamentarians might possibly be confronted – in an extreme case – with body-bags arriving back from the frontlines and citizens questioning the reasons for these Dutch soldiers dying. Parliamentarians will be held 'co-responsible' for these calamities as the parliament gave its consent to these extremely important decisions, which are ultimately about 'life and death'.

So, in the latter part of the 1990s, a doctrine of parliamentary sovereignty over peacekeeping decisions gradually evolved. Many debates were fought over the exact premises of this doctrine, and over the exact phrasing of government obligations. A compromise was reached on the rule of 'first parliamentary approval, then the actual, physical departure of troops', with some notable exceptions, such as, emergency operations and missions consisting of very few military personnel. In practice, the doctrine worked. A striking example was the debate in parliament on the Saturday before Christmas 2001 (having been recalled from recess), where Dutch participation in the International Security Assistance Force (ISAF) in Afghanistan and the US-led operation on international terrorism in Afghanistan 'Enduring Freedom', were discussed and finally approved. There are many other examples, such as the United Nations Preventive Deployment Force in the Former Yugoslav Republic of Macedonia (UNPREDEP), the United Nations Mission in Ethiopia and Eritrea (UNMEE), where the doctrine was successfully applied. After long and detailed debates, parliament gave its approval to participation in these operations, with a vote taken to ensure that at least a majority are in favour. In itself a majority is by the nature of the political process sufficient, but there is still a general desire to have a consensus or at least a sizeable majority. Military affairs in general and peacekeeping in particular, therefore, are considered as 'special' subjects, where the simple majority rule is not perceived to be entirely applicable.

Dutch Involvement in UNPROFOR 1992 - 1995

Prelude to the Safe Areas

The Netherlands jumped on the UNPROFOR bandwagon in an early phase, in 1992, when UNPROFOR I was set up for protecting the so-called safe areas in Bosnia. In military terms, and for various reasons, the Netherlands' government was not able to offer the UN a strong and large military contingent, in terms of the nature and number of troops. The first reason for this state of affairs is that the Netherlands Royal Armed Forces were in an almost continuous process of reorganisation after the enormous changes set in motion by the events of 1990. Secondly, the Netherlands' armed forces were heavily committed in other peace support operations, notably in Cambodia with over 1,000 troops and some 300 troops were assisting UNPROFOR already.

In the Dutch parliament large, if not unanimous, support existed for this participation, as well as for the deployment of a transport battalion of some 400 military to serve in a combined Dutch-Belgian battalion later in 1992. The parliament met frequently – usually in sessions of the Defence and Foreign Affairs standing committees, but on occasions also in plenary session – and intensely debated the deteriorating situation in the former Yugoslavia and the humanitarian disaster that was taking place. The atrocities in Bosnia got even more attention than the preceding ones in Vukovar and elsewhere. The images of concentration-type camps in Omarska reminded many of World War Two and shocked the nation. Many Dutch people had youthful memories of holidays in the formerly peaceful Yugoslavia. The rise of nationalism spurred by Slobodan Milosevic and the outbreak of hostilities in the imploding Federation in 1991 surprised many and confronted the Dutch with a war on the doorstep of 'civilised' Europe, just a two-hour flight away from the Netherlands. In the parliamentary debates, the call 'to do something' could be heard frequently. Many creative but sometimes also naive suggestions were voiced in those parliamentary debates, including the deployment of extremely large UN forces to enforce peace. Interestingly enough, spokespersons for the right-wing liberals and the Green Left to some extent made the same pleas for 'massive interventions'. A journalist from a centre left-wing daily paper, the *Volkskrant*, said she 'deplored the conversion of generals to pacifism' (NIOD, 2002, p. 878 and 784). The problem, however, was that nobody knew exactly what sort of peace was to be kept and how that should be done. The same parliamentarians were quick to criticise and reject proposals like the Vance/Owen Peace Plan and others – because these contained elements of rewarding and sealing ethnic cleansing, i.e. partition according to monolithic ethnic lines of division.

In 1991-1992, the government of the Netherlands basically faced two problems: the lesser problem was to react to far-reaching proposals coming from parliament and groups in society to do something such as the deployment of intervention forces. These options were, in the international reality, simply not available because of the lack of political will of the international community (i.e. the militarily relevant UN member states) to consider an outright military intervention in the former Yugoslavia to help end the war. The more acute problem was the limited availability of army troops for the smaller-scale operations launched by UNPROFOR. Only with great difficulty could two units of 200 and 400 men be made available.

Only in early 1994, after the reorganisation of the Army and the creation of the airmobile brigade for rapid reaction purposes, could Dutchbat be made available for service in the, as it turned out to be later, ill-fated enclaves.

The Call for Action

When one observes the many debates in the Dutch parliament on the former Yugoslavia in general and UNPROFOR in particular, one is struck by the almost constant opposition between the call for 'action' and the remedies offered. The word 'action' was, remarkably enough, used by both the spokesperson for the market-liberal party, VVD, in the first plenary debate on Yugoslavia on 21 November 1991 and by the representatives of the far (Green) left, wary as the latter were of military intervention, e.g. in the Gulf conflict (Everts, 2002). The broad political coalition between the (far) right and left was created by a shared feeling of anger, combined with a sense of powerlessness. For example, in a parliamentary debate, the spokesperson for the Green Left Party (Groen Links) stated that: 'It is absurd that we should accept that there is nobody who can stop or prevent this senseless bloodshed' (NIOD, 2002, p. 503). These were words, uttered after the dramas of Vukovar and Dubrovnik, but prior to the even bigger Bosnian tragedy. Still, that was exactly what would happen in the following years and this frustration constantly came back, voiced in different ways, in parliamentary debates. The fact that journalists sometimes joined the call for action by publishing pamphlets asking for intervention could also be considered remarkable. A broad consensus existed, both in politics as in society, that 'something has to be done' about Yugoslavia.

Powers of Parliament

As far as the formal powers and rights of parliament were concerned, in the first half of the 1990s – the relevant period for UNPROFOR – the customary legal doctrine indicating a need for the government to inform parliament before taking decisions on deployment still prevailed. Only later, as mentioned above, was the right of parliament to be consulted and to give prior consent established in the Constitution's text. In practice, however, no major decision on UNPROFOR and the deployment of Dutch troops was taken without parliament being informed beforehand. Formal voting, however, as developed later on with the change in the Constitution, did not take place in the UNPROFOR period 1992-1995. However, the opinion of the parliament was rather clear, despite many different questions asked and solutions suggested. In fact, all the parties represented in Parliament in 1993-1994, supported the UNPROFOR-decisions. Only the Socialist Party (SP), which until the elections in 1994 was not represented in parliament, spoke out against any Dutch participation in UNPROFOR (NIOD, 2002, p.1085). The Party claimed to be 'adamantly against the mission because military interventions would lead to an extension and escalation of conflicts'. That party has grown over the past years, which has further contributed to the lessening of consensus on peacekeeping issues in parliament, in addition to the Christian Democrat Party's (CDA) resistance to any participation in UNMEE.

In order to establish and secure a broad political consensus, ministers used various techniques, such as informal consultations with their party fellows in the parliamentary group. In the typical Dutch political culture of political debates being 'pre-cooked' and thoroughly prepared informally, this was a well established and working practice. In this way, ministers had advance warning about difficult questions in Parliament, and could be better prepared to answer them. In his memoirs, Former Defence Minister Relus ter Beek (Labour Party – PVDA) often refers to conversations with party friends in parliament which took place *'binnenskamers'* (behind closed doors) (Beek, 1996, p.200). The purpose of these informal and secret sessions between the Cabinet Minister and his party friends in Parliament was to pre-arrange parliamentary debates and its outcomes. Notably, just before the decisive parliamentary debate on dispatching Dutchbat to Srebrenica in November 1993, the Defence Minister and his party fellows in parliament convened informally behind closed doors in order to plan the parliamentary debate and its possible consequences (NIOD, 2002, p. 1083).

Also, close contacts between (high) officials of the Ministries of Foreign Affairs and Defence and MPs were not uncommon, especially to bring them up-to-date with the latest developments both on the ground in the former Yugoslavia and in the international arena, i.e. the WEU, the EU, NATO, OSCE and other international organisations. MPs were usually not privy to the deliberations in these international fora, and only received sketchy reports of these meetings. In addition, some MPs – usually those from the parties represented in government – received informal briefings and/or information from either officials and/or ministers about latest developments.

From Small Units to the Dutch Battalion

Gradually the emphasis shifted from the concept of humanitarian relief by UNPROFOR to a possible peace plan enforcement and/or implementation force. In the first phase of the war in Yugoslavia, sanctions were seen as one of the main tools, next to political pressure, to bring Serbia to reason. The Netherlands played its part in bringing these sanctions into effect through various modes (air, sea, land) with, for example, military means. This contribution was uncontroversial, despite involving all branches of the armed forces. Combat forces were, however, at that time, still not made available to UNPROFOR. Various political parties, and not only on the left (PVDA, D66, Groen Links), made pleas for using the Netherlands' combat forces. In the following months the thought of a more robust and sizeable Dutch contribution to UNPROFOR swiftly gained ground.

In May 1993, an important debate took place at a joint meeting of the Standing Committees on Defence and Foreign Affairs with the two ministers concerned. The discussion centred on the possibility of air strikes and the establishment of so-called 'safe areas'. Almost all MPs called on the Dutch government to make available military units – other than those already engaged with communications and transport – to either secure a peace settlement or at least alleviate the suffering of the population. This trend in the debate is an interesting example of what could be phrased the third core function of any parliament next to law-making and controlling the government: that of policy review and even policy-making. This might even be a striking feature of the Dutch parliamentary system in general. While other Western European parliaments have a tendency to limit their business somewhat more to controlling policies and notably budgets, in the Netherlands there is a trend towards parliament acting as a sort of 'co-government' by developing policy initiatives. Of course this was already possible in the area of legislation – the core business of any parliament – but, with the frequency and intensity of parliamentary debates increasing, the tendency for parliament to act as a sort of policy-maker was greatly increased.

In that same month of May 1993, parliament accepted an important motion, asking the Minister of Defence to prepare a new airmobile brigade for peacekeeping missions and more specifically to train and equip the battalions as soon as possible for deployment in an armoured operation in Bosnia. Later on, in June 1993, the UN Security Council accepted the famous Resolution 836 on safe areas and the European Council in June in Copenhagen explicitly and forcefully called on EU member states, including the Netherlands, to contribute troops to these safe areas. The gathering of troops went extremely slowly. For a force able to deter through strength, a number of 34,000 military was estimated, for a force able to deter through presence, a number of 7,600 was found to be sufficient. The weakness of the latter concept – despite the element of air strikes as an essential complement to protect the troops on the ground – was shown in Srebrenica some two years later. For all these reasons, pressure mounted, in political and official circles, for the Netherlands to contribute a fully-fledged airmobile battalion from the new brigade, i.e. Dutchbat.

On 7 September 1994, the Dutch Defence Minister Relus ter Beek offered United Nations Secretary-General (UNSG) Boutros Boutros-Ghali, a reinforced airmobile battalion of some 1,000 men. Boutros-Ghali was extremely pleased with this new offer which he called 'very good news'. In the preceding weeks, the defence minister had more or less convinced his chief military advisers that this was the way to go. Some of them had hesitations, but no one said flatly no. As Relus ter Beek writes in his memoirs, he also launched an effort – and a successful one – to 'win the Foreign and Prime Minister over to the idea'. As he writes, they were 'enthusiastic' (Beek, 1996, p. 193).

Parliament played a minor role in the decisions on the mandate, location, and type of forces. This limited role is somewhat in contrast with, as mentioned before, the 'co-governing' role of the Dutch parliament. The clear intention to contribute to a peacekeeping operation and the wish to involve the airmobile brigade were explicitly formulated by parliament, and in a way the government was tasked to implement this. The details of this, however, were left to the bureaucracy and the ministers. This phenomenon has to do with the various phases of decision-making on peacekeeping. Partly due to the traditional summer recess of parliament but also due to the rather unclear and very informal decision-making process in the government bureaucracy (surprisingly no discussions took place in the Cabinet about the Dutch offer), parliament was informed at a very late stage about the exact plans for deployment and its location. There was (and still is) a lot of ambiguity about the conditions attached to the Dutch offer. Although, the defence minister had made efforts in an earlier phase to avoid giving the impression that the Dutch offer was a 'blank cheque', in practice the way the offer was brought to the attention of the UN (Secretary-General), meant that the UN was able to employ the airmobile battalion for any use, be it the safe areas or the peace plan. By and large, the Dutch parliament agreed to this open-ended use, including the option of making blue helmet troops available for the safe areas, be it more for simply being present and by virtue of that deterring, than for effective protection. For this, the number of troops and the conditions for their operation were simply not sufficient. With the benefit of hindsight, former Defence Minister Relus ter Beek writes in his memoirs, that in his inner circle, including the two main military advisers, there was not much enthusiasm and that 'no one was keen to start this operation' (Beek, 1996, p. 195). He refers to 'great pressure in politics and in society', and that 'for parliament it was clear that the airmobile battalion had to go to Bosnia'.

On 12 November, the Dutch cabinet formally agreed to the deployment of a Dutch battalion, with merely general conditions like the single area of operations and a period of 18 months attached to it. Four days later, on 16 November, a debate took place in the Foreign and Defence Standing Committees of Parliament. In that debate, broad agreement between the parliamentary committee members and the cabinet was established, although the Labour Party (PVDA) asked for another committee meeting once the cabinet knew more about the exact location and tasks of Dutchbat. In a review of the 16 November parliamentary debate, the official Srebrenica-report by the Dutch Institute for War Documentation (NIOD, 2002, p.1084) notes, interestingly, that parliament was following rather than initiating and that the quality and intensity of the debate was limited, concentrating on details like the weapons and other material for the unit than on the broad question of whether the unit should be sent at all. The NIOD goes on to say that MPs were seldom militarily qualified, with one or two exceptions.

The parliamentary debates were closely scrutinised by the prime minister and deputy prime minister as well as the parliamentary group leaders and the chairmen of the political parties belonging to the government coalition. The leadership of both government coalition parties took care that party discipline remained intact. Party discipline was 'imposed' via the party networks in government, parliament and society. By means of informal consultations in telephone calls, lunch and dinner discussions, the political parties' networks secured strong support for the government's decisions and left little room for dissenting opinions from any MP belonging to the government coalition parties. Those MPs who put forward parliamentary questions, caused some 'irritation' with the defence minister and fellow-MPs, by making a formal reservation on the decision to participate with Dutchbat in the safe areas, because the exact location was at that time not fully known (NIOD, 2002, p. 1,084). In this context, parliamentarians refer to the culture at that time of consensus, habit and good sportsmanship not to raise (too many) questions and not to register reservations in these sort of debates (NIOD, 2002, p. 1,084).

Still doubts lingered in the MPs minds, albeit be it beneath the surface. Smaller parties like the two mainstream Christian ones, were traditionally reluctant to agree to send out troops, especially on risky missions like this one. The debate did not have a second stage. No plenary debate took place, no motions were tabled. The debate received little attention in the press, as it was superseded by more important affairs of domestic policies. The prevailing atmosphere was two-fold: satisfaction with the fact that the Netherlands was a 'front runner',[2] and an inclination to decide by consensus, i.e. to get support from the population at large and the relatives and friends of the military due for missions abroad in particular.

---

2   In the words of foreign minister (NIOD, 2002, pp. 954 and 995-998).

Doubts were not felt to be useful in a debate on a peacekeeping mission, precisely because of these arguments.

The Deployment of Dutchbat

Somewhat later, on 21 December 1993, the Dutch parliament was unexpectedly informed by the deputy Defence Minister Ton Frinking (NIOD, 2002, p.1120) about the Safe Area in Srebrenica as the definitive location for the Dutch UNPROFOR troops as well as their armaments (.50 mm machine guns). In a special procedure, the then Chief of the Defence Staff, General Arie van der Vlis, was allowed to speak in parliament on 1 February 1994. Normally, only ministers speak. Very rarely officials were questioned in hearings, which changed later on as one of the results of the commotion about Srebrenica, and the resulting changes in the parliamentary procedure. Not many questions were asked during the committee debates, neither on the location, nor on the equipment. In a much-quoted phrase, military leaders were said to believe that stationing Dutchbat in Srebrenica (or the adjacent Zepa) enclave was an 'honourable, not easy but feasible' mission (Beek, 1996, pp. 202-203).

In the run-up to the deployment, resistance was felt, even at that stage, from the Bosnian Serb Army (VRS), which prevented an early reconnaissance-mission into the area to prepare for full deployment later. These aspects were discussed internally in the bureaucracy and with the UN. In the parliamentary debate just before Christmas 1993, the defence minister was ambiguous about the final location and destination of Dutchbat which could well have been (initially or definitively) Central Bosnia instead of East Bosnia (Srebrenica). The parliamentary debate did not go very deep (NIOD, 2002, p.1143). The vulnerability of (Dutch) blue helmets vis-à-vis the Bosnian Serb Army (VRS) was only vaguely touched upon, but this element was not expanded upon. More discussion took place about the equipment in general and the weaponry in particular. Questions were asked, both during the debate on 21 December and the following debate on 1 February (1994), about the reasons for the use of the relatively light .50 machine guns instead of the .25mm canons. More specifically, the Market-Liberal Party (VVD) spokesman, made a plea for the .25mm canon, in view of the possibility of 'robust' operations (NIOD, 2002, p. 1128). The Labour Party (PVDA) spokesman asked whether the choice of .50mm instead of .25 mm was caused by Serb pressure. This was explicitly denied by the defence minister – although what was probably not known to MPs, was that the Dutch MoD had used that same argument (risk of escalation, possible problems with the VRS) along with more operational arguments not to choose the .25mm. In the parliamentary debate – again with the benefit of hindsight – the important question of whether the safe areas really were defendable, was not posed as such. Hardly anyone really believed in the possibility of outright Serb aggression towards the enclave(s), and if anyone did, reliance on air support and air strikes served to ease unrest about it.

The main focus of the debates was on the possible evacuation and self-defence plans for Dutchbat, again not unsurprisingly, because traditionally this was an important issue in peacekeeping. The doubts about the air weapon were widely circulating in military circles, and sometimes brought out into the open. The Dutch Chief of Defence Staff voiced serious doubts in an interview in a leading Dutch newspaper in November 1993 about the air weapon ever being used in Bosnia in order not to endanger the UNPROFOR troops or the humanitarian relief work and the lack of concrete proof, i.e. the 'smoking gun' which would trigger either close air support or air strikes. These observations later turned out to be true, but did not serve to block deployment because of the 'security guarantees' given by the UN in general and the UNSG in particular during his visit in mid-January 1994 to the Netherlands. In official circles, doubts existed about the nature of these guarantees on the availability of air power in case fighting erupted, and (self-) defence became necessary in circumstances when a deliberate attack on UNPROFOR was being carried out. Complications in this connexion were the dual key procedure for using air strikes, in view of the involvement of both NATO (to actually carry out air strikes) and the UN, and the role of the Security Council as a possible slowing down factor. The assurances supplied by Boutros Boutros-Ghali on delegation of the authority to invoke air power did not reassure the Netherlands side completely (NIOD 2002, pp.1139-1146). In the parliamentary debate on 1 February, many MPs raised this issue, but seemed to be content with the letter from the Netherlands government of 26 January 1994, and the reference by the government during the debate to the letter of the UNSG dated 28 January, in which he notified the Security Council that the authority to invoke air power was delegated to the United Nations Secretary General's Special Representative, Yasushi Akashi (NIOD 2002, p.1143). Later, during interviews with MPs and the parliamentary commission of inquiry on peacekeeping, some of them, when confronted with the apparent failure of the air weapon during the fall of the enclave, referred to the 'trust' they had in the Netherlands government when it pointed to the assured supply by the highest authority of the UN of air power in case of an attack on UNPROFOR. The different nature of close air support and air strikes, and the possible complications caused by the privileged position of the three Western member states of the Security Council and leading NATO member states, the US, UK and France, were somewhat overlooked. That said, here as well, the benefit of hindsight plays a role. In the aforementioned debate on 1 February, even critical parliamentarians, speaking about air power, said: 'It does not make much sense to constantly speculate about things which are not very likely to happen' (cited in NIOD, 2002, p.1143).

In Search of a Way Out

Between the decision to deploy Dutchbat in the Srebrenica enclave, the actual deployment itself (in February/March 1994, with one company not in Srebrenica, but close to the airfield of Tuzla) and the dramatic fall of the enclave in July 1995, things developed in a difficult way. Before the deployment, the terrible attack on a Sarajevo market on 5 February 1994, caused international indignation. Ultimatums were issued, but air power in the end was not used because, among other reasons, of the great political difficulties both in the EU itself and in the Security Council, with an opposing Russian Federation. The vulnerability of UN personnel on the ground was one of the arguments used, not without logic as later developments – the taking of UN personnel hostage – proved. After heavy losses of life, the Sarajevo crisis was 'solved' because the Serbs under Russian pressure agreed to an exclusion zone. In a little noted remark in March 1994, the US Secretary of Defence William Perry said that airpower alone would not be sufficient to protect the safe areas because this would not counter the Serb artillery and infantry (NIOD, 2002, p. 1149). William Perry, turned out to be completely right one and a half years later.

The next crisis, a Serb attack on the enclave of Gorazde, provoked a limited use of airpower by NATO F-16 and F-18 US aircraft. A stronger air attack by NATO was stopped by the UN. Criticism from various UN member states demanding more pressure on the Serbs from the UN Secretary-General's Special Representative Yasushi Akashi was voiced. Some influence in Dutch politics was felt. A visit by the Dutch defence minister to Sarajevo and Srebrenica was cancelled. The Dutch foreign minister expressed great concern for the lack of adequate reaction by 'us' to the Gorazde events. But in the Netherlands the parliamentary elections of 17 May 1994 prevailed.

A government of PVDA, VVD and D66 (Labour, Market and Social Liberals, excluding for the first time ever the Christian Democrats) was formed in late August 1994. In these months, basically the period leading up to the fall of the enclave in July 1995, the newly-elected Dutch parliament was much preoccupied with Srebrenica, but more with the dire conditions for the Dutch troops than with the contingency of an all-out attack. The attention paid to the operation lessened because many in the Netherlands – including MPs – saw peacekeeping operations in general and UNPROFOR in particular, once they were launched and once Dutch troops were participating on the ground, as a running, operational affair for which the organisation, in this case the UN, was mainly responsible. In parliament an informal agreement existed to be consulted in the case of 'major changes' in either the mandate or the location of the mission. For the rest, MPs were, both in debates and in many more or less informal contacts with parents, friends, etc of the soldiers preoccupied with things like the personal welfare of soldiers, the delivery of mail, the facilities for telephone contacts, the food, welfare and entertainment arrangements, availability of social workers, spiritual advice from the clergy, etc.

Later on, in autumn/winter 1994, attention shifted to the options for evacuation of Dutchbat. The new Minister of Defence, Joris Voorhoeve, was very much aware of the complexity of the situation in Srebrenica. Soon he had established that a proper strategy to defend Srebrenica was more or less impossible. Scenarios for evacuation were drawn up. In doing so, it became more and more evident that Dutchbat was 'trapped' between Muslims (who would not be keen to see UNPROFOR disappear) and the Serbs. The following months showed, at least in the internal Dutch political context, a great measure of attention to the options for withdrawal of Dutchbat from UNPROFOR. In parliament, the call for an early withdrawal of Dutchbat became louder. This had less to do with fears about body bags containing Dutch soldiers arriving in the Netherlands – although there were incidental casualties, usually not fatal ones – than with a growing feeling that 'enough is enough'. The dire conditions for Dutchbat with supplies blocked by the Serbs and almost no way of getting in and out were perhaps the most important driving force. And of course, the generally worsening situation in Bosnia and the total stalemate in the peace process were responsible for a feeling of frustration which strongly contrasted with the high (moral) expectations in 1993. The question was how to withdraw the Dutchbat in an orderly fashion, because even the strong proponents in parliament of withdrawal (like the VVD and CDA) felt somehow responsible for the fate of the Bosnian population. It was extremely difficult to find a (NATO) partner for Dutchbat. More successful was the search for a successor to the entire NL battalion: Ukraine was found ready to take over Dutchbat's task. The Ukrainians were already in the neighbourhood, and – probably even more important – badly needed the extra dollars connected to UN peacekeeping.

The Drama of Srebrenica

However, it was never to get that far. With the UN agreeing to the principle of rotation, but not acting upon it, the Dutch defence minister went out on a search mission, which ended successfully with the Ukrainian contingents, already present in Gorazde, Zepa and Croatia. With this last mission ending in spring 1995, the possibility existed of asking Ukraine – with the promise of increased Dutch assistance to the Ukrainian armed forces – to accept this totally unattractive task. The preparations for the actual replacement of Dutchbat by the Ukrainian battalion were enormously complex on all sides, involving the UN (which probably preferred the Dutch staying on to their replacement by the lower quality Ukrainian soldiers), Ukraine, which made a lot of requests, including on the finances and the material to be left in Croatia, and the Netherlands itself. The government had, in view of the uncertainty of an early switch to Ukraine, continued preparations for replacing Dutchbat by new Dutch troops. This fact might have prompted the UN and Ukraine to act slowly. Parliament was informed at the end of June 1995, just before the traditional summer recess, about the impending takeover, and was – knowing that very little was settled at that date – content that at least the expectation existed that Dutchbat after a long and extremely difficult period would go home. The questions of when and of who would succeed it remained unsolved. As is well known, the fall of Srebrenica rendered these questions irrelevant.

In this last part, the focus is on the aspect of parliamentary involvement. The expression parliamentary control does not seem adequate in this regard, especially in the days of the fall itself. Many important developments took place in the period from May to July 1995 which largely escaped parliament: violence flared up in Bosnia, from both sides (the ABiH and the VRS), hostage-taking of UNPROFOR soldiers occurred (the famous pictures of a Canadian soldier tied to a lamppost), and signals were received about an impending Serb attack on Srebrenica. This is, however, not the place to go into great detail about these events. They have been documented in many reports in the meantime, including the UN evaluation report, the French parliamentary enquiry report and the already mentioned NIOD report in the Netherlands (United Nations, 1999b; Boyer, et al., 2003; NIOD, 2002). The apparent lack of knowledge of MPs of preceding events might be explained not only by the daily shifting perspective and sometimes contradictory (and either not reliable or military secret) information, but unlike in the later Kosovo campaign, there was no standing procedure to inform parliament by way of confidential letters or confidential briefings. During the deployment of Dutchbat, this was done only in one or two cases, the fall of the enclave excepted. The Dutch defence minister was diligent in observing the rules of military secrecy and would share some of his concerns at most with individual MPs. This did not lead to any formal debate in parliament at the end of June, when preparations for the attack – also using the benefit of hindsight – were more and more visible. The role of the media should also be mentioned in this respect. Strangely enough the violence that flared up at the beginning of July 1995 in Srebrenica (with the start of the attack on 6 July) did not get much attention, compared to other events in Bosnia.

As the days went by, it became clear that the Serbs basically wanted to take the whole enclave, and that Dutchbat was not in a position to do much to thwart that intent. The limited airpower – too little and too late – did not change much. The enclave fell on 11 July, and the population tried to find refuge in the Potocari UNPROFOR-base. The ensuing drama of enormous proportions is well known. Many thousands of young and older men were either killed during their flight to Tuzla or on the spot. The biggest humanitarian drama in Europe since World War Two was developing. In the meantime, the Dutch government informed parliament in the morning of 12 July, the day after the fall, at a secret meeting down in the defence ministry bunker where the Crisis Staff was located. That same afternoon, an open meeting took place between the parliamentary committees and the ministers. As much was still in flux and the humanitarian drama was only beginning to unfold, this debate was stocktaking and exchanging information at best. In the beginning, parliamentarians biggest concern was that Dutchbat, which was under direct attack and in fact was kept hostage after the fall, would share the fate of the local population. Here again, the benefit of hindsight plays a role in reviewing this period. It is arguable that parliament should have done more, e.g. in pressurising the government to try to do more to secure the lives of the thousands of male refugees, and later on to investigate what really happened in the enclave. The question whether that had meant anything in terms of changing the conduct of the war can almost certainly be replied to in a negative way. The same more or less applies to the Dutch government and Dutchbat itself. As has been concluded in both the report of the NIOD and the Parliamentary Inquiry of January 2003, much went wrong, but there is no objective guilt to be found in the actions or lack of actions of the Dutch and UN authorities. Mistakes have been made, and more could have been done to try to save individual lives, but the basic guilt is for the Bosnian Serbs and the Belgrade and Pale leadership, and in addition to the concept of weakly-defended secure areas which were meant to act as a tripwire and not as a real defence.

In any case, as far as the Netherlands is concerned, things have taken too much time. The handling of Srebrenica has been piecemeal. In the period between July 1995 and now (July 2003), the Dutch parliament has spent numerous debates on various aspects of this drama. Only in 1997 did the Netherlands government commission the 'NIOD' to research the events leading up to and during the fall. This was done (and agreed upon informally by the government parties and the government) to prevent a full parliamentary Inquiry and to calm down the often heated debates about various separate aspects of Srebrenica, including the behaviour of individual members of the Dutch military. The widely-acclaimed report of more than 3,000 pages (without attachments) took a long time to produce, but was published in April 2002, and led to the fall of the government. The reasons for the fall being – in the words of then Prime Minister Wim Kok – that at least some politicians had to take the responsibility (i.e. something different than guilt) for the events of July 1995, the international community being considered as a sort of artefact. The Srebrenica affair was one of the last subjects to be handled by the outgoing parliament. Finally, in the summer of July 2002, the long-awaited parliamentary inquiry was set up. The inquiry did not reveal new insights, but more or less cleared Dutchbat, and pointed the finger at various spots in the consideration and preparation of the safe area concept. Some years before, the UN had already concluded that soft power, i.e. blue helmets, would no longer be used in dangerous and complex operations, but only in situations where a peace agreement was subscribed to and was likely to hold.

One thing is sure: for the Dutch people and those politicians responsible, this has been a painful period of efforts to find the truth (or '*waarheidsvinding*' in Dutch), and probably in keeping with a deep-rooted feeling of at least responsibility for and for some maybe even some feelings of guilt about the events in Srebrenica. The outgoing Prime Minister Wim Kok, in one of the last weeks of his office, in July 2002, paid a visit to Srebrenica, where he could hardly hide his tears. This would be hardly conceivable in any other country, but is, in turn, in keeping with a deep and long-standing tradition of Calvinism and strongly-felt idealism and engagement in international affairs in the Netherlands.

Conclusions

The involvement of the Dutch parliament with the Dutch military participation in UNPROFOR has been deep and frequent on the one hand, and superficial on the other. After the fall of the enclave, many recommendations were drawn up and brought into effect to improve the quality of the debate and control. Detailed rules were laid down in a new 'Toetsingskader' or White Paper (1995) on procedures for approval of peacekeeping operations.

Looking back, it might be concluded that the decision to deploy Dutch troops in Srebrenica was taken with a mixture of naivety and moral responsibility. Naivety because of the extreme scenarios which were possible and in a way unavoidable, given the set-up of the safe areas concept, guided by the principle of 'deterrence by presence' instead of 'deterrence by force'. Moral responsibility because many, if not most, people in the Netherlands felt an urgent need 'to do something' in the extremely distressing situation in former Yugoslavia. In this process, Dutch civil society, from churches to refugee organisations as well as journalists appealed for intervention. No large-scale demonstrations, but a debate in intellectual circles, the informed public and large parts of the press, inflamed by the 'CNN factor'. Parliamentarians, being the representatives of the people, and with antennae for the prevailing climate in society of engagement with the war in Yugoslavia, quickly followed the dominant mood in society. Electoral motives did not play a role, because politics seemed almost completely part of the prevailing consensus in public opinion which tilted strongly towards involvement in Yugoslavia. Party congresses called for action, and a groundswell for early action and relief for the innocent population swept over the Netherlands. The possibility was hardly mentioned that Dutch soldiers could be killed during this operation, which was put forward by the top military commanders as 'honourable, not simple, but feasible' (Beek, 1996, p. 203).

The role of Parliament in this process was extremely critical and difficult. The pressure from society was immense. Party members were adamant that their MPs had to call for international action with a prominent Dutch role. The Netherlands were seen, both externally and internally, as a country with a long-standing record in peacekeeping. It was unthinkable that the country would let the international community down at this crucial stage. The government on occasions thought about different options and a more modest role, but by and large was following the same lines as the overwhelming majority of parliament. During the European Council of June 1993, the Dutch prime minister was at the forefront of EU calls for a prominent role for EU member states in the implementation of the safe areas concept. The Dutch foreign minister was a respected professor of international law with a strong commitment to the UN. The Dutch defence minister was proud to present the reorganised and modernised Dutch armed forces as fit for new, challenging tasks in the new and promising area of peacekeeping. Parliament not only followed suit but explicitly called for deployment of the new Dutchbat, the symbol of the new Dutch army. Many of the decisions were informally pre-cooked by a typical Dutch mixture of informal political gatherings and processes, and a brief and not too sharp public debate to seal the deals which were more or less made behind closed doors. Opposition and too extreme questions were not appreciated on a subject, which seemed to require an automatic consensus. Warnings by the military were listened to, but they did not really change the contents and pace of the debates leading to the participation of Dutchbat. MPs did not see themselves as military experts, and neither did they formally call on those experts, e.g. to give public testimony in parliament, as in later peace support operations (e.g. UNMEE operation).

The intentions to do good and to contribute to peacekeeping and humanitarian relief were abundantly clear. As a middle-power, the Netherlands did not bear the responsibility that other major powers like the US, the UK, France, Germany and the Soviet Union had for advancing a peace settlement. The Netherlands was not a member of the Contact Group, although the Netherlands' government had wanted to become a member.

The international organisations did their work with great energy, but with rather unclear concepts of how to forge a peace in Yugoslavia, but they were all busy in their own way. The Netherlands as an active member in the frontline of many initiatives, was rather offended not to be included in the Contact Group, perhaps the most important international coordinating body on operations in Bosnia, at least in operational terms. In the end, the international community in 1995 – directed by the US – just had enough of it. Bombs and an imposed peace (Dayton) did the rest as we know.

In this context, the Dutch parliament, driven by the need to be humanitarian and to maintain consensus, tried as much as possible to at least follow the government which, in turn, was not in a much more privileged position. 'Muddling through' was the watchword. Questions were asked about the viability of ideas and concepts, but the overriding idea was that some sort of humanitarian intervention and protection had to be given. The instruments were limited and unexpectedly failed at the very end. But at least discussions took place on these essential matters of life and death of the people of Yugoslavia, and quite possibly also of the Dutch military. The few but tragic losses of life on the Dutch side, showed that these were no hollow words. Compared with many West European neighbours, the Dutch parliament was not the worst in terms of control, or efforts toward it. However, very much has changed and improved. The deeply sobering impact of the Srebrenica events has had a lasting effect on the way parliamentary debate has been and will be organised. The famous words 'lessons learned' were applicable, and the UNPROFOR experience has meant a watershed in many ways in Dutch politics in general and on peacekeeping in particular. The will to be the number one participant in peacekeeping, has given way to a sober review of the pros and cons of participation as parliamentary debate. This, at least, is a small positive aside to the drama of Srebrenica.

Chapter 6

The Public Inquiry into the Canadian Peace Mission in Somalia

Donna Winslow and Christ Klep

Introduction

In December 1992, the Canadian Airborne Regiment Battle Group (CARBG) was deployed to Somalia as part of a coalition force (Unified Task Force, UNITAF) led by the United States. The core of the battle group consisted of the Canadian Airborne Regiment (CAR), augmented by a number of armoured and service units. On the night of 16-17 March 1993, near the village of Belet Huen, soldiers from the Canadian Airborne Regiment beat and tortured a bound 16-year-old Somali youth, Shidane Arone.[1] About two weeks before, on 4 March, soldiers from the same regiment had killed a suspected Somali thief and had seriously wounded another.

The consequences of the incidents have been far-reaching not only for the Airborne Regiment, but also for the Canadian Forces (CF) as a whole. The investigations, media coverage and political debate that followed shook the Canadian military establishment to its core. For a middle-range country like Canada, peace operations represent an inherent aspect of foreign policy and national character, which is doing good and helping others. Thus when events overseas took a sour turn in Somalia it was not only the reputation of the army that was at stake; it was also a question of national pride. Public reaction led to the eventual disbanding of the Canadian Airborne Regiment in March 1995 and the creation in that same year of a government-sponsored public inquiry: the Commission of Inquiry into the Deployment of Canadian Forces to Somalia. As we will see, the Inquiry was eventually truncated just as it was beginning to examine the deadly incidents in Somalia and possible attempts at cover-up within the Canadian Forces and the Department of National Defence (DND). What the Inquiry did expose, however, were not only flaws, inconsistencies and weaknesses in the military organisation and leadership, but also the many problems faced by parliament with regard to civil control of the armed forces. After a brief description

---

1   It is important to note that Canadians were not the only ones involved in serious human rights abuses in Somalia. Belgian and Italian paratroopers were also accused and scrutinised by inquiries in their own lands. See Omaar and De Waal, 1993.

of the pertinent events in Somalia and the initial reactions of the military, media and government, our attention will turn to the Somalia Inquiry and the role of parliament.

At this point, some introductory remarks about the Canadian political system will help clarify the actions of the Liberal government which came to power in October 1993, just as the Somalia affair was taking off. In Canada's Westminster-type parliamentary system, the cabinet has traditionally held a tight grip on the executive aspects of government. Although the concept of ministerial responsibility is widely acknowledged, it may be said that the cabinet dictates executive policies, with little interference from parliament. In other words, the executive government is notionally responsible to parliament, but when party discipline is strong, as it is in Canada, checks on the use of executive power diminish because governments are formed from parliamentary majorities.

In this respect, Canada has often been described as an 'elected dictatorship'. In fact, several political scientists have adopted the position that cabinet power (and prime ministerial power itself) has only been enhanced in the last decades vis-à-vis parliament (Savoie, 1999).[2] Experts have also pointed to the fairly uninspired record of parliament as the civil authority and overseer in matters of national defence.

The basic reason behind this weak oversight lies in a distinct civil-military gap in parliament. This gap consists of elements such as a lack of concern over specific defence-related events, habit, weak parliamentary structures, partisan politics and the 'distance' between parliamentarians and the Ottawa Defence bureaucracy (Bland, 2000-2001, pp. 35-43). MPs have often remarked that they have neither the information nor the resources and expertise to monitor and debate defence policy adequately, whether generally or with regard to specific operations.[3] Defence specialists in parliament are at times prisoners to the defence minister's agenda, with little freedom to develop strong non-partisan policy positions. Defence committees lack the resources in personnel to research deeply into the many issues they consider, and are often overly dependent on government experts.

The civil-military gap in parliament is mirrored in Canadian society itself. Although parliamentarians often referred to public opinion as an important factor in the Somalia debate – and the Canadian public appeared genuinely shocked by the incidents and revelations about the Canadian military – it showed little interest in the Somalia affair as a whole and in its implications for Canadian defence policy. Many authors have pointed to the comparatively low political and media value of defence issues in Canada. There are several reasons for this. Canadians perceive no immediate military or political threat to their territory. Indeed, the most recent invasion of Canada was during the 19th century. Also, Canadians do not have the military tradition that many other countries have and the concept of

---

2   The description 'elected dictatorship' was often used since the early 1970s, for instance by Simeon, 1972. More recently, Docherty, 1997, notes that the dominance of parliament by the executive is more pronounced in Canada than elsewhere, in good part due to the relative inexperience of MPs as a result of high turnover at election time.

3   Commission of Inquiry into the Deployment of Canadian Forces to Somalia, 1997a.

military subordination to civil authority is so ingrained in Canada that it stands unchallenged. This all fits in nicely with a long tradition of 'Pearsonian' peacekeeping (Kenny, 1998; Morton, 1999). Obviously, the Canadian public was still drawn to the 'human interest' side of the Somalia affair: the stories of individual violence, racism, cover-up and deceit. But the un-military (though not necessarily pacifistic) attitude translates into a lack of interest in the broader issues of defence policy and the future of the Canadian Forces.

In other words, parliamentary control and public interest with regard to defence issues appear to be weak in the Canadian political system. In the Somalia case, this translated into a struggle not so much between government and parliament (assisted by public opinion), but between government and the independent and energetic Commission of Inquiry into the Deployment of Canadian Forces to Somalia.

The first part of the chapter describes briefly the main events in Somalia in 1992-1993, leading to the death of Shidane Arone. Afterwards, the public reaction to and the media coverage of the scandal are analysed. The chapter continues to examine the independent Commission of Inquiry, which the government initiated after strong pressure from parliament, the media and the public. The two latter parts discuss how the Canadian government and parliament dealt with the official inquiry. The chapter ends with some general assessments and conclusions related to official inquiries and the role of parliaments.

The Somalia Deployment

In April 1992, the Security Council of the United Nations sought international help to restore some semblance of law and order in Somalia and feed its starving citizens. Canadians were shocked by media images of the impending humanitarian crisis in Somalia and many felt that their country should act quickly to prevent further misery. However, it would seem that the decision to sent troops was, in the end, based more on political imperatives and the desire to secure a high-profile mission for the army rather than a clear evaluation of the tasks at hand and the Canadian Airborne Regiment's state of operational readiness, training and equipment for the job. High-level officials appeared to be responding to media opinion: that Canada had played a minor role in the First Gulf War (1990-1992) away from significant action.

In the original plans, Canada was to have participated in Operation 'Cordon', a traditional Chapter VI peacekeeping-type mission in support of humanitarian relief distribution in the northern area of Somalia around Bossasso. This was changed only weeks before the December 1992 departure to participation in a Chapter VII enforcement mission, the US-led Unified Task Force. The concern with securing a high-profile mission led the Canadian in-theatre commander to reassign the Canadian Airborne Regiment Battle Group to security in the Belet Huen Humanitarian Relief Sector. Thus Canadian troops were now being sent to a much more volatile area for which they had not been trained. The Belet Huen region was known for its extortion, banditry and intricate clan rivalries.

By the time the events of March 1993 rolled around, the Canadian Airborne Regiment Battle Group had been in-theatre for about three months and was subject to severe stress from the harsh living conditions (heat, hard rations, illness and dehydration, limited communication with families back home, etc). Infiltration by Somalis into the camps and nuisance thefts only added to the tension and the troops' resentment of the local population.[4] To counter the thefts, the Airborne Regiment's commander stated that deadly force was permitted against any Somali caught inside the compounds. On 4 March 1993 members of the Reconnaissance Platoon shot two unarmed Somalis in the back, killing one. On the morning of 16 March the commanding officer of one of the Regiment's companies gave instructions 'to capture and abuse prisoners'. At about 9 o'clock that evening the unarmed Shidane Arone was captured and detained in a bunker, where he was blindfolded, severely beaten and burned with cigarettes. The Canadian soldiers involved in the beating took 'trophy photos' of themselves with the Somali detainee. Shortly after midnight Shidane Arone died. It is believed there were members of the Battle Group, including officers, who were in or around the bunker that night and who did nothing to stop or report it. Military police were not called in until 19 March 1993. Shortly afterwards, the two Canadian soldiers most involved in the beating of Shidane Arone were arrested. One of them attempted suicide while in detention. He suffered brain damage from this attempt and was judged unfit to stand trial. By 1 April 1993, military police investigators had arrested several others.

Public Reactions to 'The Events' and Official Investigations

As media coverage of the events in Somalia took off in April 1994, a distinct pattern soon emerged. Until then, the Canadian media had been relatively uninterested in military matters in general and the Somalia operations in particular. But now journalists reacted strongly to what was perceived to be the government and military downplaying the Somalia events. This caused the media to be even more suspicious and the military and defence officials to be even more tight-lipped. In the eyes of the media, the amount of evidence lost – e.g. misplaced documents – could simply not be explained away by bad luck or mere coincidence. In many cases, this feeling translated into press stereotyping of the military, and, in extreme cases, into vicious attacks on its credibility, professionalism and integrity.

---

4 Some Somali detainees were kept in the sun, bound and blindfolded, with signs over their heads labelling them as thieves. The Officer Commanding 2 Commando (Major Anthony Seward) wrote: 'Just now I am in the Command post. Five Somali teenagers have been caught stealing from Service Commando. They have been passed to me for security and transfer to the Somali police. The troops are, however, taking advantage of the situation to put on a demonstration. They're pretending that their intentions are to cut off the hands of these kids with machetes. It sounds awful, but if you were sitting here, you'd be laughing too. Soldier humour is infectious', Major Anthony Seward in a letter to his wife, 1993, cited in Commission of Inquiry into the Deployment of Canadian Forces to Somalia, 1997b, Vol. 1, p. 291.

There was also a strong public reaction to the disturbing events of March 1993. In particular, the trophy photographs of a bloodied and beaten Shidane Arone and later home videos of repugnant 'hazing' rituals – involving racist remarks, homo-erotic behaviour, human excrement and vomit – within the Airborne Regiment appalled Canadians. Publications began raising serious concerns about the Department of Defence's ability to screen and prepare personnel for peace operations.[5] Many people felt this was indeed 'Canada's national shame,' not least because of the good reputation and proud heritage of the armed forces. One editorial comment in *The Toronto Star* newspaper read: 'These are painful but necessary questions [about the Somalia affair, ed.] that must be answered in the name of all our peacekeepers whose unceasing discipline and dignity have done Canada proud for so long' (Toronto Star, 1994).[6]

Once the Somalia crisis had started to escalate, the Ministry of National Defence and the Canadian Forces had little choice but to react by ordering their own investigations into what had happened. Thus began a long series of investigations at ever-higher military and political levels and of ever-increasing scope. First, shortly after the events, the units themselves initiated investigations and debriefings whilst still in theatre. As mentioned before, a number of Airborne soldiers were arrested for their role in the torture. But these efforts were considered too limited and only strengthened the belief among the media and the public that the military was attempting to keep a lid on the facts.

While the Canadian Airborne Regiment Battle Group was still in Somalia, the Chief of Defence convened a military Board of Inquiry under the direction of a Major-General. Because there were military police investigations going on at that time, this inquiry was unable to investigate the death of Shidane Arone itself. The absence of 'independent' outside investigators further aroused suspicion. The Board of Inquiry released its report in July 1993. It found that discipline had broken down in the Airborne Regiment and that proper training had been lacking in preparing the unit for the mission in Somalia.

However, what was more disturbing were the things that the Board of Inquiry did *not* find lacking. For example, it concluded that commanders had taken reasonable steps to screen out unfit and undesirable personnel from the mission, even though there were one or two white supremacists under investigation in the Canadian Airborne Regiment. The inquiry did not find any systemic problems of racism. Use of derogatory words for Somalis such as 'nignog', 'raghead',

---

5   For example, information came out that a member of the Airborne Regiment – and close friend of one of the soldiers involved in the Arone beating – was a member of a white supremacy group (see Kinsella, 1994). Kinsella devoted a chapter – entitled 'Matt MacKay's Youthful Folly' – on the soldier involved, Matt MacKay, who first became publicly known on 13 September 1992 when the *Winnipeg Sun* published an exposé on white supremacy in Winnipeg. The article included a photo of MacKay giving a fascist salute.

6   During the court martial against 2 Commando's commanding officer, Major Anthony Seward, military prosecutors remarked: 'He [Seward, ed.] has blemished 40 years of exemplary service by members of the Canadian Forces in the conduct of United Nations peacekeeping', quoted in Vancouver Sun, 1994.

'gimmies' and 'smufties' were considered to be 'inappropriate' but not racist. In fact, the Board of Inquiry found that the Canadian soldiers in Somalia had shown remarkable overall tolerance and professionalism (Board of Inquiry, 1993).

On 14 March 1994, one year after the death of Shidane Arone, a military tribunal found one of the Airborne soldiers guilty of manslaughter. He was sentenced to five years in prison and was discharged from the army with disgrace. As mentioned earlier, the other soldier suspected of the beating of Shidane Arone was not fit to stand trial after his suicide attempt. The other members of the Canadian Airborne Regiment involved were either acquitted or found guilty of negligent performance of duty and sentenced to detention and reduction in rank. Although charges were brought against the regiment's commanding officer for negligent performance of duty twice, he was acquitted. No person above the rank of Lieutenant-Colonel was ever charged. These outcomes were considered unacceptable by the public and the political storm continued to rage. Both media and parliament were now calling for an independent inquiry.

The Commission of Inquiry

In Canada the main political effort to uncover the truth of what had happened in Somalia was the government-sponsored independent Commission of Inquiry into the Deployment of Canadian Forces to Somalia, by far the largest investigation of the Canadian military ever. To many observers, parliament would have been the primary institution to conduct such a wide-ranging and politically volatile investigation. However, in Canada the tradition is to hold a 'Royal Commission' of inquiry with wide-ranging investigative powers. These Royal Commissions have a long history in Canada. The first dates from 1870 and concerned itself with water communications and trade with the United States (Royal Commission, 1870).

The government often appoints these Royal Commissions (in recent years the name Public Inquiries has become more commonplace) to examine matters of public concern, most often a specific, contentious and protracted national problem. A good example is the Royal Commission on Aboriginal Peoples, which started work in August 1992. It focused on the controversial issue of the position of the 'First Nations', the aboriginal peoples of Canada. The commission heard from many individuals and organisations across the country and offered a host of recommendations on issues like education and health care in its report, which was published in 1996. The government reacted by presenting new and expanded aboriginal programmes.

Charlotte Ku (see her chapter for more information) identifies three categories of techniques for parliamentary oversight of military operations under international auspices: legislative authorisation, political consensus and inquiries (including parliamentary question periods). It is not easy to class Canadian Royal Commissions of inquiry under one of these three headings. Even though Royal Commissions are independent public inquiries, power over them lies in the cabinet and not in parliament.[7] Details and revelations from these inquiries – often broadcast live on public television – would usually be debated in parliament within days or even hours, including tough questions being asked and calls for resignation. But the real power over the inquiries ultimately resides in the cabinet. It is a cabinet decision ('Order-in-Council') which begins, ends or changes the mandate of an inquiry. The inquiry commissions are appointed by cabinet under the Inquiries Act and report their findings to cabinet and the prime minister for appropriate action.[8]

Still, the core of any Royal Commission's work lies in its independence and objectivity. This is the foundation for the prestige that surrounds them and for the seriousness with which the public views their undertakings, as compared to other investigative institutions. This prestige is enhanced by the commission members, who are usually eminent people in their fields. In the case of the Somalia Inquiry, three commissioners were appointed (two judges and one distinguished journalist), assisted by a large staff of lawyers, researchers and a number of Royal Canadian Mounted Police investigators. Outside experts were also commissioned to do independent studies on issues like the military justice system, training, racism in the Canadian Forces, military culture, etc.

The Commission of Inquiry into the Deployment of Canadian Forces to Somalia started work in March 1995. The Commission's mandate was very broad, allowing it to investigate nearly all aspects of the events in Somalia. The terms of reference were divided into two parts. The first charged the Commissioners to inquire into and report generally on the chain of command system, leadership, discipline, operations, actions and decisions of the Canadian Forces and the Department of National Defence in respect to the Somalia operation. The second part of the terms of reference required the Commission to look at specific matters relating to the pre-deployment, in-theatre and post-theatre phases of the Somalia operation (Order in Council, 1995, Vol. 1, pp. 1503-1507). The Inquiries Act provides the authority to subpoena witnesses, hear testimony, hire expert counsel and advisers and assess evidence. The power to compel testimony was the principal mechanism for determining what transpired in Somalia and at the Department of National Defence. Some 116 witnesses offered their evidence to the Inquiry in open sessions broadcast on public television across Canada.

The Chairman of the Somalia Inquiry, Judge Gilles Létourneau, recognised the need for this wide approach, when at the outset of the Commission's hearings, he stated: 'We are primarily concerned with the decisions, omissions, if any, and actions of those superior officers who could have influenced the course of the whole Somalia operation as opposed to a single incident. (...) We are going up the chain of command, not down at the level of the junior ranks where various corrective measures have already been taken'.[9]

---

7   In Canada, cabinet members are at the same time Members of Parliament.
8   Inquiries Act, R.S., c-1-11, available from: http://laws.justice.gc.ca/en/I-11/text.html [accessed 27 April 2003].
9   Commission of Inquiry into the Deployment of Canadian Forces to Somalia, 1995, Vol. 1P, p.3.

Public Inquiries in Canada are not intended to be trials, although the Somalia hearings did include an examination of the institutional causes of, and responses to, incidents that had previously resulted in the charge and trial of individual soldiers. The Inquiry's primary focus was on institutional and systemic issues relating to the organisation and management of the Canadian Forces and Department of National Defence, rather than on individuals. However, this focus inevitably required the Somalia Inquiry to examine the actions of individuals in the chain of command and the manner in which they exercised leadership.

Critics claim that Public Inquiries are frequently opportunistic political stop-gap measures, established by a government unable to handle some serious and tenacious problem (see Beaudoin, 1998; Brodeur, 1998; Centa and Macklem, 2001). Moreover, recent inquiries have tended to become expensive, drawn-out affairs because of the ever-complicated quasi-judicial proceedings, which take great care in respecting the rights of all involved. Each witness, for instance, can be represented by individual counsel. Also (as the Somalia Commissioners noted themselves), even with access to the significant procedural powers of a public inquiry, answers may prove elusive if those involved refuse to be held to account or to tell the whole story (Commission of Inquiry into the Deployment of Canadian Forces to Somalia, 1997c, p. ES-3). When the Somalia Inquiry was established, however, government spokespersons stressed that there was nothing to hide. The Minister of National Defence at that time told the House of Commons that 'to get to the bottom of all the sorry events that unfolded in Somalia [the Inquiry] has been given the most wide-sweeping investigative powers probably in Canadian history'.[10]

The public hearings began in May 1995. Much time was spent on understanding policies, rules and regulations. Evidence on pre-deployment was presented beginning October 1995. At this time, however, disturbing facts were surfacing. For example, the Inquiry quickly brought to light that although Somalia proved to be the Airborne Regiment's most troubled deployment; there had been earlier signs of indiscipline in the Regiment, including alcohol problems and violent crime.[11] Little was done to implement change and the disciplinary problems in the Regiment continued unchecked. Nevertheless, the Airborne Regiment was considered the Canadian UN stand-by unit and it should have prepared to go anywhere as a light infantry battalion for peacekeeping, operating in highly ambiguous foreign environments.

More importantly, especially with respect to the progress of its work, the Inquiry soon became side-tracked because it found that there had been document-tampering by the Somalia Working Group, convened at the Department of Defence in September 1993 to coordinate all activities with regard to the Somalia affair. It was this group which eventually released doctored documents to the press, precipitating a crisis for the Director of the Group, who by the time the story broke had been promoted to Chief of the Defence Staff. This caused the Somalia

---

10 Canadian Defence Minister quoted in: House of Commons, 1995a, pp. 1235-1236.
11 These signs of indiscipline were well-documented as early as 1985 in a report by Major-General C. W. Hewson.

Commissioners to organise an impromptu six-month investigation into the activities of the Working Group (tampering with documents released to the media), problems in the production of military documents (missing and altered documents, discrepancies in operational logs) and the failure of the Department of Defence's Somalia Inquiry Liaison Team's (SILT) – set up to deal with the Commission's request for information – to disclose essential documents. This considerably delayed the inquiry's investigation into the torture-death of Shidane Arone. Nevertheless, in April 1996, the prime minister and defence minister again expressed confidence that the Somalia Inquiry was doing the job it was supposed to be doing. The prime minister told the House of Commons that the earlier deadline had been extended to 'make sure that everything is in the open and that the people of Canada know what happened'.[12]

This government strategy – to stress its support for the inquiry's work – turned out to be an effective means of sidelining parliament. As mentioned, after the start of the Somalia Inquiry, revelations about the Canadian Airborne Regiment in Somalia and the handling of the affair in the Department of National Defence kept emerging in the press. This would usually result in critical questions being raised by the opposition parties in the House of Commons and – to a lesser extent – in the Senate, the media and pressure groups. However, in such cases the government would then fall back on the strategy of using the Somalia Inquiry as a means of averting and postponing all criticism and tough questions, claiming it did not want to interfere with the work of the Somalia Commission.

The Truncation of the Inquiry

In October 1996 government public support for the inquiry fell. The change in government attitude occurred after the resignation of the defence minister. And although the reasons for his resignation involved a breach of ethics not related to the Somalia Inquiry, some editorialists and opposition parliamentarians felt that it was a convenient way for the prime minister to let go of a very hot potato, particularly since the defence minister had personally endorsed the controversial Chief of the Defence Staff, who was also forced to resign a few days after the defence minister's departure from cabinet, when his role in the tampering with Somalia-related documents came to light (see above).

The new defence minister was known in political circles as being very forceful. One of his first statements was that he was prepared to ask the inquiry to report 'as quickly as possible on what happened, why it happened, and who was responsible for what happened in Somalia'.[13] In fact the new minister frequently stated that all that was needed to be known about Somalia was already known, a radically different position from the endorsement held earlier by the government. The Somalia Inquiry's original reporting date to parliament had been December 1995. The scope of the mandate and the sheer volume (over one million

---

12 Prime Minister quoted in: House of Commons, Debates, 1996a, p. 1369.
13 Defence Minister quoted in: House of Commons, 1996b, p. 5243.

documents) of material provided by the Department of National Defence made this impossible and extensions were requested as the hearings progressed.[14] The Somalia Inquiry was on its third request for an extension when the Commissioners were told that further delay was 'not in the best interest of the country or the institution [the Canadian Forces, ed.]', and should not 'go on for years'.[15] The minister stressed that Canadians already knew all the important facts and that the whole process was keeping open a wound for an unnecessarily long period of time. He ordered that the Commission complete its hearings within three months and submit a report by the end of June 1997.

    The government eventually revised the inquiry's terms of reference and the Commission was instructed to fully report on the pre-deployment phase of the mission to Somalia only. The Commission was also given the 'discretion' to report on other matters in the original mandate 'if possible' (Order in Council, 1997). This effectively meant that the death of Shidane Arone as well as allegations of a cover-up leading from in-theatre to National Defence Head Quarters (NDHQ) in Ottawa and the responsibility of officers and officials at National Defence Head Quarters would never be investigated. The Somalia Inquiry's response to the truncation was clear: 'We saw this decision as unwarranted interference with the independence of a public inquiry, interference that is also alien to our political traditions and endangers principles of democratic accountability'.[16]

    In addition to 10 analytical monographs, the Somalia Commission of Inquiry produced a lengthy five-volume report on 30 June 1997, identifying 12 major areas of deficiency.[17] The Commissioners made no secret of the fact that they felt betrayed by the government: 'Obviously, we were mistaken in our belief, as the government abandoned its earlier declared interest in holding to account senior leaders and officials who participated in the planning and execution of the mission and responded to the problems that arose. Once again, history repeats itself: only the lower ranks have been made to account for the marked failures of their leaders'.[18] The inquiry also assessed 'blame' by naming 11 senior executive or military leaders (from the rank of Major to General) whose behaviour during the crises was found wanting. Some of these senior leaders went on to take the Commissioners to court, but without success.

    At the same time the defence minister ordered the Somalia Inquiry to submit its report, he announced the creation of two 'blue ribbon' panels to propose reforms to the Canadian military. One committee, comprised of four well-known

---

14 For details on the three extensions granted to the Commission of Inquiry into the Deployment of Canadian Forces to Somalia, 1997d, Vol. 5, pp. 1403-1406.

15 Prime Minister, quoted in: CBC Television News, 1997.

16 Commission of Inquiry into the Deployment of Canadian Forces to Somalia, 1997b, Vol. 5, pp. 1407-1408.

17 According to the inquiry 12 areas needed reform: Leadership, Accountability, Chain of Command, Discipline, Personnel Selection and Screening, Training, Rules of Engagement, Openness and Disclosure, Military Justice System, Operational Readiness, Mission Planning and the Military Planning System.

18 Commission of Inquiry into the Deployment of Canadian Forces to Somalia, 1997b, p. 1910.

historians, was asked to provide individual papers on what should be done to furnish Canada with efficient and effective military forces in the future. The other committee was to propose reforms to the military justice system and was chaired by a former Chief Justice of the Supreme Court of Canada. Both groups were ordered to report a mere three months later. Critics felt this was a ploy to 'disarm' the Somalia report even before it was published, since the work of these two committees overlapped to a large degree the mandate of the Commission of Inquiry. Issues such as accountability of leaders and the need to reform the military justice system were problems that the Somalia Inquiry was already examining. One of the commissioners of the Somalia Inquiry predicted that the defence minister would 'launch a whole series of reforms of the military within the next few months to show that he is in charge and that the inquiry isn't necessary. This will eventually overshadow concern about our inquiry' (Desbarats, 1997, p. 221).

Both blue ribbon committees reported to the Minister of National Defence by the end of March 1997 (Bercusson, 1997; Granatstein, 1997; Legault, 1997; Morton, 1997). The reports by the historians were on an average only 36 pages long (as compared to the Somalia Inquiry's five-volume report which encompassed over 1,600 pages).

Basically all four reports argued that the Public Inquiry on Somalia was not the best method to improve the morale or quality of the Canadian Forces. The authors stressed the need to rediscover the values and traditions that had once made the Canadian Armed Forces a proud institution. Suggestions were made to improve the quality of the officer corps, e.g. by providing them with a university education.

Shortly after receiving the blue ribbon studies, the defence minister published his own 57-page report (Minister of Defence, 1997). Without even waiting for the findings of the Somalia Inquiry, he praised the work of the panel of historians and immediately fully endorsed the recommendations of the panel on military justice, which were less far-reaching than those of the Somalia Inquiry.[19] For example, the minister rejected the creation of a powerful Inspector General Office, as is the case in the US Army. He recommended instead, among other things, that an Ombudsman Office be set up outside the chain of command to provide information, advice and guidance to all personnel in need of help. The minister's report also recommended that a formal statement of values and beliefs be integrated into all recruiting and training programmes of the Canadian Forces; that a university degree be made a prerequisite to commissioning as an officer and that each graduate of the Royal Military College be given a broad-based education well-grounded in the sciences and the humanities; that current cooperative programmes with civilian institutions of higher learning be strengthened; that measures be taken to increase job mobility in the higher ranks, to improve the selection process and accountability for leadership positions for command and senior leadership positions.

For its part, the Department of National Defence maintained that most changes that the Somalia Commission proposed were being implemented or were

---

19 Special Advisory Group on Military Justice and Military Police Investigation Services (Dickson Committee), 1997.

already standard procedure or standard practice for some time. In fact, of the 160 recommendations of the Somalia Inquiry, the Canadian Forces stated that 132 (83%) had been accepted. As for the other 28, most of the objectives could be achieved through other means (Minister of Defence, 1997, p. 1). The Department of Defence's response was soothing and encouraging and it appeared as if the Department and the Canadian Forces were in a genuine process of reform.

To underline this approach, a special Monitoring Committee was set up to keep track of the implementation of recommendations that came out of the Somalia Inquiry and the other panels. The Monitoring Committee, headed by a former House of Commons Speaker, released its final report in February 2000.[20] The Committee did find the military deficient in two areas: the lack of education for officers and the unclear role of the reserves, but improvements in other areas were proceeding well. The Committee believed the armed forces and the Department of National Defence had changed enough to be confident that events such as the ones in Somalia could never happen again (CBC News, 2000). Even though two of its seven members did have a parliamentary background (one Senator and a former Speaker of the House of Commons), the Monitoring Committee could hardly be seen as a form of parliamentary oversight of the armed forces. The other members had a background in business, academia, the military and the Department of National Defence.

The Role of Parliament

With a Liberal majority firmly in control of parliament, there was very little that the opposition could do to counter the government's strategy to defuse the potentially explosive Somalia Inquiry. Criticism on the content and scope of the Ministry of National Defence's policies and reforms was simply stonewalled. Sometimes tempers flared during parliamentary debate. A Reform Member of Parliament was ejected from the House of Commons during a tumultuous question period in February 1997, shortly after Somalia Inquiry Commissioner Judge Létourneau had accused the government of political interference by cutting short the inquiry's work. After the MP's expulsion, one Liberal and three Reform parliamentarians nearly came to blows in the Commons foyer.

In the eyes of the opposition parties, the Somalia affair was just one more example of 'Liberal arrogance of power'. They claimed that the Somalia controversy was similar to the Liberal Party's handling of other high-profile issues, like the Krever Inquiry. In 1993 Justice Horace Krever was appointed to head a Commission of Inquiry with the mandate to investigate the blood system in Canada, including events surrounding the contamination of that blood system, which had caused many Canadians to contract the HIV-virus and hepatitis C. Legal manoeuvring – which many critics felt was part of an official policy of obstruction – delayed the report. By the time Krever revealed his 50 recommendations for

---

20 Minister's Monitoring Committee on Change in the Department of National Defence and the Armed Forces, 1999.

revamping the blood system, many had already been embraced by the government and acted upon, thus defusing the inquiry's findings.

The government's early strategy to limit debate in parliament on Somalia consisted in fact of three separate 'lines of defence'. First, it could claim – when confronted with criticism or new revelations about Somalia – with some credibility that an independent and well-respected Commission of Inquiry was dealing with the issue. 'Mr. Speaker, I am a little frustrated', the defence minister said in March 1995. 'For a year now members of the opposition have asked for a public inquiry into these matters. They have their inquiry. Will they please let the commissioners do their job and report, and then we will look at it'.[21] Time and time again the prime minister and top defence officials repeated that they did not want to interfere with the work of the commission, which was 'doing a good job'. Similarly, the defence minister had been able to dodge awkward questions in parliament and the media during the initial stages of the Somalia affair by refusing to comment as long as the court-martials against soldiers and officers involved in the March 1993 incidents were still in progress.

Also, and following naturally from the first argument, government stressed that anyone who continued to express doubts about the integrity of government and the leaders of the armed forces, was in fact at the same time raising doubts about the professional quality of the Somalia Commissioners themselves. After all, men of such eminent standing as the three commissioners – two of whom were experienced judges – would undoubtedly be able to get to the bottom of the affair, the defence minister claimed. The government, therefore, had nothing to hide and as long as the inquiry continued there was no need for any minister to resign over the Somalia affair within the framework of ministerial responsibility.

Finally, the government could ward off criticism by stating that opposition members of parliament were in fact (further) undermining the morale of the Canadian Forces at a time when the number of deployments abroad was increasing and resources were getting smaller, all for the sake of scoring political points. This then resulted in what looked like 'matches' between the Liberals and the opposition as to who could lavish most praise on the 'ordinary soldier in the field' and the proud tradition of the Canadian military.

These Liberal tactics were backed by an absolute Liberal majority in the House of Commons. If the opposition wanted to launch an offensive against the government and the Liberal Party on the Somalia front, the Senate – traditionally a place of reflection, more so than the Commons – was the only viable alternative. The Liberals had a one-seat majority in the Senate. From March 1995 onwards the Senate became the scene of a last-ditch attempt by the opposition to finish the work of the truncated Somalia Inquiry. Shortly after the government's decision to prematurely end the inquiry, the Conservatives tabled a motion that the Standing Senate Committee on Foreign Affairs complete the work of the Somalia Commission. The Senate Committee, 'would pick up where the Létourneau commission [Somalia Inquiry, ed.] is leaving off, that is essentially the post-

---

21 Defence Minister quoted in: House of Commons, 1995b, p. 10832.

deployment phase'.[22] It would call witnesses the Somalia Inquiry had no time to hear, including former top defence officials. Obviously, attention would automatically focus on issues like accountability and the rumours of cover-up, especially with regard to the torture-death of Arone and the question of whether the defence minister at that time had been kept in the dark by her own department.

On 20 March 1997, to the surprise of many, the Liberals appeared indeed to have a change of heart and agreed to the Conservative proposal. The defence minister, who had repeatedly insisted that Canadians knew all they needed to know about the Somalia deployment, now said that Senate hearings might be useful: 'Gosh, I don't know. I have no reason to think that the Senate would embark on something that they don't think useful, so why not'.[23] The Conservatives then withdrew their motion, which was replaced by a similar Liberal motion to hold Somalia hearings in the Foreign Affairs Committee. The Committee would have the right to subpoena witnesses and to call for documents. With the Liberals and Conservatives dominating the Senate, the motion was supported unanimously. The government stressed the need to move quickly, in order not to delay much-needed reforms of the armed forces. The other opposition parties described the motion as a 'cruel joke', an attempt to neutralise a very controversial issue before an election was called (an election call by the government was expected in April). The Reform Party called the initiative to have Senate hearings 'a whitewash and a smoke-screen'.[24] The Bloc Québécois was equally critical: 'Now we'll have Tories and Liberals at the Senate, judging what happened under a Tory Government and under a Liberal Government'.[25] Despite this criticism, the Conservatives accepted that the Liberals would be in control of procedures and voting and stressed the lack of any alternative: 'I think we should take the [Liberal] offer and run', one of the Conservative Senators said'.[26]

The Special Committee of the Senate on the Canadian Airborne Regiment in Somalia first met on 9 April 1997. The Chairman was a Liberal Senator and a Conservative Senator was appointed Deputy Chairman. Outside parliament the idea for a Senate Committee on Somalia met with much scepticism. Many felt the Committee would never be able to organise an in-depth series of hearings. The Canadian Airborne Forces Association described the idea as 'laughable, if it was not so sordid' (Canadian Airborne Forces Association, 1997, para. 37). The Conservatives were indeed quickly disappointed. Soon after the first meeting of the Special Committee, the Liberals proposed to start the Somalia hearings in a matter of days, i.e. from 21 April. The first round of hearings was to take just one week. The defence minister at the time of the March 1993 events in Somalia and a number of (former) top aides would be the first to be called to testify.

---

22 Conservative Senator Lowell Murray in Canadian Senate Debates (Hansard), 1997a, p. 1550.
23 Defence Minister Doug Young quoted in: CBC News, 1997.
24 Reform Senator Jim Hart, quoted in: CBC News, 1997.
25 Bloc Québécois leader Gilles Duceppe quoted in: CBC News, 1997.
26 Senator Lowell Murray quoted in: Canadian Senate Debates, 1997b, p. 1440.

The Conservatives denounced the Liberal plan to invite witnesses for just one week as 'indecent haste' and 'a quick and dirty whitewash' (Canadian News Digest, 1997). It was pointed out that even though the Somalia scandal was an extremely complex case involving torture and allegations of cover-up, the Committee had, till that day, done no research into the matter. The Conservatives suspected that the Liberals would get a few high-profile witnesses before the Senate Committee and then shut it down after the election announcement expected at the end of April. That would give the Liberals an opportunity to claim they tried to get to the bottom of the Somalia affair, but also to effectively sideline the issue during the election campaign. The Conservatives also complained that the Senate Committee had not even hired legal counsel or research staff yet.

Despite Liberal assurances that it was important to complete this process and get at the truth, the Special Committee came to an abrupt end even before it had really started. On April 17 Conservative Senators announced they would boycott the proceedings that they said had become nothing but a farce and an insult to the witnesses. Several shouting matches between Liberals and Conservatives marked the debate. 'We won't be part of the circus', a Conservative Senator remarked sourly.[27] The surprise move by the Conservatives meant that the hearings, scheduled to begin in four days, were cancelled. The earliest the Senate could now proceed with the Somalia hearings, if at all, was September 1997. The Liberal Senators countered with charges that the Conservatives were needlessly trying to delay the Committee for political gain.

After the elections of 2 June 1997 – which again resulted in a parliamentary majority for the Liberal Party – the Conservatives indeed tried once more to revive the Special Committee of the Senate on the Canadian Airborne Regiment in Somalia. By this time, however, the Liberals had changed their strategy. Both in the House of Commons and the Senate, Liberal parliamentarians now stressed that the Somalia affair had outlived its political importance and usefulness. The time had come to look towards the future and leave the Somalia controversy behind, for the benefit of the armed forces and because there were other, more pressing matters to be dealt with. Also, Liberal Senators underlined that a Senate Committee on Somalia would no longer serve a purpose anyhow, as the truth would never be fully known after all these years.

In 1998 and 1999 the Somalia issue continued to resurface at regular intervals. Even though Conservatives kept calling for a rebirth of the Special Senate Committee on Somalia, the Liberal majority would not concede. It could now use the added argument that things at the Canadian Forces and Department of National Defence had indeed changed for the better. For instance, substantial changes were being made to the military-judicial system and the office of the Ombudsman had been introduced. By the end of 2000, the Conservatives had thrown in the towel. There would not be a Special Senate Committee and the mandate of the Somalia Inquiry was indeed left unfinished.

---

27 Conservative Senator John Lynch-Staunton quoted in: Canadian News Digest, 1997.

Conclusions

'Canada has begun a new relationship with its armed forces, one that arguably requires greater involvement by members of Parliament and Canadians generally in the direction, supervision, and control of the Canadian Forces (CF)' the Somalia Commissioners noted in the final chapter of their report.[28] Tragic as it is, the death of Shidane Arone and the shooting of two Somali youths by members of the Canadian Airborne Regiment Battle Group in March 1993 did indeed precipitate a real soul-searching in the Canadian Forces. This soul-searching was prolonged and deep, partly because Canada had invested heavily in peace operations as an instrument of foreign policy, because of the high moral standards expected of the peacekeepers and because the ministry and armed forces felt reluctant to disclose all details, especially the unpleasant ones, from the very beginning. Paradoxically, the media, public and parliamentary attention to the Somalia crisis put the military 'on the map' for the time being. Public, media and parliament were more alert to the military than they had been for a long time.

But it is particularly important to note that the main semi-judicial/semi-political attempt to discover the truth – the Somalia Public Inquiry – equally showed just how difficult is was for parliament in Canada to hold those in authority accountable for the events in Somalia. The Liberal strategy to downplay the importance of the Somalia affair and to keep structural political debate isolated to a limited number of well-controlled debates in parliament was facilitated by the civil-military gap (i.e. a lack of interest in military affairs and defence policy) in both parliament and society. Even though Canadians were appalled by photos of beatings and torture and shocked by revelations about (mis)conduct in the Canadian Forces, this never translated into a genuine increase of civilian interest into defence matters. As noted earlier, the media have become more alert about defence issues, but again it is scandal hunger rather than an improved appetite for wide-ranging defence matters.

Aided by this civil-military gap, the Liberal Government and the Liberal majority in Parliament could apply successful tactics. The Liberals could easily deflect criticism on the handling of the Somalia affair by referring to the work of the Public Inquiry. Once the Commission reached the point where it was starting to investigate the actions of top military and government officials, the government simply truncated the inquiry. The opposition could do nothing to prevent this. Attempts by the Conservatives to continue the Somalia hearings in the Senate failed to have any result. In fact, after the publication of the Somalia Commission's report and the announcement by the government that strong reforms would be implemented (fully supported by the Liberal majority in the House of Commons) to prevent a recurrence of the Somalia debacle, the affair soon died down. There has been no further attempt to answer the questions raised concerning the deployment and post-deployment phases of the Somalia mission. The exact circumstances surrounding the death of Shidane Arone will remain obscure.

---

28 Conservative Senator John Lynch-Staunton quoted in: Canadian News Digest, 1997, p. 1453.

In their *Dishonored Legacy* report, the Commissioners noted that there is 'a perceived need to strengthen the role of parliament in the development and scrutiny of defence' (Canadian News Digest, 1997, p. 1453). In the eyes of the Commissioners, conducting inquiries of this nature should be parliament's responsibility. This could be achieved, among others things, by establishing an effective mechanism in parliament to oversee the defence establishment, including a special parliamentary committee housed in the Senate or the House of Commons (or a joint committee with members from both chambers). At the time of writing (Spring 2003) this ambition remains unfulfilled.

PART IV

THE NATO CONTEXT

Chapter 7

Decision-Making in the Atlantic Alliance and its Parliamentary Dimension

Willem van Eekelen

Introduction

Among intergovernmental institutions NATO takes pride of place. Over the years it developed into a permanent consultation machinery for its members and through its 'Partnership for Peace' (PfP) programme extended security cooperation throughout the Euro-Atlantic area, which now includes the republics emerging from the former Soviet Union. Its integrated military structure provided a role for all allies and achieved impressive results in terms of common practices, joint operating procedures and rules of engagement. Even in operations which were not commanded by NATO as such, but conducted on the basis of a coalition of the able and willing, NATO procedures were the fabric facilitating joint action. This paper analyses the characteristics of the NATO system and its decision-making with special emphasis on the parliamentary dimension. For illustrating the parliamentary dimension, three case studies are selected which dominated NATO's decision-making in the last decade: the enlargement process, Kosovo as an example of a NATO military intervention, and the adaptation of NATO's Strategic Concept (with special emphasis on out-of-area operations). In each case, special attention is given to the role of the NATO Parliamentary Assembly (NATO PA) and how it tries to influence NATO decision-making. In each case it was apparent that parliamentary control in the strict sense of the word exclusively rested with national parliaments. In this respect NATO was not different from other intergovernmental organisations. Where it differed, however, was US leadership, the emphasis on multilateral review procedures which put national commitments in a comprehensive system of defence planning and a well-oiled bureaucratic system capable of dealing with crises in problem-solving. The international parliamentary dimension grew into a consensus-building network of committee meetings, visits and reports within the NATO PA which, until 2001, was called the North Atlantic Assembly, providing national parliamentarians with important information they could use in their own parliamentary debates. The contacts between parliamentarians from Europe and North America in particular, provided a basis of common understanding and assessment which became essential in mustering political support for the major decisions taken by the North Atlantic Council.

The chapter concludes with some comments on the November 2002 Prague Summit, which not only dealt with the next round of enlargement, but also took decisions in the light of changed strategic realities and the new significance of the fight against terrorism.

Decision-Making in NATO

Decision-making in NATO is an intergovernmental negotiating process with special characteristics. It is regular and frequent; with bottom-up and top-down elements; its Secretary General and secretariat have a strong position but at the same time the US exercises a leadership role; it is consensus-based, but usually a great effort is made to find a compromise between different views and interests; it is politico-military in nature with both parallel lines of authority and cross links between the political and military bodies; it contains significant mutual examination and review processes; it does not depend on meetings of ministers, as the Permanent Council possesses full decision-making authority in between ministerial sessions; and, finally, it has a parliamentary dimension (see NATO, 2001; Gallis, 2003). All these points will be examined below.

Regular and frequent   Foreign ministers and defence ministers meet twice a year in formal session, heads of government at irregular intervals, normally of several years. Defence ministers meet in the Defence Planning Committee (DPC) when they discuss the integrated military structure, i.e. without France. Occasional ministerials are possible and defence ministers have resorted to informal brainstorming-type meetings. At the headquarters in Evere, the North Atlantic Council (NAC) in permanent session meets every Wednesday morning, preceded by a luncheon of the ambassadors on the previous day. They also convene in a DPC configuration. Their deputies meet weekly in the Senior Political Committee or other configuration and their staff members meet in committees ranging from the political committee, defence review committee, nuclear planning staff group, information committee, civil and military budget committees, infrastructure committees and a host of some 400 specialised committees, groups and panels often requiring the presence of experts from member state capitals.

Bottom-up and top-down   Routine matters follow a bottom-up course. The Political Committee regularly reviews developments in all parts of the world on the basis of inputs by member states and reports to the NAC. The Defence Review Committee follows a defence planning cycle based on ministerial guidance (which it has drafted itself), force goals, force proposals (developed in conjunction with the military authorities) and examines countries on their implementation. This process of setting targets which exceeded past performance could be described as 'mutual arm twisting' or in modern jargon as 'bench-marking' and 'peer pressure'. Everybody examines everybody else and as a result everybody does somewhat better than he originally intended. However, this is only the case up to a point, because ultimately decisions on the size of the defence budgets and the composition of the armed forces remain national prerogatives. At the height of the Cold War a commitment to raise defence budgets by 3% annually was accepted as ministerial guidance, but only a few countries were willing to implement it fully.

A strong secretariat The Secretary General of NATO chairs the North Atlantic Council and DPC both in ministerial and in permanent session. He prepares the sessions, sets the agenda and introduces the individual items. On occasion he is mandated to undertake important missions, such as negotiating a new relationship with Russia. All important committee meetings are chaired by the Assistant Secretary Generals. They sum up, prepare minutes and draft policy papers. The Assistant Secretary General for political affairs chairs the drafting committee at ministerial sessions (consisting of the deputy Permanent Representatives and often senior policy officials from member state capitals).

US leadership All incumbents of the post of Secretary General try to maintain a constructive relationship with the US, without becoming its mouthpiece. The Secretary General frequently visits Washington to explain emerging European views to the US administration, whilst hoping to exert a soothing influence on sensitive issues such as the gap in defence expenditure between Europe and the US and the rift between them over the Iraq war, as well as the competition between European Security and Defence Policy and NATO. By and large, most sensitive issues are related to the dominance of the US as opposed to West European lack of unity. Obviously the Secretary General and his staff pay much attention to American views and often rely on inputs from Washington. The NATO Situation Centre very much depends on US intelligence, as NATO possesses no intelligence-gathering capability of its own. In the military chain of command this reliance is even greater as both Major NATO Commanders (MNC) are Americans and are double-hatted with US commands. The degree to which Washington exercises its leadership varies considerably, but it is omnipresent. The US representative in the Council or in its committees does not necessarily speak first, but his words carry considerable weight and often set the tone for the ultimate decision. Obviously consensus remains necessary, but the American views often determine in which direction a decision be achieved. The large financial contribution of the US and its preponderant military contribution and political clout in the world add great weight to these views. In some cases the US has lobbied actively for certain decisions it felt necessary. Examples are the acquisition of the NATO Airborne Warning and Control System (AWACS) aircrafts as a NATO asset in the 1970s, the deployment of cruise missiles in the 1980s and the NATO enlargement in the 1990s. The fact that the two Major NATO Commanders, i.e. Supreme Allied Commander Europe (SACEUR) in Mons and Supreme Allied Commander Atlantic (SACLANT) in Northwood, and a Major Subordinate Commander, i.e. the Commander-in-Chief Allied Forces Southern Europe (CINCSOUTH) in Naples, are American and double-hatted with national American commands, was a powerful link with the military might of the US and its nuclear arsenal which during the Cold War enhanced the credibility of NATO's deterrent and defence posture. At present the command structure is under consideration again, probably eliminating SACLANT as a major NATO commander, and streamlining it to enable shorter lines of command for peace support operations.[1]

Consensus-based Decisions are rarely in one go. The only recent example is the decision in principle to invoke article V on 12 September 2001, i.e. the day after the terrorist attacks on the World Trade Centre and the Pentagon. Usually several rounds of discussion follow each other, allowing for a reporting-instructing traffic of communications between Permanent Representatives and their capitals. Important issues are first explored informally at a Tuesday luncheon, followed by a non-minuted meeting of Permanent Representatives plus one assistant in the meeting room next to the Secretary General's Office. Subsequently the International Staff prepares a memorandum or a policy paper which then follows a more formal course, either through the committee structure or directly in the Permanent Council. Consensus grows during the succession of discussion rounds. The Permanent Representatives state their positions, report on the views of others, suggest possible middle ground and ask for some flexibility in their instructions. If still in doubt, they agree to a compromise subject to a reservation which could be lifted after further consultation with the home country. Over the years a certain practice has grown of not using a veto when you are in a minority of one. There have been exceptions, however, such as repeated French objections and the Greek – Turkish controversies. Other countries have resorted to a dissenting footnote to communiqués, without preventing their adoption, mainly in cases where their parliaments would have difficulty in following the agreed line. In this respect, the rift between the US-led coalition in the Second Gulf War (2003) on the one hand and NATO states such as France and Germany and other countries on the other hand, signified a serious breach of the consensus approach.

A politico-military organisation The main purpose of NATO was collective defence against aggression affecting the territorial integrity of its members. Soon after its creation in 1949, an integrated military structure was created to plan, organise and if necessary command the collective response. Consequently, much hard work took place on the military side with considerable success in joint planning, standing operating procedures and rules of engagement. At NATO Headquarters in Evere, however, most of the work is political. In theory a Military Committee (MC) with its own International Military Staff renders independent military advice to the NAC. In practice, most of this advice already has a political colouring, because the Military Representatives receive their instructions from their national Chiefs of Defence, who are subject to the ministerial responsibility of their political masters at home. A good argument could be made for streamlining the organisation at Evere by merging the International Staff (IS) and the International Military Staff (IMS) and turning the Military Committee into a senior committee under the NAC. Today the relationship between NAC and MC is ambiguous, as is the relationship between MC and the Major NATO Commanders (MNC). The Chairman of the Military Committee has a tendency to see himself as

---

1   As decided at the NATO Defence Ministerial Meeting, Brussels, 12-13 June 2003.

superior to the MNCs when he communicates instructions of the NAC to them, but in the final analysis both are subjected to the political control exercised by the NATO Council. The organisation is at its most cumbersome in respect of the defence planning cycle. The defence review committee is attended by representatives of the IS, IMS and the MNCs but their respective roles should be clarified better.

Delegated power of the Permanent Council NATO as a collective defence organisation has always been aware of the need for rapid decision-making in a crisis and mandated the Permanent Council to take all necessary decisions that are obvious. Permanent Representatives will be in constant communication with their capitals, including a secure voice network, but their status is different from their colleagues in the European Union. Due to the supranational 'communitarian method', EU decisions can only be taken by the Ministerial Council, albeit in different formats, and are not delegated to the EU Committee of Permanent Representatives (COREPER).

A parliamentary dimension Last but not least, the NATO Parliamentary Assembly (NATO PA) does not rest upon a clause in the Washington Treaty of 1949, but has gradually grown in stature, thanks to frequent reports and debates, which have often drawn attention from the press and figured in national debates. The members of the Standing Committee meet with the North Atlantic Council for an afternoon session on an annual basis. The Secretary General responds in writing to the resolutions which are adopted by the Assembly. The NATO PA has also been instrumental in raising support for major activities of NATO, often before the NAC had formally endorsed them. The enlargement process is a case in point, which will be discussed more fully below.[2]

Parliamentary Oversight over NATO Decisions

In any intergovernmental organisation, parliamentary control rests with national parliaments. Their ministers are accountable for the positions taken in international negotiations. The EU is the only organisation which has a directly-elected international assembly which oversees the functioning of the European Commission. In the field of foreign trade, the European Commission has its own competence, but in most other areas of foreign policy and in the entire field of security policy, international cooperation remains intergovernmental and is therefore not subject to multinational parliamentary control.[3]

The parliamentary assemblies of the Council of Europe, WEU, NATO and OSCE do not exercise parliamentary control as such, but rather contribute to consensus-building among parliamentarians of the participating countries. Working

---

2   Information on NATO PA is available from: http://www.nato-pa.int/
3   Such as in the European Parliament, see European Parliament, 2002; see also Chapters Nine and Ten.

together on reports and resolutions enhances mutual understanding and provides a valuable basis for positions taken in national debates at home. Detailed knowledge of the arguments advanced by parliamentarians from allies and partners is a prerequisite for an informed and responsible debate. But these international assemblies do control very little, at best their own budgets (Van Eekelen, 2002). Contrary to the directly-elected European Parliament, the other Assemblies consist of delegations appointed or elected by their national parliaments in a representative manner. They are therefore a fairly good reflection of public opinion in their countries taken together. After each election national delegations change, so the Assemblies' membership is continually in flux. Although elected as a national contingent, members participate in multinational party groups, primarily the Christian Democrats, Socialist and Liberal groups, but many more in the European Parliament.

A major drawback in parliamentary oversight of the security sector is the unevenness of national practices.[4] In some capitals, the parliament has very little influence on foreign affairs and defence. In France it is the reserved domain of the President of the Republic (Assembly of the WEU, 2001a). In the UK, the prime minister has considerable freedom of manoeuvre (see Van Eekelen, 2002). In both cases equipment decisions hardly figure in parliamentary debates. This is also one of the reasons for the reluctance to give the European Parliament more say in these matters; if national parliamentarians have little authority, why should Members of European Parliament (MEPs) get more?

The powers of these assemblies are advisory in as much as they are the parliamentary component of intergovernmental organisations which take their decisions by unanimity. Interestingly enough, even in these cases, the parliamentarians apply majority voting to the adoption of their reports and resolutions. Only the European Parliament (EP) has attributions resembling those of a national parliament, particularly in the budget procedure and co-decision with the Council of Ministers on legislation which the latter has approved by a qualified majority (i.e. approximately 71% of the votes allotted). The consent of the European Parliament (EP) is required, on a number of important decisions by the Council of Ministers, such as the structural funds, cohesion funds, international agreements and the admission of new member states. These do not, however, relate to the second pillar with its common foreign and security policy which now includes European security and defence policy after the transfer of WEU functions to the EU. The Amsterdam Treaty of the European Union (Amsterdam Treaty, 1997) provided for the European Parliament to be informed on the main lines of the Common Foreign and Security Policy and the right to ask questions (see Chapter Eleven).

The NATO Parliamentary Assembly started in 1955 as the North Atlantic Assembly and remains independent from NATO, lacking a treaty basis. The NATO PA derives its value from its role as a forum for legislators from North America and European countries to consider issues of common interest and concern. After the end of the Cold War, the Assembly has significantly broadened

---

4   See, for example, Chapters Three and Four.

both its membership and its mandate. The traditional aims of the NATO PA as stated by the Secretary General in his annual report of 2002 are, among others, as follows:

- to foster dialogue among parliamentarians on major issues; as well as to facilitate parliamentary awareness and understanding of key security issues and NATO policies;
- to provide NATO and its member governments with an indication of collective parliamentary opinion;
- to provide greater transparency of NATO policies, and thereby a degree of collective accountability;
- to assist the development of parliamentary democracy throughout the Euro-Atlantic area by integrating parliamentarians from non-member states into the Assembly's work;
- to assist directly those parliaments actively seeking NATO membership (Lunn, 2002).

In addition, the important aspect of direct contact between parliamentarians from Europe and North America should be stressed. Moreover, the NATO PA now has 19 associate members[5] and maintains contacts with Cyprus, Malta and seven countries of North Africa and the Middle East.[6] The 2001 NATO Handbook adds a useful note to this analysis:

> The Assembly is completely independent of NATO but constitutes a link between national parliaments and NATO which encourages governments to take NATO concerns into account when framing national legislation. It also acts as a permanent reminder that intergovernmental decisions reached within NATO are ultimately dependent on political endorsement in accordance with the due constitutional process of democratically-elected parliaments. The Assembly was thus directly concerned with assisting in the process of ratification of the Protocols of Accession signed at the end of 1997, which culminated in the accession of the Czech Republic, Hungary and Poland to NATO in March 1999 (NATO, 2001).

NATO PA's role in developing relations with Central and Eastern European parliaments was recognised in the NATO-Russia Founding Act and the NATO-Ukraine Charter. These documents called for expanded dialogue and cooperation between the North Atlantic Assembly and the Federal Assembly of the Russian Federation and the Ukrainian Verkhovna Rada (parliament) respectively.[7]

The NATO PA's outreach programme is separate from, but reinforces, the work of the Euro-Atlantic Partnership Council (EAPC) and NATO's Partnership

---

5   Albania, Armenia, Austria, Azerbaijan, Bulgaria, Croatia, Estonia, Finland, FYROM (Macedonia), Georgia, Latvia, Lithuania, Moldova, Romania, Russian Federation, Slovenia, Slovakia, Switzerland, and Ukraine.

6   Algeria, Egypt, Israel, Jordan, Mauritania, Morocco, and Tunisia.

7   NATO-Russian Founding Act, 1997, section II; NATO-Ukraine Charter 1997, section 13.

for Peace initiative (PfP). Particular emphasis is placed on helping to achieve a key PfP objective, namely the establishment of democratic control of armed forces. NATO PA activities aim to provide the expertise, experience and information that will help CEE parliamentarians to become more effective in influencing the development of national defence policies and in ensuring that the control of their armed forces is fully democratic.

Enlargement Process

After the fall of the Berlin Wall all international assemblies have advocated enlargement of their respective organisations and doing so more rapidly than their governments were ready to move. NATO enlargement was relatively slow in taking off. Secretary General Manfred Wörner was personally in favour of admitting new members and envisaged the Visegrad countries, but saw it as a lengthy process following the Partnership for Peace programme which was initiated in 1994.[8] Very few statesmen in Western Europe paid more than lip service to the enlargement of NATO. The only clear exception was the German Defence Minister Volker Rühe, who advocated enlargement as early as 1993 in his Alastair Buchan lecture for the International Institute of Strategic Studies (IISS) in London (Rühe, 1993, pp. 129-137). A breakthrough came with President Clinton's speech in Detroit on 22 October during his re-election campaign in 1996 in which he stated that by NATO's 50th anniversary in 1999 the first group should be invited to join, i.e. Poland, Hungary and the Czech Republic.[9] At the NATO summit in Madrid on 8-9 July 1997, Romania and Slovenia were also mentioned, the former country being strongly advocated by France, but the debate was settled by the argument that the US Congress would not be willing to admit more than three countries.[10]

There had been a debate in member-parliaments with a fairly wide spectrum of opinion. Some thought it their duty to take in the new democracies, others wanted to project stability eastwards. Opponents did not see the need in a no-threat situation and feared traumatic reactions in a Russia still accustomed to think in terms of correlation of forces; they would see NATO enlargement as American power moving eastward, threatening Russian interests rather than establishing a zone of stability of interest to both sides. In the end it was a clear case of American leadership. An extension of US guarantees to a wider Europe could hardly be questioned by Europeans who themselves thanked their freedom to those very guarantees. Nevertheless, the decision was clearly a political one, not based on concrete criteria, but intended to show these countries that they belonged to the Western world. Militarily the arguments were unconvincing: none of the three was ready with their reforms and the fact that Hungary did not border on another NATO member state clearly showed that no military threat was taken seriously. In

---

8   Based on author's personal communication with Manfred Wörner.
9   Available from: http://www.usemb.ee/clitond.php3
10 Radio Free Europe/Radio Liberty, 3 June 1997.

fact, NATO had moved away from the traditional threat analysis to a new jargon of 'risks and responsibilities' (Coker, 2002).

The Washington Summit of 1999 welcomed the three new members but did not issue new invitations and adopted an extensive declaration and a new strategic concept.[11] The NATO Parliamentary Assembly had advocated the admission of Slovenia to demonstrate that the door indeed remained open for other candidates. The NATO PA adopted a report submitted by its president Senator Bill Roth of Delaware to this effect but without success (NATO PA, 1998, p. 62 and annexes). Since then the momentum for further enlargement has been growing and now seems to encompass seven candidates: the Baltic Countries, Slovenia, Romania, Bulgaria and Slovakia.

At first, some doubted the wisdom of taking in the Baltic countries in the next round, which might be a bridge too far to cross for the new President Vladimir Putin and kindle opposition against him. A reintroduction of strategic arguments in the internal Russian debate might deviate scare resources from the necessary economic reforms. These arguments were countered, however, by pointing at the smooth entry of Poland into NATO without much impact on East-West relations. Putin was wise enough not to stake his prestige on preventing the admission of the Baltic countries, as in the final analysis he could do little to prevent it without disturbing completely the newly emerging atmosphere of cooperation (The Economist, 4 April 2002).

The other side of this coin was the constructive role played by Russia in the Afghan crisis, which might have caused hesitation in the West to antagonise Russia and lose her valuable support against the Taliban. This dilemma was resolved by British Prime Minister Tony Blair's initiative to create a NATO-Russian Council at Twenty in which Moscow would move beyond the Joint Partnership Council (where it was confronted with positions previously agreed by the 19 NATO member states) and obtain equal status in decision-making on a number of subjects (The Guardian, 13 May 2002). The chances of Romania and Bulgaria, which had been slipping in the years after the Madrid Summit, rose again with the introduction of serious military reforms and active participation in peace support operations. Moreover, the post 9/11 'war' on terrorism and the heightening tension in the Middle East enhanced the strategic position of these countries (The Economist, 4 April 2002).

The NAC was intentionally slow in discussing candidates by name because nobody wanted to be definitive long before the deciding moment at the Prague Summit in November 2002. To soften the disappointment of the 1999 Washington Summit, a Membership Action Plan (MAP) was launched listing actions which would have to be taken and subjected to annual reports on progress made. Candidates would have to be providers of security, not just consumers, a notion which did not excel in precision. The MAP had the advantage that ultimately it would remain a political decision.

---

11 See the NATO Press Release on the Washington Summit Communiqué, 24 April 1999, available from http://www.nato.int/docu/pr/1999/p99-064e.htm [accessed 25 June 2003], and, see for example, Washington Post, 1999, p.A1.

The NATO Parliamentary Assembly did not wait for governments to draw in new participants. It brought delegations of the Partnership for Peace countries into its midst as associates or observers and was positively inclined towards the notion of 'security through participation' starting in 1999. Spring sessions of the Assembly were held in candidate countries and their parliamentarians were invited to act as rapporteur for committee reports. Additionally, training seminars for young parliamentarians and their staffs of Eastern European countries provided useful information and managed to remove misconceptions about the role of NATO in the new security environment (NATO, 2001).

On enlargement there were two schools within the NATO PA. One focusing on criteria and progress made, the other already wanting to become specific by mentioning names. At the Berlin plenary in November 2000 the latter group, led by general rapporteur Markus Meckel, lost narrowly in advocating entry of the Baltic states, Slovakia and Slovenia. Subsequently, the German delegation took a wider view and included Romania and Bulgaria in the light of their recent progress. Those countries are also favoured by the Southern tier of member states but the UK seemed more reluctant. In Washington the momentum seemed to veer towards a 'big bang' in spite of some reservations in the Pentagon about seven countries coming in at the same time and overburdening the process of military adaptation.[12]

The plenary meeting of the 2002 Spring session took place in Sofia on the very day that the ministerial NAC decided on the new relationship with Russia and created a Council at Twenty where Russia would have equal status with the other NATO member states on a range of subjects. In the autumn of 2002 in Istanbul the Assembly was able to become more precise and called for the admission of the seven countries by name in a 'broad and regionally balanced enlargement' (NATO PA 2002a, para. 3.1). The November 2002 NATO Summit in Prague acted accordingly, and the member states signed the protocols of accession on 26 March 2003. Ratification is expected to be concluded within a year.

NATO enlargement requires the ratification in parliament of all NATO member states, which puts national parliaments in the position to oversee the enlargement process. The procedure varies from parliament to parliament along the following lines (Kay and Binnendijk, 1997). In some countries, eg. Canada, France, Germany, Iceland, Italy, the Netherlands, Portugal and Spain, a simple majority vote would suffice. In other countries, such as Belgium, Greece, Luxembourg and the US, a two-thirds majority is required, giving a powerful voice to opposition parties in parliament, which can lead to complicated negotiations between government and opposition parties. Since most parliaments vote on a draft law, the law enactment can be a time-consuming process, between two months in the UK up to twelve months in the Netherlands. When debating NATO enlargement in 1997, various parliaments of NATO member states were primarily concerned about the impact on relations with Russia. Additionally, budgetary consequences, NATO command structure reform, relations with the EU, as well as

---

12 For more information on NATO enlargement, see, for example, Hopkinson, 2001.

changes in the Conventional Forces in Europe (CFE) Treaty were on the parliamentary agenda (Kay and Binnendijk, 1997).

The Kosovo Crisis

The escalation of the crisis in former Yugoslavia since 1991 had all the trappings of a Greek tragedy. Events were predictable and seemed inevitable, harbouring the potential for a much larger conflagration involving all countries in the region. Starting with fighting between Serbs and Croats – particularly bloody in the Vukovar area – then the eruption of Bosnia-Herzegovina, the spectre of an explosion in Kosovo as the third act, finally crowned by the disintegration of Macedonia with the neighbouring states fighting over the pieces.

In 1995, events in Bosnia came to a head with Serbians holding UNPROFOR soldiers hostage, the massacre at Srebrenica (see Chapter Five) and finally NATO air strikes against Serbian military installations. Dayton ended the war, but could not achieve the structures of a comprehensive peace. The agreement brokered by Richard Holbrooke owed much to last-minute concessions made by President Slobodan Milosevic and his willingness to sign on behalf of the Bosnian Serbs. At the same time his constructive role made it impossible for Dayton to include Kosovo in an overall settlement. In fact, Milosevic seemed to believe that Dayton would have brought him a guarantee of territorial integrity, including Kosovo. Nevertheless, in 1996 the situation on the ground seemed to improve when Kosovo's President Ibrahim Rugova and Milosevic agreed to end the six-year Albanian boycott of schools. High hopes were short-lived, however, and in 1998 the Kosovo Liberation Army (KLA) made its violent entry after a decade of peaceful action and demanded independence.

On 13 October 1998, US Secretary of State Madeleine Albright summoned the NATO foreign ministers to approve the Activation Orders (ACTORDS) that would allow for air strikes against Serb targets in Kosovo and elsewhere in Serbia, if Milosevic failed to comply with UN Security Council resolution 1199 on withdrawing his forces from the field of battle (Albright, 1998, p. 12). The US obtained the Activation Orders, but the same evening the North Atlantic Council despatched Holbrooke to Belgrade for a last attempt to avert war. Once again he succeeded. Serb forces would be withdrawn and NATO did not have to act. In Brussels the permanent representatives heaved a sigh of relief as, in spite of the activation orders, NATO was poorly prepared for an air campaign. Milosevic was aware of NATO's lack of readiness, which probably hardened his stance six months later. But then he misjudged NATO's determination to uphold its credibility by military action, even, if necessary, without an explicit mandate of the UN Security Council.[13]

In October, Belgrade promised to withdraw substantial numbers of security forces, to allow 2,000 unarmed OSCE 'verifiers' to monitor a ceasefire and to negotiate the details of restored autonomy to the province. The 'verifiers' would be

---

13 See Albright, 1998, p. 12.

backed up by an extraction force stationed outside Kosovo. The agreement had something in it for the Albanians in as much as it would allow refugees to come down from the hills and – more importantly – in taking an, albeit feeble, step towards internationalisation of the conflict through OSCE. The Serbs were allowed to keep 10,000 police officers and 11,000 army personnel, which was a recipe for disaster as the KLA predictably made progress in resuming control of Kosovo. A massacre of 40 Albanians outside the village of Racak brought matters to a head.

The draft settlement presented to the Serbs at Rambouillet in January 1999 left no obligatory links to Serbia but only some to the Yugoslav Federation. On the final status a mechanism was proposed that would take into account the will of the people after three years. A side letter from Madeleine Albright to KLA leader Hashim Thaci indicated that the mechanism would include a referendum. In return he gave up his claim to immediate independence. The Serbs got some safeguards in favour of their minority, including a disproportional representation in the Kosovo parliament. Apparently Milosevic was furious that the Albanians swallowed their pride and were prepared to sign. For him the real stumbling block was the presence of a NATO military force to guarantee the constitutional and political arrangements. His refusal led to a 78-day air war in June 1999.

President Clinton offered three aims for NATO's bombing campaign: (1) to demonstrate the seriousness of NATO's purpose, (2) to prevent further violence against the Kosovar population and (3) to preserve regional stability.[14] Against all expectations Milosevic managed to cleanse north-western Kosovo of Albanians and at the same time consolidated his authority at home. Those who had argued that after a few days of bombing Milosevic would give in, proved terribly wrong. In fact, Kosovo almost became a case of 'operation successful, but patient died' as the region was being emptied of Albanians. The bombing campaign ran out of targets and the lack of ground troops to turn the tide in the field became painfully obvious. The matter was exacerbated by public denials in Washington of every intention to despatch ground forces, thus facilitating Serbian military planning. Once again democracies appeared poor war strategists in foreclosing options which could have constrained the enemy. Only the Blair government in London was prepared to keep the option of ground forces open.

The North Atlantic Council did not give a free hand to their military authorities. Targets for the bombing campaign were frequently discussed in detail. President Jacques Chirac publicly prided himself on stopping the selection of certain targets. In addition, other states, including the US and UK, were very careful and sought delay before selecting more sensitive civilian targets such as bridges and police headquarters (Clark, 2001). This was greatly resented by the US military which, during the Afghanistan crisis, cited these complications as a reason for not involving NATO more closely in the campaign against the Taliban. In any case the North Atlantic Council, the most important decision-making body of NATO as it decides on political-military strategy, is difficult to oversee for outsiders, such as the general public and parliaments. The main obstacle is secrecy,

---

14 Address to the Nation by the President, 11 June 1999 following up an earlier address of April 28, see http://www.nato.int/usa/pres-archive.html [accessed 28 July 2003].

as the Council's deliberations take place behind closed doors and its decisions are confidential. Another factor is that the lead-time between decision and action can be very short, giving little space for oversight by parliaments or the general public.

The lack of concrete involvement and the absence of casualties on the NATO side restrained political reactions to the long duration of the bombing without the desired effect on Serbia. There was a serious debate on the question of legitimacy in the absence of a clear UN mandate and whether grave violations of human rights could provide their own legitimacy for coercive action. On the whole this legitimacy was recognised. This was the case in Canada – usually the most insistent on UN mandates. It also applied to Greece where the population was overwhelmingly against the bombing, but the government nevertheless managed to join the NATO consensus. In the words of the IISS Strategic Survey 1999-2000 (International Institute for Strategic Studies, 2001, p. 26) Kosovo constituted a highly significant precedent, which established more firmly in international law the right to intervene on humanitarian grounds, even without an express mandate from the Security Council. The NATO position suggested that such intervention would be lawful only when:

- A grave emergency threatens widespread loss of life;
- That emergency's existence is authoritatively confirmed; and,
- Action by the Security Council is blocked by (the threat of) the veto (IISS, 2001).

The NATO PA continually debated the situation in South-Eastern Europe and passed specific resolutions on Kosovo in 1999, 2000 and 2001 (see for example NATO PA, 1999a; 1999b).[15] On 31 May 1999, the Warsaw Declaration 294 was adopted on Kosovo, introduced by the Standing Committee on the basis of statements issued by the Standing Committee on 27 March and 7 May 1999. The Declaration supported NATO in its campaign 'to establish conditions making it possible for refugees to return in safety and to secure peace and stability in the region'. The policies of President Milosevic were condemned totally: 'This campaign of terror cannot be allowed to succeed.' The objectives of a peaceful, multi-ethnic democratic and autonomous Kosovo were fully shared, but it added: 'in full respect of the territorial integrity of the Former Republic of Yugoslavia'. Equally, the military action undertaken by NATO was fully supported, but a hand was offered to Russia by stating NATO PA's readiness to work with partners in the Russian parliament 'in order to find common ground on this crisis and on any major future challenge to Europe's security'.

Six months later, on 15 November in Amsterdam, the NATO PA adopted Resolution 286 on humanitarian intervention (as a measure of last resort and subject to the principle of proportionality) and Resolution 287 on respect for humanitarian law (to develop conflict mediation strategies and to pursue the prosecution of war crimes). In November 2000, in Berlin, Resolution 300 recognised the Stability Pact for South-Eastern Europe as a key forum for a

---

15 Available from www.nato-pa.int [accessed 28 July 2003].

comprehensive and consensual approach to centralise the region and to deepen cooperation among the countries of the region. The democratic election of a new president of the Former Republic of Yugoslavia was welcomed, but the country must meet the same visible criteria for international support as the other countries of the region, including bringing to justice those of its citizens accused of committing war crimes. More generally, the resolution urged member governments to be prepared for a long-term military and civilian engagement in Bosnia and Herzegovina and in Kosovo in order to achieve stability and respect for human rights in the region.

Concluding, NATO PA did not exercise control over NATO's Kosovo campaign, but ventilated the opinion of the members of national parliaments during its international assembly meetings. The role of national parliaments in NATO's intervention in Kosovo varied from country to country. In some states, such as Denmark, Germany and the Netherlands, governments asked their parliaments for consent to be militarily involved in NATO's intervention (Assembly of the WEU, 2001a). In other NATO member states, such as in France, parliaments played a marginal role in the government's decision to commit troops to NATO's operations in Kosovo (Lamy, 2000). In a number of other states, such as Britain, where the government has no legal obligation to engage parliament in decision-making, the choice to do so is made as the parliament can table a 'non-confidence' motion which can force a government to resign (Assembly of the WEU, 2001a). In the US, the Congress remained indecisive concerning the Kosovo intervention (Damrosch, 2003, pp. 50-51).

Adapting NATO's Strategic Concept

Originally NATO's Strategic Concept was a document drafted by the Military Committee (MC) to provide a basis for military planning, organisation and deployment. MC 14/2 embodied massive retaliation, MC 14/3 defined flexible response. The latter could be adopted only after France had left the integrated military structure. During the Cold War these documents were not made available to the public, but after the fall of the Berlin Wall and the eclipse of the Warsaw Pact and even the Soviet Union, NATO acquired an interest in a public document showing not only its defensive character (which had always been a basic precept) but also its changed orientation. As mentioned before, risks and responsibilities took the place of 'threats' and new emphasis was put on ethnic and religious conflicts within states as well as non-military challenges to society like organised crime, drugs, illegal immigration and – increasingly – terrorism (Coker, 2002).

In a no-threat environment defence planning became difficult to quantify. The problem was exacerbated by a decline in defence budgets in order to cash in on the peace dividend and the political difficulty in sending conscript soldiers on other missions than self-defence. No wonder that NATO's new strategic concepts (adopted in 1991 and 1999) emphasised mobility and flexibility, because the layer-cake defence of eight national army corps lined up along the inner German border no longer made sense. With its disappearance went an important yardstick for measuring national contributions as each corps area should possess comparable defensive capabilities.

In 1991, NATO moved beyond the twin principles of the Harmel Report – defence and détente – which in 1967 had provided a conceptual injection into NATO cohesion after France had left the integrated military structure and NATO moved to Brussels. In defining the future tasks, NATO's 1991 Strategic Concept stated that security policy could now be based on three reinforcing elements: dialogue, cooperation and the maintenance of a collective defence capability. The remaining risks to allied security were multi-faceted in nature and multi-directional, which made them hard to predict and assess.[16] They would be less likely to result from calculated aggression, but rather from the adverse consequences of instabilities in Central and Eastern Europe. Nevertheless, the text was still very much oriented towards collective defence and constituted an uneasy compromise to cover the new realities. Peace support operations and especially peace enforcement would require new concepts for the use of military force. Military capabilities were a precondition for the credibility of policy objectives and Clausewitz was back, in a modern garb.

In 1999, the Strategic Concept moved further and said that 'NATO has an indispensable role to play in consolidating and preserving the positive changes of the recent past, and in meeting current and future security challenges' and 'NATO embodies the transatlantic link by which the security of North America is permanently tied to the security of Europe' (NATO, 1999, para. 4 and para. 7). Solidarity and cohesion, through daily cooperation in both the political and military spheres provided a sense of equal security among its members. The fundamental security tasks now were defined in the 1999 Strategic Concept as:

- Security: no country would be able to intimidate or coerce any other through the threat or use of force;
- Consultation on any issues that affect their vital interests;
- Deterrence and Defence.

And in order to enhance the security and stability of the Euro-Atlantic area:

- Crisis management, on a case-by-case basis and by consensus, including crisis response operations;
- Partnership with other countries in the Euro-Atlantic area.

The increased emphasis on crisis management was reflected in the guidelines for the force posture. Paragraph 52 stated:

The size, readiness, availability and deployment of NATO's military forces will reflect its commitment to collective defence and to conduct crisis response

---

16 The 1991 NATO Strategic Concept, available from www.nato-int [accessed 29 July 2003].

operations, sometimes at short notice, distant from their home stations, including beyond the Allies' territory (NATO, 1999).

The NATO PA devoted considerable time to these questions, both in the Defence and Security Committee and in the plenary. Briefings by the NATO International Staff and Supreme Headquarters of Allied Powers Europe (SHAPE) and regular visits to Washington kept the parliamentarians up to date. Their resolutions were generally supportive of the decisions reached in the Council, but pressed for accelerated action. The document 'NATO in the 21st Century' (NATO PA, 1998) initiated by Assembly President Senator Roth already mentioned in the section on enlargement, took a forward look and inspired national thinking. The same applied to the Declaration 322 on NATO Transformation of 19 November anticipating and supporting the outcome of the Prague Summit a few days later. Throughout the years special attention was given to the emergence of new threats. Defence against terrorism and weapons of mass destruction figured prominently (NATO PA, 2002a, para. 4) as well as the reform of military structures to facilitate force projection, multi-nationality and role specialisation. The debates in the NATO PA welcomed the lifting of the Strategic Concept, but sometimes questioned whether it provided a sufficient basis for concrete military planning.

Out-of-Area Operations

Already in 1992, Secretary General Manfred Wörner had declared the out-of-area debate 'out of date' in his address to the annual conference of the IISS in Brussels. The NATO operations in Bosnia and later in Kosovo confirmed this, but NATO operations in Africa or Asia still remained unlikely. This may change though. The 2002 session of foreign ministers in Reykjavik gave a preview in its *communiqué*:

> NATO must be able to field forces that can move quickly to wherever they are needed. This will require (new) capabilities within NATO, including strategic lift and modern strike capabilities, so that NATO can effectively respond collectively to any threat or aggression.[17]

The words 'wherever they are needed' and 'respond collectively' would indicate a NATO role in the fight against terrorism, but several problems remain. The day after 11 September 2001, NATO invoked its article V collective defence clause and confirmed it when the US had satisfactorily proven that the attack had come from abroad, albeit with domestic means. Yet NATO did not play a role in commanding the operation, which was conducted by the US CENTCOM in Tampa, Florida. Even the consultation opportunities were not fully used by the US which followed a policy of 'don't call us, we'll call you'. In the end some 1,000 European forces were on the ground in Afghanistan fighting the Taliban compared

---

17 Final Communiqué of the Ministerial Meeting of the North Atlantic Council, 14 May 2002, Reykjavik, Point 5.

with 4,000 US troops, but they got little credit for their participation. The ISAF peacekeeping force had substantial European contingents and no US units. Therefore, the brilliant gesture of European solidarity raised questions about its military implications. Did it erode the meaning of collective defence? Could it be remedied by double-hatting CENTCOM like SHAPE and SACLANT where the American commander exercises the double function of both NATO and national US command? Does the new orientation of NATO require the multi-tiered command structure or could the number of headquarters be drastically reduced in spite of national sensitivities? Will the fight against terrorism be sufficient as an organising principle for an alliance, especially in situations where terrorist acts cannot be linked to state-actors? Will NATO be best placed to deal with the increasingly obvious interrelationship between internal and external security and its impact on legislation? Here the EU with its cooperation in the field of justice, border control, and home affairs offers a better structure.

And finally and most importantly: would operations out-of-area require the consensus of all members (soon to be 26 or more) or could coalitions of the willing be formed within NATO, able to use NATO assets in the way 'combined joint task forces' were conceived in 1994, but never formally implemented? Clearly the US would like NATO to go global, as has been advocated consistently by politicians like US Senator Lugar, but Europeans will be more reticent about putting a NATO label on operations outside their own continent. Only if vital interests like oil supplies are at stake, might this reticence disappear.

The problem of consensus plays a role in every expanding international organisation. In the OSCE, the potentially paralysing effects have been mitigated by giving more authority to the Chairman-in-Office. In the EU, the formula of 'constructive abstention' – i.e. not obstructing a consensus by opting out of the decision and therefore not being bound by it – has been agreed but as far as is known never yet used. In WEU, there was an understanding that consensus was needed to launch an operation, but that there was no obligation for every member state to contribute forces. Some similar arrangements might be necessary in NATO in order to keep the consultation process viable. Of course, this may result in some centrifugal tendencies and reduce the sense of joint obligation and commitment. The impact on the parliamentary dimension would not be necessarily divisive, as the debate among parliamentarians will continue to be consensus-oriented, and ultimately the national decision to commit forces will remain a prerogative for national parliaments.

The crucial question will be whether the current American Bush Administration will modify its unilateralist tendencies and make an effort to act together with the European Union in approaching world problems. Clearly the US and Europe no longer have the cohesion of the Cold War period where the overriding priority of collective defence dampened irritations in other fields. Transatlantic relations will require more care than in the past, because the framework of common values could easily erode. The list of differences is increasing: on the death penalty, arms control, biological weapons convention, genetically manufactured food, Kyoto, the International Criminal Court and, recently, the Iraq war and protectionist measures on steel and agriculture. Even if the US regards the security situation in Europe as settled, consultation on world wide issues would remain of mutual interest. To be constructive, the US would have to discard its disdain for the emerging European foreign and security policy, which sceptics in Washington describe as 'Eurobabble'. A move in this direction was made by Stanley R. Sloan – one of the most perceptive American experts on NATO and currently director of the US Atlantic Commission. He not only advocated the creation of a special anti-terrorist command but also a new Atlantic treaty focusing on consultation and cooperation on a wide range of political, economic and other issues (Sloan, 2001).

The NATO PA plenary session in Istanbul adopted a declaration on transformation (NATO PA, 2002a) only a few days before the Prague Summit. It covered the full range of issues involved in NATO's adaptation from the projection of stability, the capability to take action 'wherever the security of the members is threatened' (NATO PA, 2002a, para. 2.b), the future development of special forces, to close cooperation with the European Union according to the 'Berlin Plus' formula for using NATO assets for EU-led operations when NATO itself is not involved. The Declaration also appealed for an overhaul of the internal organisation of NATO.

Conclusions

If we assess NATO decision-making in terms of parliamentary oversight, the enlargement process is most relevant. There the NATO Assembly played a stimulating role, somewhat ahead of government positions, and created political support for the decisions which ultimately were taken. The same applies to relations with Russia and Ukraine where the NATO PA through joint monitoring committees managed a substantial debate on a wide range of issues and was able to remove serious misunderstandings in both countries. The agreement with Russia on a Council at Twenty for a list of subjects was followed by a corresponding intensification of relations on the parliamentary side through a first joint session of the Standing Committee of the NATO PA with the Head of the Russian delegation and then, in Prague during May 2003, a formalisation into a NATO PA–Russia Standing Committee. Also national parliaments play an important role since the accession of new member states has to be ratified by parliament.

Other decisions have been elaborated and concluded strictly at governmental level, often in confidential negotiations (like the strategic concepts) or on the spur of the moment with hardly any time for consultations with capitals of member states (like the invocation of Article V, on 12 September 2001). As the NATO Parliamentary Assembly includes many members of national defence committees they generally supported demands for higher defence budgets although a substantial number preferred spending differently to spending more. In this respect the Defence Capabilities Initiative listing 58 areas for improvement was unhelpful and confusing. Only recently was an effort at prioritising made, but it is unclear to what extent the new demands of the fight against terrorism will undercut the earlier priorities. Here, national parliaments, like their governments, are in need of further guidance.

On some issues, such as the future importance of missile defence, national parliaments have held substantial debates. Only a few went deeply into the intricacies of arms control and non-proliferation and their significance in a changing world. Clearly, the first and foremost subject for parliamentary involvement is the despatch of troops on missions of intervention and peace support. In this respect both NATO and EU will not only remain intergovernmental in character, but ministerial commitments will remain subject to the constitutional procedures at home. Even when NATO could go global in principle, the size, composition and availability of national contributions will be different from the quasi-automatic pledges to collective defence. In any case, participation in out-of-area operations will require close consultation on the causes of the conflict, the relevance of military forces to its solution and the chances of success. Under present circumstances the chances for such a consensus on global issues are not bright as, contrary to expectations after the end of the Cold War, NATO has not become more political in nature but focused increasingly on military operations. On these questions the NATO PA focused considerable attention and its resolutions often softened the controversies at governmental level. In Kosovo this led to support for action without a UN Security Council mandate, combined with an attempt to maintain constructive relations with Russia. On the Strategic Concept, the new orientation and tasks were fully supported.

Apart from consensus-building on the main themes of security policy and transatlantic relations, the value of the NATO PA lies in the promotion of informed debate. Even with its special characteristics, NATO remains an intergovernmental organisation of sovereign nations. Therefore, parliamentary scrutiny of NATO takes place in national parliaments only. Yet it might be possible to synchronise parliamentary debates, for example by annually devoting a debate to the State of NATO and by making use of the major reports drafted by the Assembly. In such a way the national debates would be underpinned by common assessments, while conversely the consensus-building role of the NATO PA would be tested in practice.

Chapter 8

The United States Congress, the German *Bundestag*, and NATO's Intervention in Kosovo

Lori Fisler Damrosch

Introduction

The 1999 intervention in Kosovo presents fertile ground for research into the comparative politics and comparative constitutional law of military decision-making. Within a compressed time frame between autumn 1998 and spring 1999, the member states of the North Atlantic Treaty Organisation (NATO) had to reach a set of interconnected decisions: whether there would be a military operation in Kosovo, and if so, which states would participate in the action; whether the NATO vehicle or some other framework would be used for multilateral coordination; what the triggering conditions for military action would be; who would contribute what forms of support; who would exercise command and control over the operation in progress (including its military objectives, targets and choice of weaponry); and how to calibrate military pressure in relation to diplomacy and political initiatives. In the background for each of these decisions were premises about the locus of authority for democratic societies to decide to deploy and use military forces outside national territory. These issues were on some level present for all 19 of the NATO states, whether they ultimately chose to join active military operations or not.[1]

Among the many potential issues for which the Kosovo intervention provides ample raw material for comparative inquiry, the present chapter will single out one: Was there parliamentary control over the decision to apply military force in Kosovo?

---

1 Almost all NATO members did eventually join the effort. Along with the major NATO states, even tiny Luxembourg, and Iceland which lacks its own armed forces, contributed in some way to the collective endeavour. See 'Nonfighters in NATO Give Help for Raids,' *New York Times*, 27 March 1999. On the other hand, Greece made clear from the outset that it would not contribute troops; and in the case of Turkey, permission for NATO forces to use airports in Turkish territory was given only in mid-May 1999. See Kostakos, 2000, pp. 166, 167, 169. Concerning the newest NATO members (Hungary, Poland and the Czech Republic), see Tálas and Valki, 2000.

For clarity of focus, this chapter will consider only two countries, the United States and Germany. These countries were two of the most substantial military contributors to the NATO operation,[2] and also played significant roles throughout the 1990s in political discourse about the conflicts in former Yugoslavia. Equally important for present purposes, they present two different constitutional models for parliamentary involvement, with the United States as an archetype for the presidential form of organisation and Germany for one important variant of parliamentary governance.

The chapter begins with the United States as the dominant power in NATO and the leading state to organise the coalition that intervened in Kosovo. The principal question for examination will be whether the US Congress participated in any meaningful way in the decision to mount a military intervention in Kosovo or controlled any significant aspect of US involvement once the military operation began. The record shows that President Bill Clinton set the relevant policies for the United States, while Congress stayed mostly on the sidelines throughout the Kosovo operation. Then, by way of contrast, the chapter turns to the role of the German *Bundestag* in the same timeframe. The comparison of the role for the two national parliaments will show that the US Congress was confused about its own constitutional role and unable to speak with a clear voice, while the *Bundestag*, by contrast, carried out its constitutionally-mandated responsibility to give affirmative authorisation for an international military deployment.

The US-German comparison also invites attention to another aspect of constitutional practice in which the two countries differ markedly, namely the role for the judicial branch in giving definitive answers to constitutional questions in disputes between the legislative and executive branches. The US Supreme Court has by and large declined to clarify contested constitutional issues about the respective authorities of the President and the Congress concerning war powers, while the German Federal Constitutional Court does address and answer such questions.[3] In relation to the conflict at issue here, the US courts dismissed a lawsuit that sought to require the President to end US involvement in Kosovo unless he received affirmative authorisation for war from the Congress (Campbell v. Clinton, 2000). The Supreme Court did not take the case. The German Constitutional Court, by contrast, had authoritatively resolved questions of a similar type at an earlier phase of the conflicts in former Yugoslavia.[4] By virtue of that previous decision, it was entirely clear to

---

2   France and the United Kingdom undertook larger contributions than Germany to the military engagement in Kosovo. While Germany offered only 14 fighter aircraft, France carried out 12.8 percent of the air raids and more than 20 percent of aerial reconnaissance. At the peak of the military operation, 11,000 British troops were in Kosovo, while Germany had only a modest presence during the combat phase but increased its contribution in the post-conflict phase. See Duke et al., 2000b, pp. 128, 131-132, 134, 136, 140.

3   On the US Supreme Court's 'political question doctrine' and other techniques of avoiding a decision in war powers cases, see generally Henkin, 1996, pp. 143-148; Ely, 1993, pp. 54-67; Koh, 1990, pp. 134-149. On the US-German comparison concerning the judicial role in foreign affairs cases, see Franck, 1992.

4   See International Military Deployments Case, 1994, discussed further below.

German parliamentarians, and to the public in general, that the *Bundestag's* affirmative approval was needed as a condition for Geman troops to be sent to Kosovo. A complaint brought to the German Constitutional Court by a parliamentary group at the outbreak of the Kosovo war was dismissed on procedural grounds (Fink, 1999). But in contrast to the situation in the United States, the respective roles for the legislature and the executive had already been enunciated by prior judicial decision and the *Bundestag* had already cast its votes to authorise participation in the conflict.

This chapter endorses the proposition that parliaments should indeed be actively engaged in decision-making processes concerning potential military commitments. In this respect, it builds on the author's previous publications and work-in-progress concerning constitutional control over war powers, in which parliamentary control is a main focus of attention (Damrosch, 1995; 1996; 1997; 2003). In the discussion of the United States and Germany below, the comparison will show that the US Congress did not fully carry out its constitutional responsibility for shared participation in decisions to engage US armed forces in combat in Kosovo, while the German *Bundestag* did fulfill the legitimising role expected of it in the German constitutional system.

The chapter concludes with some reflections on the transplantability to new and prospective NATO member states of the divergent US and German models for constitutional control of war powers. The United States and Germany provide different sources of inspiration for countries undergoing constitutional change, including several of the newest NATO member states. Thus it may be relevant to consider what lessons could be learned from the Kosovo experience for countries that are seeking to consolidate democratic governance in general and civilian control over the military in particular. US presidentialism is a problematic model in this regard. From the viewpoint of strengthening parliament's voice in military decisions, the German model could be more attractive.

The Role of the US Congress in War Powers Decisions Concerning Former Yugoslavia

In order to understand what Congress did and did not do concerning the Kosovo intervention, it is necessary to step back for some context on the long-running controversy over the respective roles for Congress and the President under Articles I and II of the US Constitution and in recent history. More than two centuries after the framing of the Constitution, there is still no agreement in principle on how to apply the provisions that confer upon the Congress the power 'to declare war' (US Constitution, Article I, section 8, clause 11) and upon the President the power of 'Commander in Chief of the Army and Navy of the United States' (US Constitution, Article II, section 2). The basic conception of the constitution-framers was that it should not be in the power of one man, or one body of men, to take this fateful decision alone;[5] and that the

---

5   As US constitutional framer James Wilson explained to the ratification convention in Pennsylvania: 'This system will not hurry us into war; it is calculated to guard against it. It

President, who would have the greatest temptations in the direction of war, should be under effective checks and balances.[6] Thus the Constitution divides the war powers and indicates an affirmative responsibility for the Legislative Branch to share in decisions that could embroil the United States in war.

This view of the original design of checks and balances was largely respected over more than two centuries of constitutional experience, until the substantial growth of presidential power in factual terms following World War Two. The Korean War went forward on President Harry S. Truman's initiative, with only indirect and after-the-fact endorsement through congressional appropriation of funds and maintenance of authority for conscription. On a variety of occasions, presidents deployed troops to foreign countries and sent them into action without meaningful congressional involvement. Defenders of congressional prerogatives did not muster the political will to make an effective response to the Executive's position or to constrain executive war-making in specific conflicts.

The constitutional controversy reached its peak in the era of the Vietnam War,[7] when Congress decided to reassert its own position by enacting the War Powers Resolution of 1973 (United States Congress, 1973). The War Powers Resolution affirms a congressional understanding of the original constitutional intent to require congressional participation in decisions to 'introduce United States Armed forces into hostilities'.[8] But all US presidents, from President Nixon who tried unsuccessfully to block enactment of the resolution by use of the presidential veto,[9] through Presidents Ford, Carter, Reagan, Bush, and Clinton, have contended that at least in certain respects, the War Powers Resolution is unconstitutional.[10] Presidents (and proponents

---

will not be in the power of a single man, or a single body of men, to involve us in such distress; for the important power of declaring war is vested in the legislature at large: this declaration must be made with the concurrence of the House of Representatives: from this circumstance we may draw a certain conclusion that nothing but our national interest can draw us into a war.' As quoted in Reveley, 1981, p. 102.

6   James Madison wrote that the Constitution 'supposes, what the history of all governments demonstrates, that the Executive is the branch of power most interested in war, and most prone to it. It has accordingly with studied care, vested the question of war in the Legislature.' Letter from James Madison to Thomas Jefferson , 2 Apr. 1798, in Hunt, 1906, p. 312 (spelling modernised).

7   See generally Ely, 1993, pp. 12-46.

8   Outside the very limited situations of responses to armed attack on the United States or its territories, possessions or armed forces. See United States Congress, 1973, para. 1541(c).

9   For President Nixon's veto message, Weekly Compilation of Presidential Documents, 1973. Congress was able to enact the resolution despite the veto, by passing the measure by supermajority votes.

10 Damrosch, 2000. President George W. Bush has acted in conformity with the War Powers Resolution by seeking and obtaining two specific statutory authorisations under the Resolution's terms (in September 2001 for the war on terrorism and in October 2002 for the war against Iraq). It is not clear whether President George W. Bush espouses a different constitutional view from his predecessors or whether he has simply yielded to political imperatives. As that question is outside the scope of this volume, it will not be addressed here.

of strong conceptions of presidential power) object in principle to Congress's efforts to restrain the President from exercising independent initiative concerning potential uses of military power. They also object in particular to two aspects of the Resolution's procedural framework: these are the provision under which the President would be required to withdraw US armed forces from hostilities after the expiration of a 60-day period unless the Congress had affirmatively acted to approve their involvement[11] and the provision for Congress to direct the President to remove the armed forces from hostilities by passage of a concurrent resolution which the President could not veto.[12]

The constitutional issues about war powers intersect with broader questions of the political context for separation of powers in the United States, especially the tendency of American voters to elect one or both houses of the legislature not from the President's political party but from the opposite party. In the period of the late 20th-century war powers disputes, presidents could rarely count on a same-party majority in the two houses of Congress; and thus the political dynamic for asking for formal authorisation to conduct war did not usually exist. By the same token, Congress could rarely muster the bicameral, bipartisan sentiment necessary for avoiding presidential veto of legislative measures to constrain the exercise of war powers after the fact, though sometimes the purse-string control could be used for this purpose.

The controversy over the underlying constitutional distribution of war powers persisted throughout the 1990s, including in the earlier phases of US decision-making on whether to commit troops to peace-keeping or peace enforcement in former Yugoslavia. The Clinton Administration did not acknowledge any requirement of formal congressional approval for military operations in Yugoslavia. Even before ground troops were deployed to Bosnia-Herzegovina in implementation of the Dayton Agreement,[13] US military power was used in connection with the Yugoslav conflicts, including in naval interdiction operations in enforcement of the UN embargo, and in policing the no-flight zone over Bosnia-Herzegovina and protecting 'safe havens' in Bosnian territory. In each instance, the decision to apply US military force was a presidential initiative in which the Congress did not formally participate. After the Srebrenica massacre, President Clinton authorised air strikes against Bosnian Serb positions, without asking Congress for permission. Congress basically acquiesced in these measures that had been taken on presidential responsibility and did not assert itself to play a more active role in supervising or controlling them.[14]

---

11 United States Congress, 1973, para. 1544(b). The 60-day period could be extended for an additional 30 days upon certification by the President that 'unavoidable military necessity respecting the safety of United States Armed Forces requires the continued use of such armed forces in the course of bringing about a prompt removal of such forces.'

12 United States Congress, 1973, para. 1544(c). The concurrent veto feature falls in the class of measures which the US Supreme Court held to be generally unconstitutional (see Immigration and Naturalisation Service v. Chadha, 1983).

13 General Framework Agreement for Peace in Bosnia and Herzegovina, 1995, p. 75, for the military provisions, p. 92.

14 For detailed analysis of the extent of congressional acceptance of presidential initiatives in

At Dayton, President Clinton committed 20,000 US troops to the NATO Implementation Force in Bosnia-Herzegovina. Although preserving his position that congressional authorisation was not constitutionally required, President Clinton stated that he would 'welcome' an appropriate expression of congressional support (Clinton, 1995). But Congress did not exactly grant him that favour. Shortly before the President left for the signing ceremony for the Dayton Agreement in Paris, Senate Majority Leader Bob Dole obtained a favourable vote in the Senate on a resolution stating that the Senate 'unequivocally supports' the sending of the troops to Bosnia but also noting 'reservations' about the presidential decision to dispatch them (United States Congress, 1995, Res. 44, p. S18552). For its part, the House affirmed its 'pride and admiration' for the troops but expressed 'serious concerns and opposition to the President's policy' that had produced the plan for their deployment. As a leading US scholar of the constitutional law of war powers has concluded, '[i]n the end, Congress as a body opted neither to block the deployment of American combat forces to Bosnia nor to authorise it' (Stromseth, 1996, p. 904).

In the same timeframe that the Dayton Agreement was being negotiated and put into effect, President Clinton and congressional leaders tried to hammer out a budgetary compromise that would include funding for the Bosnian deployment. But because of other unresolved issues in the budget, President Clinton vetoed the authorising legislation for defence expenditures that Congress passed in late December 1995. One of the reasons cited for the veto was a provision that would have attached a certification requirement to presidential decisions to place US armed forces under the operational or tactical control of the United Nations, which Clinton characterised as an infringement on his constitutional authority as commander-in-chief (United States Congress, 1996a, p. H12). The House failed to override the veto.[15] In a legal memorandum explaining the Administration's views on the unconstitutionality of such restrictions on presidential authority, Assistant Attorney-General Walter Dellinger wrote:

> It is for the President alone, as Commander-in-Chief, to make the choice of the particular personnel who are to exercise operational and tactical command functions over the U.S. Armed Forces...Congress may not prevent the President from acting on such a military judgment concerning the choice of the commanders under whom the U.S. forces engaged in the mission are to serve (United States Congress, 1996b pp. H10061).

Ultimately, the Congress did appropriate funds for US troops to deploy to Bosnia, but it did not directly confront the terms of their mission or attempt to regulate their potential involvement in hostilities. And for as long as the situation on the ground remained basically stable, this level of congressional involvement may have been sufficient: after all, the War Powers Resolution purports to require specific

---

Bosnia-Herzegovina, see Stromseth, 1996; Tiefer, 1999; Fisher, 1999.

15 See United States Congress, 1996a, at H22. For discussion, see Committee on Military Affairs and Justice of the Association of the Bar of the City of New York, 1999, p. 63.

congressional authorisation only for those situations entailing involvement of US armed forces in 'hostilities', not for non-combat deployments.

Between the Dayton Agreement of December 1995 and the Kosovo developments that reached crisis proportions beginning in October 1998, congressional attention to the situation in former Yugoslavia was mainly limited to passive receipt of reports from the Executive Branch and periodic renewal of funding for the forces in Bosnia. Nor did Congress mobilise itself for closer engagement even as tensions mounted between October 1998 and March 1999, although the Armed Services Committee of the House of Representatives did hold hearings in mid-March 1999 (see Butler, 2000, pp. 278, 288).

At the same time as the confrontation over Kosovo was mounting, the Clinton presidency suffered an unprecedented domestic political onslaught and also confronted international challenges from terrorist attacks and a crisis over the international weapons inspection regime in Iraq. Domestically, President Clinton's romantic involvement with Monica Lewinsky and subsequent misleading testimony under oath provoked the most serious political crisis since President Nixon's resignation in 1974. For only the second time in US history (the first was in 1868), the House of Representatives voted on 19 December 1998 to impeach the President, thereby invoking the extraordinary constitutional procedure of a Senate trial in early 1999, which ended with the President's acquittal on 12 February 1999. Meanwhile, even under those domestic clouds, President Clinton continued to function as Commander-in-Chief. On 20 August 1998, he ordered cruise missile strikes against Sudan and Afghanistan in response to the East African embassy bombings earlier in the same month (Murphy, 1999a, pp. 161-167). In autumn 1998, he oversaw the intensification of diplomacy to settle the Kosovo conflict and the preparation for military action as part of the strengthening of pressures against the Milosevic regime in Yugoslavia (Murphy, 1999a, pp. 167-170). On 16 December 1998, just as the House of Representatives was preparing to vote on the impeachment resolution, President Clinton ordered cruise missile strikes against Iraq, in response to Saddam Hussein's defiance of the UN-mandated inspection regime for weapons of mass destruction (Murphy, 1999b, pp. 474-478). The tumult of the times did not enhance the atmosphere for productive presidential-congressional interactions when the time came to decide about military action in Kosovo.

On the international plane, political negotiations over Kosovo's worsening plight reached a new plateau in autumn 1998, with the adoption of UN Security Council Resolutions 1199 (23 September 1998) and 1203 (24 October 1998), under which the Kosovo Verification Mission composed of monitors from the Organisation for Security and Cooperation in Europe was to be sent into Kosovo with NATO support. The setting of US policies in these negotiations, and the decisions on the nature and extent of US military involvement belonged to the presidential domain, with only minimal attention from the Congress.[16] The NATO decision to put combat aircraft in a state of readiness for potential strikes in Yugoslavia did not elicit any

---

16 Congress was preoccupied at the time with the Lewinsky affair and with the midterm elections of November 1998.

significant congressional reaction, amidst the welter of other crises competing for the attention of American politicians and the American public.[17] In any event, although President Clinton's credibility was at its lowest ebb, the intensification of coercion concerning Kosovo as of late 1998 did not appear to push the limits of presidential Commander-in-Chief powers or to cross any clear lines necessitating direct congressional involvement.

After the failure of the Rambouillet negotiations for a diplomatic settlement of the Kosovo conflict (Independent International Commission, 2000, pp. 151-159), NATO air strikes against the Federal Republic of Yugoslavia began on 24 March 1999. That very day, the House of Representatives passed, by a vote of 424-1, a measure stating that it 'supports the members of the United States Armed Forces who are engaged in military operations against the Federal Republic of Yugoslavia and recognises their professionalism, dedication, patriotism and courage.' (United States Congress, 1999a). But neither this rhetorical gesture, nor any other measure adopted by the Congress before, during, or after the 78 days of combat, constituted a specific statutory authorisation under the War Powers Resolution. Nor was there any available mechanism for definitive clarification of whether Congress should have been constitutionally required to give affirmative approval. Notably, the constitutional issue could not be resolved by the US federal judiciary.

Within days of the outbreak of combat, some 30 members of Congress, led by Representative Tom Campbell of California, brought suit against President Clinton in an effort to obtain judicial vindication of their position that under the Constitution and the War Powers Resolution, Congress had a duty to approve the participation of US armed forces in hostilities in Kosovo. At the first stage of the suit in the federal district court in the District of Columbia, the Executive Branch argued that the case should be dismissed on threshold grounds, including that the congressional plaintiffs lacked the standing to sue the President and that the matter presented a 'political question' unsuitable for judicial determination. The district court did indeed dismiss the case without discussing its merits (Campbell v. Clinton, 1999), upon concluding that the plaintiffs could not satisfy the standards previously laid down by the Supreme Court concerning congressional standing.[18] The court of appeal confirmed the dismissal on grounds of lack of standing, and the Supreme Court declined to review the dismissal (Campbell v. Clinton, 2000).

---

17 The two steps in this process were an activation warning issued 25 September 1998 and an activation order of 13 October 1998 which signaled that air strikes could begin in 96 hours. See Whitney, 1998; Cohen, 1998; Butler, 2000, pp. 277-278. Shortly after the issuing of the activation order, the Milosevic regime agreed to the plan that was to be embodied in Resolution 1203, thereby avoiding the threatened air strikes for the time being. See Independent International Commission on Kosovo, 2000, pp. 148-149.

18 The leading case on congressional standing is Raines v. Byrd, 1997, which held that members of Congress cannot sue to vindicate abstract interests, including their institutional interest as voting representatives. The Supreme Court observed in *Raines* that some European constitutional courts do operate under a system in which members of the legislature can bring constitutional complaints, but that the US system 'contemplates a more restricted role' for the federal courts.

The record of legislative activity concerning authority for combat operations includes the following actions (or lack thereof):[19]

- On 23 March 1999, the day before the NATO air strikes began, the Senate had taken a favourable vote (58-41) on a measure that would have authorised the President to 'conduct military air operations and missile strikes in cooperation with our NATO allies' against the Federal Republic of Yugoslavia (United States Congress, 1999b; see Campbell v. Clinton, 1999). In the form and procedure under which this measure was presented (a concurrent resolution rather than a specific statutory authorisation under the War Powers Resolution), this was mainly a symbolic vote rather than one with operative significance. But the House never adopted the Senate's resolution; rather, when the House voted on it on 28 April, the measure failed by a tie vote (see below).

- On 24 March 1999, the House passed (with only one dissenting vote) the symbolic gesture of support for the troops in the field, as noted above (United States Congress, 1999a).

- On 28 April 1999, in response to Representative Campbell's invocation of the procedural provisions of the War Powers Resolution, the House took four votes concerning Kosovo, as follows: (1) It voted down a declaration of war by 2 votes in favor to 427 against (United States 1999c); (2) It voted down, by a tie vote of 213-213, the Senate's measure previously adopted on March 23 that would have authorised the military air operations and missile strikes;[20] (3) It also voted (by vote of 139-290) against a resolution that would have purported to require an immediate end to US participation in the conflict under para. 5(c) of the War Powers Resolution;[21] (4) It voted (249-180) for a bill to prohibit the use of funds appropriated to the Department of Defence for deployment of any US ground forces to Kosovo, unless specifically approved by Congress.[22]

After this sequence of votes, the White House spokesman captured the prevailing mood: 'The House today voted no on going forward, no on going back and they tied on standing still'(Mitchell, 1999, p. A1). On the occasion of these House votes, President Clinton tendered assurances that Congress would indeed be involved in any decision to introduce ground troops into hostilities:

---

19 Previously, on 11 March 1999 the House had voted (219-191) to approve a US commitment to a peace-keeping force in Kosovo if a peace settlement could be reached; but this vote did not speak to the question of combat operations. See Mitchell, 1998.

20 United States Congress, 1999b. All the Campbell plaintiffs had voted no on this measure, thereby bringing about its defeat. Their argument for congressional standing included the claim that the President had effectively nullified their votes by continuing with the very operations that the House had refused to authorise.

21 United States Congress, 1999d. This measure had been introduced by Representative Campbell under the priority provisions of the War Powers Resolution.

22 United States Congress, 1999e. The Senate never voted on that bill, so it never became law.

[W]ere I to change my policy with regard to the introduction of ground forces, I can assure you that I would fully consult with the Congress. Indeed, without regard to our differing constitutional views on the use of force, I would ask for Congressional support before introducing U.S. ground forces into Kosovo into a nonpermissive environment (New York Times, 1999).

Since ground troops were ultimately not introduced for combat purposes, this pledge did not need to be acted upon.

Later, on 20 May 1999, Congress passed an Emergency Supplemental Appropriations Act[23] which included money for Kosovo operations (up to $11.8 billion) but lacked the explicit recital of specific statutory authorisation necessary to comply with the terms of the War Powers Resolution.[24]

The rulings of the district court and court of appeals in the Campbell case came after the 'distinctly mixed messages' of the foregoing legislative record (Campbell v. Clinton, 1999). The district court ruled on 8 June 1999, more than two months into the military operation and after the 60-day period contemplated under the War Powers Resolution would have expired. Though the congressional plaintiffs argued that the district court should instruct the President to comply with the War Powers Resolution's time limit, the court found that the suit could not be maintained in light of a recent Supreme Court precedent restricting the conditions under which legislators may bring suits in federal court.

Active combat operations ceased on 10 June 1999, upon Yugoslavia's agreement to withdraw its forces from Kosovo and to accept a NATO-led peace-keeping force there. US ground troops did indeed deploy to Kosovo as part of this peace-keeping operation, but not in combat mode (United States Weekly Compilation of Presidential Documents, 1999).

About a year later, on 18 May 2000, the Senate narrowly rejected a measure that would have set a deadline of 1 July 2001 for withdrawing US ground troops from Kosovo. The effort to include a funding cutoff for Kosovo operations in a military spending bill lost on a 53-47 vote. Senator Robert Byrd, the provision's chief sponsor, explained that '[t]he intent of the amendment is to restore congressional oversight over the Kosovo mission...Of course, the administration doesn't like it. They don't want to hear a peep out of Congress.' The Administration had threatened a presidential veto if Congress had passed the measure (Schmitt, 2000a). Again in autumn 2000, the Clinton Administration had to beat back an effort by House Republicans to attach a deadline for withdrawal of troops from Kosovo in connection with the negotiations over the

---

23 United States Congress, 1999f. appropriating funds for operations against the Federal Republic of Yugoslavia 'during the period beginning on March 24, 1999, and ending on such date as NATO may designate, to resolve the conflict with respect to Kosovo.'

24 According to para. 8(a) of the War Powers Resolution, (United States Congress, 1973, 50 U.S.C. para. 1547(a)): 'Authority to introduce United States Armed Forces into hostilities ... shall not be inferred – (1) from any provision of law..., including any provision contained in any appropriation Act, unless such provision specifically authorises the introduction of United States Armed Forces into hostilities...and states that it is intended to constitute specific statutory authorisation within the meaning of this joint resolution...'

annual budgetary appropriations for the Pentagon for fiscal year 2001 (Schmitt, 2000b).

We now turn to the contrasting framework for authorisation for use of military force by Germany.

The *Bundestag's* Approvals of Military Action in Former Yugoslavia

For a long time, Germany's Basic Law of 1949 (*Grundgesetz*) was interpreted to allow German armed forces to participate in military activities in defence of the NATO area; but there was considerable uncertainty about whether the Basic Law would permit German military action other than in self-defence of Germany or its NATO partners. As amended in 1954 and 1968, the Basic Law allows the Federal Republic to establish armed forces 'for defence purposes,' with the proviso that '[o]ther than for defence purposes the armed forces may be employed only to the extent explicitly permitted by this Basic Law.' (*Grundgesetz*, art. 87a[1] and [2]). The Basic Law also allows the Federal Republic to 'become party to a system of collective security.' (*Grundgesetz*, art. 24[2]). Until the 1990s, Germany's political leaders resisted a constitutional interpretation embracing UN peace-keeping or NATO out-of-area operations (despite considerable scholarly opinion taking a different and more generous view of what was constitutionally permitted).[25] At the time of the 1991 Gulf War, Hans-Dietrich Genscher (then foreign minister) insisted that Germany could not constitutionally deploy troops outside the NATO area (Kommers, 1997, pp. 160-64). Chancellor Helmut Kohl pledged that the government would seek constitutional reform or clarification as soon as an all-German parliament had been elected (New York Times, 1990).

Soon after the Gulf crisis, with German reunification having been accomplished and with Germany being pressed to assume a more active external role, Kohl's government shifted toward a more flexible conception of the constitutional permissibility of certain military activities outside the NATO area. In 1992 and 1993, the cabinet approved decisions to allow German military units to assist NATO in monitoring compliance with the UN-mandated embargo of former Yugoslavia, to put German AWACS[26] aircraft at the service of NATO enforcement over Bosnia-Herzegovina, and to participate in the UN humanitarian operation in Somalia (Heintschel von Heinegg and Haltern, 1994, pp. 286-288). These decisions were controversial both politically and legally; and they came under attack in the Federal Constitutional Court, through actions initiated by minority parliamentary parties (Kommers, 1997, pp. 162-163; Kress 1995, pp. 414-415).

The Federal Constitutional Court eventually settled the constitutional issues in an important 1994 judgment clarifying the terms on which Germany could join in multinational military operations (International Military Deployments Case, 1994). The constitutional ruling, which disposed of general objections to German

---

25 Khan and Zöckler, 1992, and references in Kommers, 1997, pp. 162-63.
26 Airborne Warning and Control System (AWACS).

involvement in peace enforcement, enunciated principles governing Germany's participation in any collective military action. As the judgement is discussed elsewhere in this volume (see Chapter Nine), only one aspect of it will be dealt with here. That aspect is the Court's articulation of a constitutional requirement of parliamentary consent.

The Constitutional Court stressed that in principle, the *Bundestag's* prior approval is essential to the legitimacy of all external military engagements. The sole exception would be in a situation entailing imminent danger, in which case the government may take a provisional emergency decision but must immediately lay the matter before parliament and recall the troops if parliament so decides (International Military Deployments Case, 1994, I.L.R., vol. 106, p. 350). According to the Court, the constitutional rules

> seek to ensure that the Federal Army, instead of becoming a source of power solely for the use of the Executive, will be integrated as a 'parliamentary army' into a democratic constitutional system governed by the rule of law, in other words to preserve for Parliament a legally relevant influence on the establishment and use of the armed forces (International Military Deployments Case, 1994, I.L.R., vol. 106, p. 348).

The Court called on parliament to enact legislation on procedures to obtain parliamentary consent to future deployments: such legislation should 'accentuate the principle of formal parliamentary participation' but also should 'pay attention to the government's constitutionally-guaranteed exclusive sphere of executive power and responsibility in respect of foreign policy' (International Military Deployments Case, 1994, 106 I.L.R. at 351). So far, such standing legislation has not yet been introduced or enacted.

Following the 1994 decision, the *Bundestag* has carried out the responsibility envisaged in the Court's judgment in a series of affirmative votes concerning military involvement in former Yugoslavia. In June 1995, more than two-thirds of the *Bundestag's* members voted in favour of the deployment of warplanes to support UN forces in Bosnia-Herzegovina (Cowell, 1995, p. A3). In December 1995, by a vote of 543-107 the *Bundestag* approved the dispatch of 4,000 German troops to participate in the NATO Implementation Force (IFOR) to carry out the Dayton Agreement (Reuters World Service, 1995); and in February 1996, it approved the use of German warplanes in aid of the UN force in the Eastern Slavonia region of Croatia (Deutsche Presse-Agentur, 1996). In December 1996, by a vote of 499 to 93, it approved the deployment of 2,000 combat-ready ground troops to Bosnia to serve jointly with French forces in the stabilisation force that replaced IFOR (Cowell, 1996, p. A3).

Consistent with the Federal Constitutional Court's interpretation of German constitutional requirements, the *Bundestag* likewise had to authorise German participation in the Kosovo campaign. The domestic political context for the *Bundestag's* initial consideration of the Kosovo situation was the election in September 1998 of an incoming 'red-green' coalition, which inherited the Kosovo issue from its predecessor and which had to formulate a position even before officially taking office. Before the September 1998 elections, the Kohl government had already indicated Germany's solidarity with NATO's threat to use force in Kosovo;[27] but this signal of support could not constitutionally commit Germany to participating directly in any military action, unless and until the *Bundestag* could formally approve such action. The politics of the matter were delicate, since the leftist parties who prevailed in the elections were torn between their historical pacifism and their sense of Germany's moral obligation to participate in an effort to stop a European genocide.[28] As a candidate and as incoming Chancellor, Gerhard Schroeder had stressed that a government under his leadership would be a full partner in NATO (Duke et al., 2000b, p. 133). But the fact that NATO would be leading the military initiatives in Kosovo did not sit well with some of the deputies from the former eastern zone. Also, doubts had been raised about the compatibility of the proposed intervention with international law under the UN Charter, in the absence of an explicit authorising resolution from the UN Security Council. All these factors made for a parliamentary debate which has been called a watershed – 'long, earnest and searching' (Nolte, 2003, p. 247).

In an extraordinary session held on 16 October 1998, the outgoing *Bundestag* voted in favour of participation by federal armed forces with NATO in Kosovo, by a huge majority of 500 in favour, 62 against, and 18 abstentions.[29] In the parliamentary debates, issues of compliance with the international law on the use of force took on constitutional significance, because of the constitutional supremacy accorded to the rules of general international law within the German legal system.[30] The government emphasised in this connection that the Kosovo case was unique and that there would be no question of setting a precedent for other uses of force without Security Council authorisation.[31] The overwhelming margin of the vote in favour of the military action under NATO auspices, even without formal Security Council approval, may have helped calm the concerns of the German public about the impending war.[32]

Later, the *Bundestag* confirmed and specified its approval in further votes held

---

27 See Whitney, 1998, quoting Germany's Defence Minister, Volker Rühe, on Germany's preparations to contribute fighter-bombers to an air campaign in Kosovo; see also Perlez, 1998, noting that Kohl's departing cabinet would meet on October 12 to confirm a position on participation in NATO air strikes, prior to a NATO meeting at which the activation order would be approved.

28 The Green Party's foreign minister, Joschka Fischer, commented that Germany's two cardinal principles of foreign policy – 'No more war' and 'No Auschwitz again' – were in contradiction in respect of Kosovo. Interview with Fischer in Der Spiegel, No. 16, 1999, quoted in Duke et al., 2000b, p. 133.

29 Duke, et al 2000b, p. 128 at p. 133. Approval was for the 'use of the Federal Republic's armed forces in the framework of its participation in planned NATO operations in order to avoid a humanitarian disaster in the conflict in Kosovo.' Fink, 1999, p. 1017.

30 On the prominence of international law in the *Bundestag's* October 1998 debate, see Simma, 1999, pp. 12-13.

31 Simma, 1999, pp. 13-14, 20.

32 According to Duke, et al., 2000b, p. 134, a majority of Germans supported the military action, while '[t]he dispute about the war took place in the media rather than in parliament.' For the proposition that the parliamentary debate may have served as a catalyst for public opinion, see Nolte, 2003, p. 247.

on 13 and 19 November 1998 to approve participation in a NATO extraction force in Macedonia and on 22 February 1999 for use of troops in a post-crisis stabilisation force (Duke et al., 2000b, p. 133; Fink, 1999, p. 1017). In the parliamentary debate in February, the government took the position that a UN Security Council resolution would be politically desirable but not legally indispensable (Simma, 1999, p. 9). When the NATO bombing campaign began on 24 March 1999, German warplanes joined the action.

The fact that the *Bundestag* had voted did not put to rest all questions about the legal situation once combat actually began. On 25 March 1999, members of the *Bundestag* belonging to the Party of Democratic Socialism (PDS),[33] who had consistently opposed and voted against military action, brought a complaint to the Federal Constitutional Court claiming that German participation in the military operation in Kosovo was unconstitutional; their main allegation was that because the intervention had not been authorised by the UN Security Council, Germany could not lawfully participate in it (Fink, 1999, p. 1017). However, the Constitutional Court dismissed the petition on the procedural ground of lack of standing of the PDS parliamentary party to complain of a constitutional violation (Bundesverfassungsgericht, 1999; see also Chapter Nine). The Court took the view that the PDS parliamentary group could only assert a claim against the executive branch in respect of the *Bundestag's* rights; however, since the *Bundestag* had already voted more than once to approve the participation in military operations in Kosovo, the *Bundestag's* rights could not have been violated (Fink, 1999, p. 1017).

Although there is a superficial resemblance between the dismissal of the complaint of the US congressional plaintiffs and that of the minority parliamentarians in Germany, the contexts are different. In the United States, the US courts held that there was no judicial competence to rule on a claim that the executive branch had usurped the legislature's prerogative. In Germany, by contrast, the Constitutional Court had previously established the need for the legislature to act and the legislature had indeed acted.[34]

Conclusions

The Kosovo experience, and the US-German comparison in particular, suggest different ways that democratic societies can be organised to take decisions on commitment of national military forces in support of international objectives. Under the US presidential model of governance, the head of government has a power base separate from that of the legislature and a large measure of decision-making autonomy, especially in respect of external affairs. Although the legislature is supposed to fulfill a constitutionally-prescribed role of shared participation in decisions for war, the US Congress has frequently fallen short in attempting to discharge this responsibility, as in

---

33 The successor to the former ruling party of the German Democratic Republic,
34 For an illuminating comparison of the US and German systems with respect to judicial authority to resolve separation of powers disputes, see Franck, 1992.

the Kosovo case. And the US Supreme Court, notwithstanding its potency in ruling on many kinds of constitutional questions, has remained silent about the still-unresolved struggle between Congress and the President over war powers. Thus the President has been able to engage US armed forces in military conflict without the direct approval of the legislative branch, as President Clinton did in Kosovo.

Many aspects of the US constitutional model have proven highly influential as countries around the world have gone through waves of democratic transformation (see Henkin and Rosenthal, 1990). Presidentialism, however, has not been one of the more successful exports. As many commentators have observed (Linz, 1992, and other essays in Lijphart, 1992), the US model does not transplant well and has had a tendency (especially in Latin America) to give way to authoritarian rule.

German constitutionalism offers a strikingly different version of separation of powers, with significant implications for military decision-making. Under the constitutional doctrine elaborated by the Federal Constitutional Court in the 1994 International Military Deployments case, the legislature must take an affirmative decision, in principle in advance of the commitment of troops. Parliamentary deliberation provides a level of transparency and a potential for consensus-building that would be lacking if the executive could take such decisions alone.

To date, only a few other NATO countries (notably Denmark and the Netherlands, as discussed elsewhere in this volume) have followed Germany in insisting upon formal, advance parliamentary approval for participation in a proposed NATO action such as Kosovo. A fuller comparative study would reveal the extent to which indirect forms of parliamentary control have operated across a broader range of democracies, in respect of Kosovo and other conflicts involving international military enforcement.[35]

As NATO embraces its new and prospective members and revamps for the challenges ahead, questions of democratic control over military engagements will be central to the future of the alliance. Of course, there are a variety of ways in which democratic values can be pursued and consolidated; and among the NATO member states there is a variety of potential models. NATO member states include some of the oldest democracies and some of the newest; some are organised in presidential and most in parliamentary form; some function mainly on a two-party model while others require complex coalition-building, and so on.

Adequate democratic credentials and assurance of civilian control over the military are touchstones for the recent and prospective waves of NATO expansion. For several new democracies, the very processes of admission into and participation within NATO have served as a kind of tutorial in democratic consolidation and institution-building. Polities in transition have looked to diverse constitutional models in developing their own approaches to executive-legislative relations with respect to war powers. In that connection, the role of national parliaments in military decision-making deserves special attention. The most recent additions to the NATO community faced their first tests of constitutional control of war powers with the Kosovo crisis, as did

---

35 The author is currently engaged in comparative research along these lines, involving some 20 well-established democracies (not all of which are members of NATO).

several states that were aspiring toward NATO admission. Their parliaments were a key forum for considering the relevant decisions. Hungary, which had just been received into NATO when the Kosovo conflict began, submitted certain critical decisions for the affirmative authorisation of the national parliament (Tálas and Valki, 2000, pp. 202-203). Bulgaria and Romania, not yet NATO member states but eager to prove themselves to be suitable partners, had parliamentary votes to approve opening their airspace to NATO planes (Pierre, 1999, pp. 3, 5). Bulgaria cited a constitutional requirement for parliamentary approval as the rationale for denying Russia's request for overflight rights at a tense moment near the end of the Kosovo war in June 1999 (Lewis, 1999). These examples illustrate that the newly democratising members of NATO have had to pay attention to domestic constituencies and allow opportunities for transparent deliberation about decisions that could embroil those countries in military conflict. In that regard, the German model, under which the parliament must openly debate and decide before armed forces can be used for purposes other than self-defence, may hold an attraction for newly-democratising states.

Chapter 9

Parliamentary Accountability and Military Forces in NATO: The Case of Germany

Roman Schmidt-Radefeldt

Introduction

The increased influence of public international law on national legal systems has rendered it necessary to strengthen parliamentary control in the sphere of foreign affairs. The development of international law has meant that the traditional distinction between home and foreign affairs has become blurred, one example being the ever-increasing number of foreign affairs matters that are becoming part of the national decision-making process (Tomuschat, 1978, p. 7).[1] Governments feel more and more often compelled to disclose the reasons behind their activities abroad in order to create a general acceptance of their actions. All this serves to reinforce the conflict between the demand for democratic legitimacy and the necessity for governments to retain their capacity to act in the field of foreign affairs.

This chapter examines this system of potentially conflicting checks and balances in the case of Germany, using the example of integrated NATO forces. Three particular aspects of military integration will be brought to the fore and will be discussed in the context of the ability of national parliaments to exercise controlling functions. The first aspect concerns the stationing of NATO troops on the territory of NATO member states; the second deals with the deployment of integrated military forces for NATO operations; and the third examines the military cooperation of integrated NATO forces within the framework of multinational units of NATO member states.

In all three areas, it is the constitutionally-guaranteed competencies of the German *Bundestag* in the field of military affairs to which our attention is drawn. It is not least for historical reasons that the control exercised by the German parliament over the integrated forces of the German Federal Army (*Bundeswehr*) appears especially intense when compared to that of other countries. This high

---

1 This phenomenon is described by American doctrine as the 'domestication of international policy'; see Nincic, 1988, p. 57 f.

level of control has resulted in the development of the German doctrine that the power to control foreign affairs (*auswärtige Gewalt*) belongs not exclusively to the government but rather is shared between government and parliament. This is referred to as the doctrine of 'combined power' (*kombinierte Gewalt)* (Menzel, 1963, p. 179 and Friesenhahn, 1985, p. 9; Wolfrum, 1997, pp. 38-40).

The distribution of competencies between government and parliament is not only based on the explicit provisions of the constitution but has also been influenced considerably by the decisions of the German Constitutional Court (*Bundesverfassungsgericht*). In the 1980s, the stationing of nuclear weapons (cruise missiles) following the Resolution of the NATO Council of 12 December 1979 (the 'dual-track' decision) was challenged in several NATO member states (Stationing Case, 1984). During the 1990s, the engagement of the *Bundeswehr* in former Yugoslavia led to a key judgment by the Federal Constitutional Court concerning the deployment of German armed forces abroad (International Military Deployments Case, 1994). More recently, the German Federal Constitutional Court has ruled on the NATO Strategic Concept (*Organstreit* Case, 2001). All these cases raised the issue of whether or not the government was required to obtain the constitutionally stipulated consent of the legislature before being able to proceed with the foreign affairs in question.

The dominant position of the German *Bundestag* is rooted in the core competence to be able to decide on each deployment of German armed forces by means of a prior constitutive parliamentary decision. The central importance of this competence becomes especially clear when the constitutional positions of parliaments in other NATO member states are examined. The competence of the German parliament is all the more remarkable when one considers that it was not foreseen by the constitution but was rather created by the Federal Constitutional Court. This chapter aims to trigger some of the legal questions that were left open by the ruling of the Court, but which may prove to be relevant to the future military practice of German troops.

In addition, the German constitution (Basic Law – *Grundgesetz*) provides the parliament with a whole host of competencies in the field of military affairs, including budgetary powers and the appointment of the German Parliamentary Commissioner for Armed Forces. The legal mechanisms and constitutional safeguards of parliamentary control form a part of the so-called 'constitutionalisation' of the military sphere and as such should not be compromised by increasing multinational military integration. Nevertheless, as will be seen during the course of this chapter, the competencies of the German parliament can and indeed are challenged in the context of multinational units of NATO member states, for example the German-Netherlands Corps and the Multinational Corps Northeast, as these represent a deepening of the military integration structures of NATO.

Stationing NATO Forces within the Territory of Germany

The German Basic Law provides for the possibility of making German territory available for the stationing of allied forces within the framework of a Defence Alliance. A more concrete extension of this is provided by the Treaty on Stationing Foreign Armed Forces in the Federal Republic of Germany of 1954 (Stationing Treaty *(Aufenthaltsvertrag))*, which is to be regarded in the context of the NATO Treaty acting as a legal basis for the stationing of Alliance forces on German territory.

Following the declaration of the German government that it would consent to the stationing of US nuclear weapons (cruise missiles) on German territory, the parliamentary group of *The Green Party* challenged the declaration on the grounds that the parliament had not been consulted on the matter. In the resulting Stationing Case (1984) the Federal Constitutional Court found that Article 59 (2) of the Basic Law,[2] which requires parliamentary consent before the government can finally assent to an international treaty, could not be extended to cover unilateral declarations such as the assent of the government given within the framework of the Alliance. Furthermore, the court was of the view that Article 59 (2) of the Basic Law, although indicating an intention to increase parliamentary involvement in foreign relations, did not empower the legislative bodies to initiate, shape or control the actions of the executive in the sphere of foreign relations.

The principle of the separation of powers ensures that only the appropriate bodies shall take action with regard to the organisation, functioning and proceedings of government. Any extension to this was said to be an encroachment on the central formative sphere of the executive and would to a large extent transfer political power to the parliament in an area that does not constitute law-making within the meaning of the Basic Law. In this way, no democratic deficit would arise from the fact that the executive enjoys exclusive power to take far-reaching and sometimes crucial decisions in the field of foreign relations (Stationing Case, 1984, p. 1).

In the Stationing Case (1984) the court was not able to find that the stationing of nuclear weapons in Germany represented a transgression of the parliamentary Act of Consent *(Zustimmungsgesetz)* that had been given in connection with the ratification of the *Stationing Treaty* and the NATO Treaty. It was not deemed to constitute a fundamental change to the integration programme of the Alliance[3] that the federal government had enabled the president of the

---

2   Article 59 (2) reads: 'Treaties that regulate the political relations of the Federation or relate to subjects of federal legislation shall require the consent or participation, in the form of a federal law (....).'

3   The Constitutional Court used similar arguments in its 2001 judgment on the new NATO Strategic Concept. It held that the concretisation of the NATO Treaty and its underlying integration programme was a task of the federal government and that this included participating in non-formal developments within a system of mutual collective security.

United States to use German territory as a potential starting point for military reprisals against the Soviet Union (Stationing Case 1984).

With a view to the stationing of nuclear weapons on German territory, the Constitutional Court therefore declined to recognise the widely-accepted jurisprudential 'rule of essential matters' (*Wesentlichkeitstheorie*) which states that all essential matters, especially those relating to the exercise of fundamental rights, must be decided in substance by parliamentary legislation.[4]

The upshot of the Stationing Case (1984) is that the government possesses an exclusive area of competence in the field of foreign affairs that it can mould as it sees fit. This thought is characterised by the principle that those who are responsible for foreign affairs must also be capable of dealing effectively and of reacting rapidly to changing circumstances.

However, a parliament is more difficult to put into action on an urgent matter and is capable of reaching decisions only after considerable debate. It is for this reason, as a matter of principle, that actions linked to foreign policy do not have to be put in the form of an act of parliament. The parliament does not have the right to contribute to all foreign affairs by means of formal legislation but rather has only a limited right of contribution that is defined by the scope of Article 59 (2) of the Basic Law.

Although renewed parliamentary authorisation was not required for the stationing of nuclear weapons on German territory, it would be inaccurate to conclude from this that fundamental decisions can always be made by bypassing parliament, as the Basic Law foresees a number of means through which a thorough control of the executive can be exercised.[5] Furthermore, it is the generally accepted practice in Germany that the federal government explains its proposed international action before commencement of the same. In this way the federal parliament is provided with an opportunity to make its views known in advance.

It is interesting to note that such thoughts are actually ancient in origin. In Thucydides' '*History of the Peloponnesian War*', the character Pericles remarks: 'Granted, only the few are capable of drawing up and realising a political plan (of war), but all of us (the Assembly of free citizens of Athens) are capable of judging it'.[6]

Deployment of Armed Forces to NATO Missions

Ten years after the Stationing Case, the Federal Constitutional Court moved away from its previously advocated doctrine of narrow parliamentary competencies in the sphere of foreign relations. In the International Military Deployments Case

---

4   See the established case law of the Federal Constitutional Court (Justizverwaltungsakt, 1975; Sexualkundeunterricht, 1977; Kalkar I, 1978; Schulentlassung, 1981).
5   E.g. by means of investigation (Committee of Defence, Article 45a Basic Law), parliamentary interpellation and questionnaires (Article 43 Basic Law) or by budgetary rights (Article 87a Basic Law).
6   Thucydides as quoted in Landmanns, 2002, p. 142.

(1994), the Court accepted (at least indirectly) the 'rule of essential matters' where the deployment of national armed forces is concerned (Kokott, 1996, p. 937).

Constitutional Positions and Parliamentary Practice

Where the deployment of armed forces is concerned, the constitutional rights of participation afforded to national parliaments of the different NATO member states vary considerably (Assembly of the WEU, 2001a, p. 9 and Nolte, 2002). Of particular importance is the right of the parliament to obtain information from the government (as in the United States, Belgium, the Netherlands and Poland) and the formal right of approval for each deployment of national armed forces abroad (as in Denmark).

In its judgement of 1994, the German Constitutional Court held that the Basic Law posed no obstacle to sending troops into collective security operations within the scope of Article 24 (2), since the Basic Law[7] provided that the federal parliament was required to give its specific 'prior and constitutional approval' of each deployment. Although both falling within the NATO integration programme, the issues of the deployment of armed forces and the stationing of foreign weapons must be handled differently. Despite the fact that in the Stationing judgement of 1984 parliamentary consent to the ratification of the NATO Treaty and the Stationing Treaty were deemed sufficient to authorise both the integration programme and the related acts of the executive, it is important to note that this consent acted only as a general legal basis for the participation of German armed forces. However, any specific use of the federal army in international armed operations must be approved by the federal parliament.

In Germany, where memories of both the Third Reich and the Cold War serve to fuel strong pacifist tendencies, there are increasingly charged disputes over NATO operations. With a view to such debates, it may be asked whether the federal government might find itself in a position where it could not secure the necessary parliamentary support. To answer this question, the special conditions of Germany's system of parliamentary government have to be borne in mind. Unlike in presidential systems of government, the German Chancellor and his ministers all belong to the majority coalition in parliament. The federal government therefore has to reach a consensus between the coalition parties but not necessarily with the other parties with seats in the parliament. In this way, a requirement of the approval of the deployment of armed forces can often become a home affairs test as regards the reaching of a consensus between the coalition parties in defence-related matters. This very problem arose in relation to Germany's participation in the Afghanistan mission: the decision of the federal parliament of 27 September 2001 to deploy armed forces to Macedonia with a view to joining the NATO

---

7   Article 24 of the Basic Law reads: '(1) The Federation may by means of a law transfer sovereign powers to international organisations. (2) With a view to maintaining peace, the Federation may enter into a system of mutual collective security; in doing so it shall consent to such limitations upon its sovereign powers as will bring about and secure lasting peace in Europe and among the nations of the world.'

mission 'Amber Fox' was taken solely with the votes of the opposition party, that is to say, the federal government was not even supported by all members of the coalition parties. This caused Chancellor Gerhardt Schroeder to combine the voting on the Afghanistan deployment with a vote of confidence under Article 68 of the Basic Law.[8] The resulting parliamentary decision of 16 November 2001 then brought about a narrow victory for the government (Limpert, 2002).

Identifying the Requirements of Parliamentary Authorisation in Germany

Although the German Basic Law does not contain an explicit requirement that the *Bundestag* authorise each and every deployment of troops, the constitutional court has spoken out in favour of the introduction of legislation to this effect. While this has not been done so far, the requirement of parliamentary approval has instead been pronounced to be a new and unwritten constitutional principle. This principle can be regarded as having derived from several different sources.

Firstly, the court considered the Basic Law as a whole and in doing so referred to specific constitutional provisions concerning the constitutional regime for the armed forces (*Wehrverfassung*). The *Bundestag* decides about 'War and Peace';[9] a member of the government possesses supreme command over the armed forces,[10] parliamentary control over the armed forces may be exercised by means of a special Committee of Defence (*Verteidigungsausschuß*) and parliament is assisted by a Parliamentary Commissioner (Ombudsman) for the Armed Forces.[11] Furthermore, the court invoked historical[12] and systematic considerations to reach a requirement of constitutional parliamentary approval (*Parlaments-vorbehalt*) that extends to every 'armed operation'.

The Court reasoned that the Basic Law *in toto* conceives the armed forces not as a tool of power for the executive, but rather as a 'parliamentary army' (*Parlamentsheer*). The federal parliament has the task of securing the integration of the *Bundeswehr* into the democratic order under the rule of law by controlling both the establishment and the use of the armed forces. In other words, the Basic Law has the role of preserving for parliament a legally relevant influence on the establishment and use of the armed forces (International Military Deployments Case, 1994).

---

8 Article 68 of the Basic Law reads: 'If a motion of the Federal Chancellor for a vote of confidence is not supported by the majority of the Members of the *Bundestag*, the Federal President, upon the proposal of the Federal Chancellor, may dissolve the *Bundestag* within 21 days.'

9 Basic Law, 1949, Cf. Article 115a (1) and Article 115 I (3).

10 Article 65a of the Basic Law reads: 'The command of the armed forces shall be vested in the Federal Minister of Defence.'

11 *Wehrbeauftragter*, Basic Law, 1949, Cf. Article 45a and 45b.

12 In the Weimar Constitution (1919), Article 45 contained the requirement of parliamentary authorisation for each deployment.

Formal Conditions of Parliamentary Authorisation

On the national level, parliamentary decisions to deploy German armed forces do not have to be taken in accordance with the usual legislative process; it suffices for the *Bundestag* to take a vote by simple majority on a motion by the government to approve the deployment (Basic Law, 1949, Article 42). The decision of the Court left no doubt that parliamentary participation in foreign affairs does not always have to be solely on the basis of legislation but rather may be by means of anticipated assent. This shifting of parliamentary consent is an innovative mechanism that could be developed further in order to close the gap between the development of international law and the problem of parliamentary legitimacy.

In Germany, it is regarded as political common sense that the *Bundeswehr* should not be deployed abroad except under international auspices and leadership. As the 'collective security clause' in Article 24 (2) of the Basic Law only permits the deployment of troops by a system of mutual collective security, the crucial question is whether NATO qualifies as a sufficient source of international authorisation for the purposes of German constitutional law, at least when implementing resolutions of the UN Security Council (as in the case of Security Force [SFOR]). In its decision of 7 November 2001, which aimed to support the collective defence mission of the United States in Afghanistan, the federal government referred explicitly to Article 24 (2) of the Basic Law. From a constitutional point of view, it is sufficient that a mission is formally conducted within the framework of a system of mutual collective security; it is not necessary for NATO headquarters to be directly involved in the mission concerned. However, problems may arise where NATO acts without the authorisation of the UN Security Council. This was the case in 1999 during the Kosovo conflict, where NATO actions relating to humanitarian intervention had not been authorised by the Security Council. The situation raised issues about the court's broad interpretation of a 'collective security system'. Indeed members of parliament from the Party of Democratic Socialism (PDS) challenged the constitutionality of German participation in Kosovo on this very ground (*Zur Zulässigkeit von Anträgen im Organstreitverfahren*, 1999).

Scope and Limitations of the Parliamentary Prerogative

In the context of NATO, the approval requirement applies to armed operations of collective self-defence (North Atlantic Treaty, 1949, Article 5) as well as 'non-Article 5 missions' (crisis management tasks). Apart from mere relief deliveries, the requirement would only be dispensable in the case of an attack on the territory of Germany following the declaration of a State of Defence (Basic Law (Grundgesetz), Article 115a).[13] The prerogative of parliament to decide on the deployment of troops is not unlimited. Against the background of the principle of

---

13 The attacks of 11 September 2001 have demonstrated that the State of Defence (*Verteidigungsfall*) and a threat to the Alliance (*Bündnisfall*) are not necessarily identical as was supposed at the time of the Cold War.

the separation of powers, a delimitation of responsibilities between 'if' and 'how' would be fully consistent with the 'rule of essential matters'. According to this rule, the legislature would have a prerogative as regards to the deployment itself, and the executive would enjoy sufficient discretionary power to ensure the government's capability to act in the international sphere. As the Federal Constitutional Court pointed out in the Stationing Case, executive decision-making power in the field of foreign affairs and defence could be justified in a view of the special character of these matters, as they require rapid decision-making and a competent assessment of complex situations (Stationing Case, 1984, p. 106). This would seem to lead to the conclusion that parliament is to be considered structurally incapable of resuming full responsibility for decision-making in armed missions abroad. As far as questions of specific conduct of operations are concerned, it is for the executive to take responsibility.

The following aspects of the approval requirement aim to illustrate the distribution of responsibilities between the executive and the parliament with regard to the deployment of armed forces:

- The role of parliament is necessarily restricted to providing an initial legitimising function since it cannot make meaningful determinations concerning the scope, methods or tactics of the operation involved (Nolte, 2002). Parliament may not force the government to deploy troops and furthermore, that it may neither determine decisions concerning the modalities, the dimension and the duration of the operations nor the necessary coordination within and with the organs of international organisations (International Military Deployments Case, 1994).

- The democratic legitimacy and the military effectiveness of armed missions would seem to be inversely proportional to one another: the more the time factor becomes important in cases of urgent deployments, the less can be achieved by demanding parliamentary approval (Menzel, 1963, p. 593). In order to be able to pursue its military policies, the government must procure speedy decisions. The Federal Constitutional Court has argued that 'the participation of the *Bundestag* must not interfere with Germany's military capability and her ability to fulfil her obligations within NATO' (International Military Deployments Case, 1994, p. 350). This is an indication by the court that in emergency situations, the executive is permitted to make provisional decisions on the deployment of armed forces without the prior consent of parliament. Nevertheless, the government is required to address parliament immediately and to seek its approval as soon as possible.

- The argument of non-interference with the military capability can also be drawn upon when certain decisions usually debated in parliament need to be delegated to parliamentary committees for reasons of security.[14] The deployment of German Special Command Forces (*Kommando*

---

14 The German Federal Constitutional Court argued similarly in a case concerning the budgetary means of secret services (*Haushaltskontrolle der Nachrichtendienste*, 1986).

Spezialkräfte) with the task of searching for Al-Qaeda terrorists in Afghanistan, raised the question of parliamentary consent in cases of secret deployments. It seems evident that in such cases the entire parliament cannot be concerned with deployments that are subject to NATO security classification. In order to ensure parliament's rights of participation, the possibility of delegating powers to the Defence Committee as an 'assisting organ' of the *Bundestag* should perhaps be considered, as its meetings are not held in public and its members are bound to strict secrecy (Muench and Kunig, 2002, under Article 45a, at n. 10).

- The increasing length of international missions raises the issue of recalling troops from abroad. In its 1994 decision on deployment, the constitutional court held that the federal armed forces are to be recalled if parliament so demands (International Military Deployments Case, 1994, p. 350). However, it is by no means undisputed among German scholars as to whether the parliament possesses a right of initiative to terminate the missions of armed forces abroad. It may be argued that a revoking competence of parliament is not necessary because a parliamentary system like that in Germany provides the parliament with other means to express dissatisfaction with the state of a certain mission abroad; as a last resort it retains the power to elect another government. Yet, the ability of the parliament to revoke its consent would be advantageous from the perspective of the soldiers as they would no longer have to constantly question whether or not they were still acting within the scope of the framework consented to by the *Bundestag*.[15] Furthermore, parliament would be more willing to agree to the deployment of troops if it was assured that it could revoke its consent at any time. It seems to be unacceptable for parliament's initial vote to irrevocably legitimise a decision of the executive if the operation is developing unsatisfactorily. Parliamentary approval can therefore not be taken as a 'blank cheque'.[16] Essential deviations or modifications relating to the identity of the mission (e.g. ground troops are becoming necessary) may instead require a completely new parliamentary consent (Wild, 2000, p. 620). From a constitutional point of view, the provisions concerning the State of Defence (Basic Law (Grundgesetz), Article 115a) could reasonably support the alleged parliamentary competence. The constitutional court itself has explicitly interpreted the principle of 'parliamentary army' in the light of the constitutional rules concerning the State of Defence when identifying a general principle of constitutive participation of parliament in relation to the deployment of armed forces from Article 115a (1) of the Basic Law. The State of Defence is determined by the federal parliament, with the consent of the Federal Council, on the application of the federal government. It may be declared

---

15 The deployment of German Tornado fighters in Bosnia in 1993, subjected to strict controls in every phase illustrates the difficulties associated with a deployment when the mandate of the *Bundestag* falls behind that of the United Nations.

16 Statement of Lamers, Member of Parliament, cited in, *Bundestag*, 2000, p. 10155.

terminated at any time by a decision of the federal parliament that is to be promulgated by the federal president (Basic Law Article 115 (l) (2)). This constitutional position could easily be applied to the recalling of armed forces, thus enabling the initiative to derive from parliament alone (Nolte, 1994, p. 652).

The Role of Parliament in Collective Defence Activities

The former president of the Federal Republic of Germany, Roman Herzog, once described the military decisions during the Cold War as the 'time of the executive – not even of the German executive but of the American President' (Herzog, *et al.*, 2001, Article 115a, at n. 98). The threat to the Alliance presented by the attacks of 11 September 2001 has shown that the circumstances of today are very different to the conditions that were prevalent during the Cold War – indeed, they are more similar to the 'crisis operations' provided for by the NATO Strategic Concept of 1999. Whereas military reaction was deemed to be the only appropriate response to a Russian attack, this is not the case as regards the struggle against international terrorism. The events of the 11 September 2001 have led to the realisation in Germany that collective defence need not necessarily be synonymous with the State of Defence under Article 115a of the Basic Law. It was indeed remarkable that military action was not taken until a month later. This was due to the fact that the legal issues surrounding an Article 5 case, namely the link between the terrorist structures of *Al-Qaeda* and the state of Afghanistan as a subject of international law, needed to be resolved before any such action could be taken.

For security reasons, the information made available to NATO member states' governments by the NATO Council between 12 September and 7 October 2001 was neither disclosed to the public nor to national parliaments. While the main obstacle to effective parliamentary participation in military affairs during the Cold War was the inability of parliament to react rapidly, it is possible that the lack of information available to parliament will become the main obstacle of the 21st century. On the other hand, it is not unthinkable that the German parliament may make its approval of collective-defence deployment dependent on receipt of all the relevant information concerning the background to the mission. This has the potential to lead to controversial parliamentary discussions about NATO's Article 5 decisions (determining the State of Defence of the Alliance) that have been taken by the government in the NATO Council. It is for these reasons that the role of national parliaments in future defence cases cannot yet be predicted.

Multinational Units of NATO Member States

Multinational military cooperation is intended to promote European integration and in particular the common European Security and Defence Policy (ESDP) as the European pillar of NATO. Since the London Declaration (NATO, 1990), NATO has expressed itself to be in favour of the creation of multinational units. In doing so, aspects related to cost-cutting, strategic reorientation (in the field of 'crisis management') and the general cohesion of the organisation have clearly been influencing factors. Above all, it enables participation in military operations at corps level that would not be otherwise possible in most European countries (Fleck, 2001, p. 33).

Between NATO member states at least three different models of multinational military cooperation have been developed. The two German/US Corps follow the so-called lead nation model, with Germany and the US taking turns to perform command functions and occupy key positions in each of the corps. The second or so-called framework model is realised in the Allied Rapid Reaction Corps (ARRC) in which British forces provide the framework, including the command, administration and logistic support of the headquarters. However, it is the third deepening integration model that raises questions of legal integration and parliamentary oversight. It is used by the German-Netherlands Corps with headquarters in Münster, Westphalia, and the Multinational Corps Northeast, comprising troops of Germany, Denmark and Poland, with headquarters in the 'Baltic Barracks' in Szczecin, Poland. Both the multinational corps in Münster and in Szczecin consists of forces of each participating state stationed on the territory of the partner state.[17] The military cooperation that exists within multinational units is based on intergovernmental agreements. The principles of organisation and cooperation as well as the location of the headquarters are laid down in the Conventions of each corps[18] whilst the details of organisation are dealt with by special Corps Agreements. The Corps Conventions require ratification by the relevant national parliaments and it is the usual practice for Corps Agreements to be taken note of but no objections are usually raised.

Multinational units are not legally independent of the national executive. Therefore the use of armed forces in multinational units is subject to the constitutional rules of parliamentary oversight of each contributing state. However, in the case of Germany, certain parliamentary control functions foreseen by the German Basic Law can be challenged when viewed in the context of multinational military cooperation. Firstly, it is paramount to guarantee national sovereignty as regards the deployment of national troops. Secondly, the setting of budgets for multinational corps must respect the budgetary rights of parliament.[19] Moreover,

---

17 The Corps in Munster comprises German main forces (1st Armed Division) and a substantial part of the Netherlands Army (1st Division '7 December'). The bi-national Command Support Group including more than 1,400 German military and civilian personnel is stationed in Eibergen (Netherlands). The Multinational Corps Northeast is reinforced by a Danish Division, the 14th German Mechanised Infantry Division and the 12th Polish Division. Permanent deployment in foreign countries is restricted to the Danish and German elements of the Corps headquarters in Szczecin (Poland).

18 German-Netherlands Corps Convention, 1997. Multinational Corps Northeast (MNC NE) Convention, 1998.

19 Basic Law Article 87a (1) reads: 'The Federation shall establish armed forces for the purposes of defence. Their numerical strength and general organisational structure must be shown in the budget. Budgetary competences of parliament in the military sphere are to be found in the constitutions of every NATO Member State and can therefore be considered a part of the common European constitutional legal order'.

financial matters are subject to control by the national board of auditors in all NATO member states. Thirdly, a number of NATO member states have a general parliamentary Ombudsman whose responsibilities are increasingly extended to military affairs.[20] However only the German Basic Law provides for the existence of a special Parliamentary Commissioner (Ombudsman) for the Armed Forces. (Basic Law, Article 45b). He is entrusted with the task of investigating the observance of fundamental rights of soldiers and then reporting his findings to parliament. Questions arise however, when German soldiers lodge complaints about the conditions in a multinational unit or about the behaviour of a foreign superior. Ultimately, multinational chains of command may challenge the national supreme command of the armed forces. Unlike in other NATO member states' constitutions,[21] the German Basic Law provides explicitly that the supreme command over the Federal German Army is vested in the Federal Minister of Defence (Basic Law Article 65a) who is of course responsible to parliament in his capacity as a member of the government. In particular, four aspects of multinational units are relevant to parliamentary oversight, i.e. deployment of multinational troops; control of multinational budgets; and investigation carried out by the parliamentary Ombudsman on multinational units.

Deployment of Multinational Troops Multinational units may only operate within the limits of national constitutions and pursuant to the decisions taken by the competent organs of the contributing states. This kind of 'constitutional proviso', to be found in each Corps-Convention,[22] ensures that the requirement of parliamentary approval (to be found e.g. in the German and Danish constitutions) is met where the deployment of troops is concerned.[23]

However, the integration of armed forces in a European corps heavily restricts the ability of the individual national components of the corps to be deployed separately from the corps itself. The multinational corps can only be put into operation when all the partner states are in agreement. In this way, the lack of any such agreement with regard to the Iraq War prevented Polish troops belonging to the Multinational Corps Northeast from being deployed at all.

---

20 E.g. Belgium, Denmark, the Netherlands, Poland and Spain. See for example, Born, 2003, pp.90-94.

21 For example, in Belgium the prerogative of command over the armed forces that is possessed by the King is exercised by the minister of defence. In Poland, the president exercises the command and control through the minister of defence (Constitution of the Republic of Poland Article 134 (2)). In the Netherlands, it is the organ of government (through the Raad vor Europese en Internationale Angelegenheiden) that exercises the highest command over the armed forces, Article 97 (2) of the Constitution of the Kingdom of Netherlands.

22 See German-Netherlands Corps Convention, 1997 and the Multinational Corps Northeast Convention, 1998 Article 3.

23 According to Article 3 of the German-Netherlands Corps Convention, 1997 and the Multinational Corps Northeast Convention, 1998, the tasks of multinational units comprise e.g. common defence purposes under Article 5 NATO Treaty as well as multinational crisis management purposes within the Alliance's framework.

Control of Multinational Budgets Part of the deepened integration in all fields of military cooperation is the multinational budget provided for in the Corps Conventions.[24] The budget covers costs arising from the implementation of the Conventions and Agreements with respect to the multinational elements of the Corps and is set after the mutual consent of the competent national authorities has been secured.[25] As the financing of the Corps is entirely dependent on the budgets of the respective member states, national parliamentary control has to be ensured by means of specialised multinational auditing bodies established within the framework of the Corps. These bodies consist of national representatives who are responsible to their national authorities and, more importantly, to their national parliaments.

Within the Multinational Corps Northeast, a special Budget and Finance Group was established to act on behalf of the Corps Committee with respect to all financial and budgetary matters.[26] Moreover, the execution of the multinational budget is audited annually by the competent national audit institutions on a rotational basis and in accordance with mutually-accepted auditing standards and procedures. For the purposes of supervision and of auditing the bi-national budget of the German-Netherlands Corps, a bi-national board of auditors was established in accordance with the NATO auditing procedures. The bi-national board of auditors works alongside the national auditors and so does not encroach on their rights and responsibilities. National auditors are entitled to request from the bi-national board of auditors any information they consider necessary for informing their respective governments and parliaments and are able to examine any relevant files.[27]

Investigation carried out by the Parliamentary Commissioner on Multinational Units According to paragraph 3 (4) of the 1982 German Parliamentary Commissioner (Ombudsman) Act (*Wehrbeauftragtengesetz*, 1982), the Ombudsman (*Wehrbeauftragter*) can carry out investigations in all contingents of the German Armed Forces, as well as within multinational units. As the service within multinational armed forces does not in any way alter the status of a German soldier or his relationship to the *Bundeswehr*, the soldier's right to petition according to paragraph 7 of the Act (*Wehrbeauftragtengesetz*, 1982) is not inhibited by his membership of multinational armed forces. To date, however, no cases from multinational units have officially been mentioned in the annual reports of the Parliamentary Commissioner delivered to Parliament in accordance with paragraph 2 of the *Wehrbeauftragtengesetz*. Therefore, it is only possible to speculate on problems that may occur when conducting investigations within multinational units. It is important to realise that military contingents of other nations are not

---

24 German-Netherlands Corps Convention, 1997, Article 7; Multinational Corps Northeast Convention 1998, Article 10.
25 German-Netherlands Corps Agreement, 1997, Article 34 (1); Multinational Corps Northeast Agreement, 1998, Article 27 (2).
26 See Multinational Corps Northeast Agreement, 1998, Article 27 (3).
27 German-Netherlands Corps Convention, 1997, Article 7 (2).

subject to the control of German constitutional organs or the parliamentary commissioner. The ability of the commissioner to make inquiries does not stretch to the investigation of the acts of foreign superiors, as these are not generally regarded as falling within the field of German sovereignty. He also has no right whatsoever to inspect documents of foreign partner states, not even if they are the subject of the application and as such decisive in a full investigation of the matter in hand (Klang, 1986, p. 103). In practice, the parliamentary commissioner strongly depends on the cooperation and diplomatic partnership of the national defence ministry with the ministry of the partner nation. This means that the political independence of the parliamentary commissioner is extremely difficult to maintain when investigating multinational military units.

Conclusions

Hence we can conclude that the political legitimacy of multinational military activities is to be derived solely from national parliaments as no international control bodies exist within the context of multinational units. When compared to the legal provisions of other European states, the German Basic Law provides for strong parliamentary control of the national armed forces which in turn results in a particularly high level of parliamentary legitimacy. The structure of the constitutional instruments available for the purposes of parliamentary control and regulation (for example the accountability of the defence minister to parliament, the parliamentary approval of international treaties, the control function of the Parliamentary Commissioner for Armed Forces and the budgetary and informative control of parliamentary committees) remains untouched by the international process of military integration.

The complexity of integrated leadership structures and the fact that intergovernmental cooperation is not all based on treaties means that it is not possible to fully guarantee parliamentary control at the national level. The effectiveness of such parliamentary control is dependent on the extent to which the international process of military integration is based on treaties, transparent decision-making procedures and accountable institutions. The more diverse the multilateral cooperation in the field of defence and security policy becomes, the more effective the allocation of responsibilities, the parliamentary control of decision-making procedures and the access to information must be. Legally institutionalised international regimes and bodies with clear areas of responsibility and transparent rules of procedure are easier to make the subject of parliamentary control than sporadic and more informal forms of executive cooperation. Yet this requires more than simply an increase in legal bases and transparent decision-making procedures. In the long run, it is essential that the interaction and communication functions of parliament also be strengthened, in particular in the case of the European Parliament. The combination of European and national levels is capable of producing and guaranteeing adequate parliamentary control of the integrated armed forces.

PART V

THE EU CONTEXT

Chapter 10

The European Union as an International Security Actor: Challenges for Democratic Accountability

Giovanna Bono

Introduction

The ability of the European Union (EU) to directly command and control military and police forces for external security engagements is a recent novelty. Since the end of the Second World War, some European countries had a vision of European integration involving cooperation not in the economic and political spheres alone, but also in the foreign, security and defence fields. An expression of this desire was the signature of the Brussels Treaty in 1948, which resulted in the establishment of the Western European Union (WEU).[1] Yet from the creation of the European Economic Community (EEC) in 1957 to the end of the 1980s, the EEC did not coordinate the security and defence policies of its member states.

Even when the EEC was transformed into a project of the European Union (EU) in the 1990s, the role of the EU in external security and defence was limited. The signing of the Maastricht Treaty in 1992 provided the European Union with a Common Foreign Security Policy (CFSP). It established a three-pillar structure that remains in place to this day. Pillar I comprises economic cooperation and trade, Pillar II deals with CFSP and Pillar III with Justice and Home Affairs.[2] It was agreed that whilst Pillar I was to be dominated by a supranational approach in which the European Commission would take the lead in shaping policy initiatives, the other two pillars would follow an intergovernmental approach. A muddled clause in the Treaty on European Union stated that CFSP could only 'eventually'

---

1 The Brussels Treaty, 1948, was signed by Belgium, France, Luxembourg and the United Kingdom on 17 March 1948.
2 Since Pillar III, which holds responsibility for Justice and Home Affairs, is concerned with *internal security* questions, no reference is made to its working in this chapter. Pillar III does contribute to the ability of the EU to project power externally in that some of the lessons learned in developing an internal police capability (EUROPOL) spill over to Pillar II and contribute to the overall development of an EU security identity.

give the EU a role in defence.[3] The Amsterdam Treaty which was signed in 1997 did not change this state of affairs substantially, though it incorporated the WEU peacekeeping tasks into the EU Treaty (Article V).

Due to this history, until recently the EU was perceived as a 'civilian power' in that it acted externally mainly through the tools available under Pillar I and II: its trade links, humanitarian aid and diplomatic initiatives. The nature of the EU came to be described as that of a hybrid system including both supranational and intergovernmental aspects.[4]

It was only with the St. Malo Declaration of 1998, which was signed by France and Britain, along with a number of other key decisions taken by the WEU and EU Councils during 1999 and 2000, that the EU endowed itself with political and military structures to undertake external police and military operations. These decisions have given shape to what is currently known as the European Security and Defence Policy (ESDP). The ESDP has resulted in the transfer of most of the WEU's functions to the EU. A number of new political and military institutions have been created under Pillar II. In addition, the EU has agreed to develop the Headline Goal (HG): a military force of up to 60,000 men, known as the Rapid Reaction Force (RRF); a police force of 5,000 to be deployed in external engagements and the introduction of a formal process of discussions and peer-reviews to ensure that EU member states acquire military equipment and assets to allow for the existence of the RRF. To date, by 2003, EU member states have launched three ESDP military operations: one in Bosnia-Herzegovina, another in the Former Yugoslav Republic of Macedonia (FYROM), and a third in the Congo (Operation Artemis).

This chapter argues that the ESDP is as much an expression of the desire of EU member states to strengthen the ability of the EU to act during external crises and by so doing to project its power regionally and globally, as it is an attempt to re-forge the transatlantic security relationship. The development of the ESDP needs to be understood in the broader context of a shift in the nature of the international security system and at present competing trends in operation exist, which will shape its future. Although the ESDP has strengthened the ability of the EU to coordinate the external security engagements of its member states, the extent to which the EU will develop as a security actor is as yet not known. The ESDP has given the EU a role in defence but has not, at present, changed its hybrid nature. In fact, the Intergovernmental Conference (IGC) 2000 failed to reform the EU's pillar structure. Hence the ESDP is currently a policy that sits alongside the CFSP in a policy-making system that cuts across the pillars. Most of the financial

---

3	Article B of the European Union Treaty, 1992, stated that the Union was 'to assert its identity on the international scene, in particular through the implementation of a Common Foreign Security Policy including the *eventual* framing of a common defence policy, which *might* in time lead to common defence'.

4	The notion of the EU as a hybrid system – neither political system nor international organisation, but something in between – is captured by one of the dominant EU integration theories of the moment: multilevel-governance. For a review, see Rosamond, 2000, pp. 109-113.

and human resources required for non-military external security engagements remain under Pillar I. For the most part, instruments of a military nature remain under national control or available through other multilateral frameworks. At present, the development of the ESDP has worsened the already existing 'democratic deficit' of the EU and made it more difficult for parliamentary bodies at the national and EU levels to scrutinise the decision-making process.

The chapter presents these arguments in two sections. In the first section, a description of the background leading to the creation of the ESDP is presented and the nature of the military and police cooperation is explained. The political structures that were established are also mentioned as are some of the key issues in the ESDP project that remain unresolved. The second section focuses on examining the consequences of these developments for democratic accountability. To simplify a complex issue, democratic accountability is examined on five levels: administrative (the existence of a clear division of labour between executive and legislative), parliamentary (the role of parliamentary assemblies in scrutinising policy-making), political-military (the existence of clear political guidelines for the military), external (vis-à-vis the population and governments of countries in which EU/NATO member states intervene) and internal (vis-à-vis EU citizens).

The European Security and Defence Policy (ESDP)

Immediately after the end of the Second World War, there was the belief on both sides of the Atlantic that the creation of peace and stability in Europe required the development of an independent role for Western Europe in security and defence matters alongside a process of economic and political integration. This vision found its first expression in the Treaty of Dunkirk, signed between France and Britain in March 1947. Then, a year later, the signing of the Brussels Treaty (17 March 1948) gave birth to the WEU. The vision of the process of European integration having a security and defence dimension was embodied in the Pleven Plans of the late 1950s and the early 1960s. Such plans foresaw the creation of a European Defence Community (EDC) in which the EC would have political and military structures at its disposal, including a standing army (Fursdon 1980; Duke 2000a). However, the dynamics of the Cold War and differences among European states on the nature and extent of the integration process prevented the creation of independent European political and military structures in the security and defence field. In fact, throughout the Cold War period, the majority of European security and defence issues were coordinated within the North Atlantic Treaty Organisation (NATO), despite the existence of the WEU.

The predominance of NATO in European security remained intact throughout the 1950s. Then, between the late 1960s and the 1970s some EC member states' desire for a European security identity found their expression in attempts to 'Europeanise the Alliance', through the establishment of the Eurogroup

(Laird, 1991). The Eurogroup[5] aimed to demonstrate greater European unity within NATO, improve relations with the US and allow a second tier of communication for Britain with the six member states of the EEC within the NATO context. It also facilitated meetings between the defence ministries of its member states. Another attempt to strengthen a European security identity was made in the late 1980s with the creation of a Franco-German brigade and a revamped role for the WEU (Duke, 2000a, pp. 72-78). EEC member states also strengthened their level of cooperation in foreign affairs by developing formal and informal political structures in the EEC, known as European Political Cooperation. However, it was only with the end of the Cold War that new opportunities for rethinking European security emerged.

In the early part of the 1990s, a debate erupted about the nature of the European security architecture. The end of the Cold War raised doubts about the future of NATO and gave an impetus to the process of European integration. To simplify a complex issue, three visions emerged. One group of policy-makers led by US and British officials wanted a future role for NATO to include 'out-of-area' tasks and for the EU to remain an essentially political and economic organisation with no substantial role in defence matters. Another group of policy-makers, located mainly in France and Germany, aspired to a fundamental reform of NATO and wanted to give the EU the ability to undertake external security tasks. There was also a group of policy-makers among which were leading sections of the German Liberal Party (FDP), sections of Western European social democratic parties, communists and green parties who demanded a more drastic change to the European security architecture. They envisaged substantial decreases in military spending and the creation of the CSCE, later known as the OSCE, as the epicentre of the European security system. From this perspective NATO was, in the short term, to retain a primarily political role and later disappear. Within this latter group there was no consensus on the extent to which the EU should assume a defence and security role.

The battle between these three perspectives was shaped by the outbreak of the Gulf War and armed conflicts in Croatia and Bosnia. The ad hoc reactions to these events, domestic shifts in the traditional right-left divide in Europe over the use of force, along with renewed divisions over the nature of the EU project and the transatlantic security relationship resulted in the defeat of the third perspective and a mixed compromise between the other two views.

In fact, between 1990 and 1997, NATO managed to assume peacekeeping and peace-enforcement tasks in the Balkans and thus retained the leading role in European security, sidelining the project of giving the OSCE such a task (Bono, 2003a). However, NATO's supremacy was only maintained by embarking on an enlargement process, by reforming its posture and by making formal concessions to those Europeans who wanted more responsibility for European security. This latter development took the form of discussions between NATO and the WEU for closer military cooperation, embodied in NATO's Combined Joint Task Force

---

5   The Eurogroup was composed of 12 member states: Belgium, Denmark, the Federal
    Republic of Germany, Greece, Italy, Luxembourg, the Netherlands, Norway, Portugal,
    Spain, Turkey and the United Kingdom.

(CJTF) concept, and in an official agreement to allow the WEU to have access to NATO assets and planning capabilities, the so-called Berlin Plus Agreements, signed by NATO member states in 1996.[6] At the same time, EU member states agreed to give new political and military capabilities to the WEU and to reinforce the role of the EU in the security and defence areas.

Thus, between 1992 and 1997, WEU member states endowed the organisation with a peacekeeping role, the so-called 'Petersberg Tasks'[7] that led the WEU to assume policing activities and monitoring sanctions in the Balkans. Then at the Intergovernmental Conference (IGC) during 1996 and 1997 which resulted in the Amsterdam Treaty, EU member states created new political structures in the Second Pillar of the EU to strengthen their role in foreign and security policy. They created a Policy Planning and Early Warning Unit (PPEWU), a CFSP unit and the post of 'Secretary-General/High Representative for CFSP' (Common Foreign and Security Policy), also known in French as 'Monsieur PESC'. In addition, the Amsterdam Treaty established 'qualified majority voting' (QMV) and 'constructive abstentions' in order to provide greater flexibility for CFSP (Cottey, 1998). The WEU Petersberg Tasks were incorporated into Article V of the Treaty of the European Union.

However, the Amsterdam Treaty did not make substantial changes to the role of the EU in security and defence, meaning that the WEU remained an autonomous organisation. This outcome was the result of Britain's determination not to concede to the position of countries, led again by France and Germany, who wanted a closer integration between the two organisations (Morvacsik and Nicolaidis, 1999; Heisbourg, 1999; Duke, 2000a, pp. 126-144).

The tide in favour of the EU assuming a stronger role in security and defence policies turned in late 1998 and 1999 due to the convergence of a number of new long-term and short-term dynamics. The latter included: in Britain, the entry into office of a new Labour government which wanted to take a leading role in shaping a transatlantic security bargain; the impact of the war in Kosovo on the European Union, as well as NATO; a new awareness among EU member states that to have weight in dealing with external crises, one needed to combine economic and diplomatic means with military capabilities. This awareness and the tough transatlantic negotiations resulted in the creation of the European Security and Defence Policy (ESDP), which for the first time in its history allowed the EU to have political control over military and police forces for external security engagements. The next section will focus on describing the key decisions taken since 1999 chronologically to give the EU a role in coordinating military and

---

6   In reality NATO member states remained reluctant to endorse the political agreement during the late 1990s though the CJTF allowed some planning for joint NATO-WEU military operations to take place.

7   In June 1992, the WEU Council of Ministers issued the Petersberg Declaration. This stated that the WEU could be employed for 'humanitarian and rescue tasks; peace-keeping tasks; tasks of combat forces in crisis management, including peace-making' (Western European Union Council of Ministers, 1992).

police activities. This section then goes on to sketch the new political structures established within the EU.

The Rapid Reaction Force and the Headline Goal

At the EU Helsinki Summit in December 1999, EU member states established the Headline Goal (HG). In essence, these are decisions to develop, by the year 2003, an EU military force of up to 60,000 troops able to be deployed at 60 days notice and with the ability to sustain itself for at least one year. This force has to be able to undertake a large spectrum of tasks ranging from peacekeeping to peace-making. The Headline Goal also involves the introduction of programmes to upgrade European military capabilities to include, amongst others, the acquisition of new equipment, logistics and communication and control assets.[8]

Since the HG was announced, two official reviews have taken place. The first was the Capabilities Commitment Conference of November 2000. A year later, on 19 and 20 November 2001, a 'Capabilities Improvement Conference' took place to review the work undertaken (official documents in Rutten, 2002, pp. 95-100) since the previous conference. The results of the November 2001 conference were approved a month later at the Laeken Summit and came to be known as the 'European Capability Action Plan'. This plan outlined a method and guiding principles to achieve the HG (Council of the European Union, 2001a; House of Lords, 2002, pp. 16, 20). As an outcome of the summit, in the first few months of 2002, 14 working groups were set up in the EU Council to tackle the military shortcomings identified.

In relation to the military aspects of the ESDP, the EU also acquired the WEU Satellite Centre in Torrejon. This currently provides satellite images to the EU Situation Centre and makes available its information to the intelligence division within the military staff as well as the Police Planning Unit.[9] The European Commission, which traditionally contributed to enhancing the European defence industry, (particularly the aerospace sector), via its international trade negotiations and its Research and Development strategies (Moussis, 2002), has made new strides. One example is the creation of a European Global Navigation Satellite System (GNSS), also known as the Galileo Project (Dombey, 2002). Though this is mainly a civilian project, in the longer run it could be used for defence purposes. Another example is the proposal for an EU defence equipment policy (European Commission, 11 March 2003). There have also been attempts to strengthen cooperation among EU member states in the area of arms production and acquisition through ad-hoc frameworks such as OCCAR (*Organisme Conjoint de Coopération en Matière d'Armement*), and the Framework Agreement, though these bodies are not directly under the control of the EU (Brzoska, 2002;

---

8   The decision to establish the Headline Goal and the Rapid Reaction Force is reprinted in Rutten, 2001, pp 84-86. For an in-depth discussion of the Headline Goal, see Centre for Defence Studies, 2001.

9   For EU satellite centre's activities, see their webpages (http://www.eusc.org/). For the activities of the EU Situation Centre, see discussion of political institutions below.

Mawdsley, 2002). On 31 March 2003 these discussions, together with the establishment of new political structures, as mentioned below, resulted in the first EU-led military operation, named Concordia.

Concordia was formally requested by Macedonian President Boris Trajkovski and is based on UN Security Council Resolution 1371. Officially, the first EU military operation is supposed to contribute to security in the Former Yugoslav Republic of Macedonia (FYROM) so that the government can implement the August 2001 Ohrid Framework Agreement.[10] The operation is in fact part of a larger EU commitment to the FYROM and to its rapprochement with the EU within the Stabilisation and Association Process.

The mandate for Concordia, as outlined in the EU Council Joint Action agreed on 27 January 2003, has been to take over the NATO-led mission 'Allied Harmony' in the FYROM (Council of the European Union, 4 February 2003). NATO's past mission involved liaison and providing military support for the work of international monitors and giving advice on security issues to the Macedonian government. Although Concordia's mandate is built on that of NATO's Allied Harmony, the mandate remains vague at present. This might have been done on purpose so as to allow a potential broader definition of security tasks in Macedonia. Most important, Concordia, though small (it is composed of 350 military personnel), could be a test for other ESDP military operations in the Balkans. For example the EU could take over the NATO-led SFOR and KFOR missions in Bosnia and Kosovo.

Concordia is in fact the first test of a new EU-NATO relationship. It was only made possible after an agreement was reached at the EU Copenhagen Summit in December 2002 to allow EU access to NATO assets and operational planning capabilities, the so-called Berlin-Plus arrangements, which had been a thorny issue in the transatlantic security relationship for more than two and half years (NATO, 16 December 2002).[11]

As a result, Concordia involves close coordination at the political and military levels between the EU and NATO.[12] Although the EU's Political Security Committee exercises overall political and strategic direction for the operation, under the advice of the European Council, it works closely with NATO.[13] The level of cooperation established between the EU and NATO is also evident in the composition of the force. At the time of writing, 14 non-EU countries participate in the operation alongside 13 EU member states – Ireland and Denmark remaining outside (Mace, 2003).

---

10 See official website of the Council on Operation Concordia:
    http://ue.eu.int/arym/index.asp?lang=EN [accessed: 13 June 2003].
11 For a background to the ESDP-NATO issues, see Bono, 2002-2003.
12 At the Command and Control level, Admiral Rainer Feist, NATO's D-SACEUR, is the commander-in-chief of the mission. French Brigadier-General Pierre Maral is the commander of European ground forces. The operational headquarters is based at SHAPE (Supreme Headquarters Allied Powers Europe).
13 In case of a deterioration of the security environment, NATO will manage an extraction force.

The EU Police Force for International Missions

Apart from Concordia, the development of the ESDP has also allowed the EU to take over police missions for international engagements. At the Feira Council meeting in June 2000, EU member states set about establishing, by 2003 and on a voluntary basis, a police force of 5,000 police officers. The force needs to be able to undertake international missions across the range of crisis prevention and crisis management. It was envisioned that EU member states would acquire the ability to deploy up to 1,000 police officers within 30 days (Rutten, 2001, pp. 120-139). To achieve this aim, EU heads of state conceded that a number of steps had to be contemplated including pre-defining forces, reinforcing the mechanisms of rotation and putting at the disposal of the EU additional financial and logistical resources.

With regard to the potential conditions for the deployment of the force, the June 2000 EU Declaration stated that the EU police deployment could 'either be in response to a request from an international lead organization, in particular the United Nations or the OSCE' or it could 'constitute an EU autonomous police operation, possibly part of a larger EU-led crisis management operation' (quoted in Rutten, 2001, p. 137). Amongst the tasks envisaged for the force, the following were outlined: prevention and mitigation of internal crises and conflicts; involvement in post-conflict situations requiring robust force able to restore law and order; in support of local police and ensuring respect for basic human rights standards.

The impetus for the definition of tasks for the emerging EU international police force came to light in early 2002 as a result of a number of initiatives taken by the Spanish Presidency. In March 2002 EU member states agreed to send 500 EU military officers to Bosnia-Herzegovina to take over from those of the UN-led International Police Task Force (IPTF) that consisted of 1,674 officers, 535 of whom were Europeans (Bulletin Quotidien, 18 and 19 February 2002). The force was deployed on 1 January 2003 and is to be engaged in a three-year mission making use of 466 police officers, 67 civil experts and 289 local staff. The mandate of the EU Police Mission (EUPM), endorsed by the UN Security Council Resolution 1396 (5 March 2002), is to monitor and train the Bosnian police force as well as to help in building up its institutional structures in the context of a coordinated rule of law programme (United Nations Security Council, 2002). The aims of the mission are: by 2005, to seek to ensure that the police of Bosnia and Herzegovina (BiH) services will develop professional, politically neutral and ethnically unbiased law enforcement systems; to monitor, mentor and inspect BiH police managerial and operational capacities, along with the level of profession-alism. EUPM will also monitor the exercise of the appropriate political control over the police (European Union, 2002).

Institutional Aspects of Military and Police Cooperation

The ESDP has involved the creation of a number of new political and military bodies under Pillar II of the European Union, the pillar responsible for Common

Foreign Security Policy (CFSP). These bodies are: the Political Security Committee (PSC), the EU Military Committee (EUMC), the EU Military Staff (EUMS), the EU Situation Centre, the Committee on the Civilian Aspects of Crisis Management (CIVCOM) and the Police Unit. These bodies interact with already existing structures that are responsible for the CFSP, i.e. the EU Council, General Affairs Council, Presidency, the Secretary General/High Representative for CFSP, the General Secretariat, Political Committee, the Committee of Permanent Representatives (COREPER), and the PPEWU.[14]

Although from a legal point of view a separation of functions exists between the EU's Pillar I and II, the reality is that the bodies under Pillar I are also involved in shaping policies in Pillar II. Thus the posts of Commissioners responsible respectively for External Relations, Development and Humanitarian Aid, and Trade and Enlargement, along with the President of the Commission, are active in CFSP and ESDP. To add to complexity of the policy-making structure at the EU level, the ESDP has also resulted in a number of committees, working groups and ad-hoc multilateral arrangements being established so to enable an interaction between EU member states and NATO countries that are not EU members. Given the nature of the EU, policymakers have different instruments at their disposal in CFSP and ESDP that are distinct from legal instruments available under Pillar I.

In the area of CFSP, the EU Council or the Council of Ministers have a number of legal acts at their disposal for taking decisions. The key legal instruments are: Common Strategies, Joint Actions and Common Positions. The EU Council decides about Common Strategies on the basis of unanimity, with respect to those countries/regions or themes where member states share a strong common interest, and cover both Community and CFSP aspects.[15] Once a common strategy has been adopted, the Council of Ministers can take decisions on follow-up measures on the basis of QMV. Joint actions are used in cases where operational activity by the Union is considered necessary. They are decided upon unanimously (except in the framework of a common strategy) and are binding on member states. The Council of Ministers can also adopt common positions on international, regional or thematic issues. They require unanimity, except in the framework of an existing or thematic issue.[16]

---

14 A summary of the nature and functions of these bodies can be found in the following publications: Bono, 2003; and International Crisis Group, 2001, 2002. For a graphical representation of the bodies, see Muller-Wille, 2002, p. 67.

15 At the time of writing, the common strategies are: Russia, Ukraine and the Mediterranean region.

16 The exact legal and practical difference between Common Positions and Joint Actions is, however, not easy to define. To simplify a complex issue, joint actions are more important than common positions in that there are more detailed procedures for their adoption and, in contrast to common positions, they require a general willingness to put financial resources at the disposal of the Council for their implementation. See Wessels, 1999, section on 'Specific legal basis of CFSP Decisions'.

Through article 27a-e, the Nice Treaty modified the nature of enhanced cooperation in CFSP and introduced specific clauses concerning the way in which it relates to CFSP and ESDP.[17] Enhanced cooperation allows groups of states to push ahead in a specific policy area without the consensus of all EU member states. In the Amsterdam Treaty, the provisions for this stipulates that 'at least a majority' of member states have to be involved, while amended Article 24 of the Nice Treaty requires a minimum of eight member states. In other words, in the current EU of 15 member states a simple majority is required, whereas in a larger Union, the use of an enhanced cooperation mechanism could be undertaken with less than a simple majority of member states. The Nice Treaty incorporated enhanced cooperation in CFSP, but this is limited to common positions and joint actions, which need to be based on prior unanimous decisions. The area of military cooperation is excluded from this application.

The legal instruments in the field of ESDP are similar to those in CFSP with important exceptions. Any decision to launch a crisis management operation would be taken on the basis of a Joint Action. However, the Treaty (Article 23) explicitly excludes the use of majority voting in any decision having military or defence implications and the use of enhanced cooperation as previously mentioned. Since the Nice Treaty only includes references to ESDP in Articles 17 and 25, the legal provisions for ESDP are extremely vague. The legal provisions in the Nice Treaty do not facilitate a legal distinction between CFSP and ESDP. There is a danger that this might lead to a blurring of the threshold between CFSP and ESDP policy areas through piece-meal actions, following the principles of British case law.

Despite the role that the EU has assumed in peacekeeping and external police operations, there are a number of unresolved issues that will shape the EU's overall development in this area. Two of the most important issues are the interrelationship between the changing nature of the transatlantic security relationship and the impact of the current reform of the EU[18] on CFSP/ESDP matters. These issues can only be briefly sketched here.

As previously mentioned, the EU Council Summit in December 2002 formally resolved the two and half year dispute about the relationship between ESDP and NATO.[19] Some commentators maintain that this represents a new strategic relationship between the EU and NATO. There is indeed a trend that points towards a more equal redistribution of power between the USA and Europe within the current multilateral security frameworks. The ESDP and NATO agreement is in fact about ensuring that the EU contributes a fair share of military burdens and capabilities. The EU could become an equal partner of the USA in the longer-term by sharing additional costs and responsibilities within a reformed NATO. The EU could take over the full spectrum of operations in the Balkans and expand its remit internationally. By so doing, European member states may be able to 'restrain' the more unilateralist members of the US policy-making elites.

---

17 Article 27a can be found in Title V of the Nice Treaty, 2001.
18 The reform of the EU has been undertaken by the EU Convention and will be followed by an Intergovernmental Conference in 2004.
19 For background information on the dispute, see Bono, 2002-2003.

However, all of this is dependent on the current discussions about the reform of the EU giving impetus to a new consensus amongst the 25 EU member states and on the USA agreeing to an 'equal share of power' both in the Balkans and internationally.

Other trends are also evident. One such trend points to a less equal transatlantic security relationship. For some policy makers, especially in the United States and Britain, the key aspect of the ESDP-NATO relationship is about allowing the rejuvenation of the NATO integrated military structure by establishing stronger links between the NATO military planning process and the civilian capabilities at the disposal of the EU and its member states. This trend is already evident in the handling of the Afghanistan crisis and its aftermath. The USA, with the support of Britain, concentrated on war-fighting, and then European member states contributed substantially to the humanitarian aid and peacekeeping efforts. Through this 'division of labour', NATO was eventually able to take over the command and control and operational aspects of the peacekeeping force in Afghanistan, thus flexing its external military muscles to reach Asia. From this perspective, by using the EU framework and other multilateral ad hoc arrangements, European member states have provided the Anglo-American partners with additional peacekeeping and post-war reconstruction capabilities. If this pattern of 'cooperation' were to continue, the EU's role in external security engagements would remain subordinate to the international requirements of Anglo-American military strategists.

There is also a third trend that is expressed in the emergence of 'ad-hoc coalitions of the willing'. This challenges the political roles of both NATO and the EU in the security area. This trend is evident in the 'divisions' left over from the aftermath of the Iraq war. France, Germany, Belgium and Luxembourg decided to forge ahead in military affairs and establish closer diplomatic links with Russia (European Defence Meeting, 29 April 2003). Many officials in the EU Convention also called for enhanced cooperation, in the security and defence areas.[20] The hostile British and US reception of these proposals shows that the rift in the transatlantic relationship remains acute. The seeds of reconciliation may take some time to be sown because the Anglo-American 'war on terrorism' is not over yet and might lead to new external military engagements requiring support from European allies. The latter will remain reluctant to provide full support for such engagements without a more equal share of political responsibility. If this trend is strengthened by events, the European security landscape will be left with a number of multilateral institutions bereft of any political power. New military and political alliances will emerge resembling the style of Great Power Diplomacy of the second half of the 19th century.

Due to the fluidity of the current moment, predictions about the future of the ESDP can only be extremely speculative. The second and third trends are more likely if the USA and Britain continue with their policy of undermining the UN by turning it into a provider of 'post-reconstruction' services and if the reform of the

---

20 For an example, see the European Convention, 2002.

EU stalls and leads to ad hoc coalitions of the willing dictating the future of CFSP and ESDP.

The Challenge of Democratic Accountability

The introduction of the Headline Goal and of the new institutional arrangements for the ESDP has changed the EU's role in international security substantially and has created new challenges for democratic accountability. Already, prior to the establishment of the ESDP, the EU suffered a democratic deficit[21] and at the national level, the de-politicisation process that since the end of the Cold War has assumed astonishing dimensions has resulted in a general shift of the balance of power between national parliaments and the executive in favour of the latter. Through the introduction of the ESDP, EU member states have made these problems worse because they decided to deepen their coordination of foreign, security and defence policies without simultaneously changing the overall structure of the EU and giving existing parliamentary assemblies and citizens an enhanced ability to scrutinise the policy-making process. To fully capture the complexity of the issue and make explicit some of the assumptions behind the notion of democratic accountability, a specific definition of democracy, as a liberal 'ideal' type, is adopted and from it a set of questions and criteria are derived and discussed.

Models of Democratic Accountability

There are different models of democratic accountability that rely on divergent notions of democracy and on contrasting conceptions of the nature of the EU and its future.[22] To simplify a complex subject, the model based on the idea that democracy is about putting the will of the people into effect will be taken. According to this model, to be understood as a liberal 'ideal type' that synthesises the characteristics of the classical model of liberal democracy and those of liberal developmental democracy,[23] parliament embodies the will of the people in so far as citizens are able to exert political power not only through elections but also via direct forms of participatory democracy.[24] Taking this model into account, the

---

21 There is a vast amount of literature on the democratic deficit of the EU. Amongst the most recent publications that provide an overview are: Lord, 1998, 2001; Katz 2001; Hoskyns and Newman, 2000; and, Chryssochoou, 2000.

22 For a discussion on different models of democracy, see Held, 1987. For an overview of the different approaches to analysing the EU, its evolution and future: Rosamond, 2000; Eriksen and Fossum, 2000.

23 For the two models, see Held, 1987, pp. 36-102.

24 This model of liberal democracy assumes a certain level of economic equality amongst citizens. The two other models are those of the regulatory state and that based on the notion of civil society and the role of legitimacy. For literature on the former, see Majone, 1994, 1999; and on the latter, see Weiler and Netwich, 1998.

significance of ESDP for democratic accountability will be examined by posing a set of questions that seek to capture five different faces of democratic accountability. These facets are: administrative, parliamentary, political-military, external (vis-à-vis the population and governments of countries in which EU/NATO member states intervene) and internal (vis-à-vis EU citizens).[25]

1. *Administrative accountability:* is there a division between the executive and law-making bodies and are the law-making bodies in full charge of supervising the role of the executive?

2. Assuming that there are some forms of *parliamentary accountability*, we need to ask how it is exercised. What are the principles on which parliamentary accountability is based? Are these principles based on the continuous flow of information and the appraisal of the executive? Is executive power transparent? Do representatives have the power to investigate executive decisions? Are elected representatives able to exert political control?

3. *Political-military relations* In a democracy it is common practice for the military to follow the orders of elected politicians, and it is the role of governments to define the grand security strategies that should shape the work of the military. It is important to ask if the ESDP follows this model and if military planners are given clear guidelines from elected decision-makers.

4. *External accountability (vis-à-vis the population and governments of countries in which EU/NATO member states intervene)* Whose law will the EU's Rapid Reaction Force and/or international police force follow when it is deployed? Will they follow the rules present in international law and embodied in the UN Charter or will new rules be devised?

5. *Internal accountability (vis-à-vis the EU electorate)* Is the EU Council, the supreme political body responsible for CFSP/ESDP, accountable to EU citizens? Do EU citizens who are organised into political groups, have means at their disposal to scrutinise and sanction the role of the EU Council when it decides to undertake military operations?

Administrative Accountability

Administrative accountability in a liberal model of democracy assumes a clear separation of powers between the executive and the legislature. It also assumes a clear division of positions, authorities and centres of power. This clarification is essential because in contemporary Western democracies the role of the bureaucracy is pervasive. The complexity of government has led politicians to rely on the bureaucracy not purely for administrative functions but also for access to information, expertise and secrets. There is a problem with administrative accountability in the new military and police arrangements established under the

---

25 This definition has been developed by the author.

EU. This is because, as it has developed so far, the European Security and Defence Policy (ESDP) lies formally under Pillar II, the intergovernmental pillar, but in practice it also relies on the other pillars, especially on resources available in the Commission. The ESDP is exercised through a set of opaque policy-making structures in which civil servants play a disproportionate role unsupervised by the national and international legislatures. Moreover, at the EU level, the key institutions involved in authorising decisions related to CFSP and ESDP, including the deployment of the Rapid Reaction Force and the police force for international missions – that is the Commission and the Council and to a more limited extent the European Parliament (EP) – are not structured in such a way as to allow administrative accountability to occur. The Council is not able to control the work of the Commission in the area of CFSP for a number of reasons.

In the first place, the Commission has a certain level of independent political power in areas linked to the CFSP and ESDP, including external trade, humanitarian aid and accession/enlargement policies. The Commission plays a powerful role as an agenda-setting institution and has developed considerable autonomy in relations with member states. It is the only institution able to propose new European legislation and, under some circumstances, if the Council wants to amend proposals from the Commission it is obliged to do so unanimously. In contrast to national bureaucracies, the Commission has, in fact, the ability to concentrate on rule-making, rather than more labour-intensive aspects of government such as redistribution. It has the added advantage that it can rely on national administrations for information and implementation, although its role in obtaining intelligence and information in purely defence security issues is non-existent at present. The Commission obtains its autonomy from a number of other factors. Firstly, it has access to more information than national bureaucracies and is in a better position to formulate alternative policy options because it has the power to mobilise other non-state actors, it can exploit differences between its own 'time-horizons' and those of member states, and it is able to present itself as an 'impartial' agency for brokering agreements (Lord, 1998, pp. 26, 81-82).[26] Secondly, the Council has a problem in controlling and legitimising the activities of the Commission because it is not a 'neutral' actor. In fact, the working groups set up by the Council to control the work of the Commission are made up of individuals who are heavily involved in the work of the Commission itself. Hence the link between the working groups and the Commission is not one of supervision, but rather one of self-validation and self-policing (Lord, 1998, pp. 83).

Moreover, within the EU, political power is dispersed between different levels and branches of government. This means that many organisations and individuals have the power of veto in the area of CFSP. The net result can be decisions which appear non-rational, or even random: what academics describe as the phenomena of 'joint-decision trap' and 'garbage can' model of decision-making (Lord, 1998, pp. 84). In order to overcome these vetoes, the Union has allowed a great deal of policy initiation and administration to pass to a series of

---

26 There is substantial literature that supports the analysis of the Commission as an independent actor. For an overview, see Hix, 1999, pp. 52-54.

'policy-communities', which act as an interface between the national and European bureaucracies and who include 'experts' and lobbyists. They act through informal and formal processes such as the 'comitology'.[27] These networks corrode established hierarchies and lead to policy-making being characterised by the search for consensus solutions that cut across the different levels and branches of government. Experts within these networks want to preserve their credibility with one another and therefore avoid challenging established positions. There is thus an in-built mechanism for the confirmation of dominant views within the EU policy-making process.

The ESDP has made the problem of administrative accountability worse in that it has created many new working groups between NATO and the EU on a number of important topics. It has also resulted in the establishment of informal groups, for example, the Informal Ministers of Defence Meetings. These working groups and informal meetings have been established under the Council structures and the European Parliament and national parliaments are not involved in scrutinising their work. Moreover, the existence of these informal networks renders the ESDP decision-making process extremely opaque. The system of formal and informal committees has led to a blurring of responsibilities which makes it difficult for citizens to allocate responsibilities for failed policies.

The lack of a clear separation of competencies between CFSP and ESDP also has also crucial consequences for the overall decision-making process in crisis management. As previously argued, the legal instruments for ESDP are not precisely defined in the Nice Treaty. This creates opportunities for blurring the line of demarcation between purely humanitarian measures, taken under CFSP, and those with a potential military character.

Parliamentary Accountability

The national parliaments and two regional parliamentary assemblies (the European Parliament (EP) and the EU Interim European Security and Defence Assembly,[28] have the task of scrutinising the ESDP, yet there still remains the problem of parliamentary accountability. Since the limits of the role of the EP and national parliaments are examined in Chapter Eleven, the comments here are general.

It is often argued that ultimate power of scrutiny over the ESDP lies with national parliaments because the ESDP is partly intergovernmental. However, this assertion fails to take into account that as soon as national governments enter into a multilateral agreement, they are able to gain extra executive powers over their own national parliaments. The executive branches of government are able to do so because a national position, though it might be agreed in advance in consultation

---

27 For an analysis of the system of comitology, see Hix, 1999, pp. 41-44.
28 The EU Interim European Security and Defence Assembly has taken over the role of the WEU Assembly. The Assembly remains in operation because the Brussels Treaties still stand since the EU has not taken over Article 5 of the Brussels Treaty, the article that deals with the defence of its members. For a review of the history and role of the Assembly see: Lotter, 1997.

with national parliamentarians, is usually modified during diplomatic exchanges with other governments. In the area of ESDP, these exchanges take place in formal and informal meetings at the EU and NATO levels. They also take place in informal bilateral meetings or through ad-hoc groups of countries. At the EU Council and NATO North Atlantic Council levels, national parliaments are not represented and do not have access to details of discussions. The same applies for decisions taken in ad-hoc and in informal meetings. Hence, national parliaments cannot fully scrutinise the decision-making process when decisions are formulated and revised at such levels. The two regional parliamentary assemblies mentioned above have neither the formal powers to influence ESDP decisions nor have they sufficient formal powers to scrutinise the ESDP policy-making process. For example, the role of the EU Interim European Security and Defence Assembly [29] is limited to making recommendations and asking questions in written and verbal format once decisions have already been taken.[30]

Political-Military Relations

Nation states have grand strategies that define their political principles towards other states and multilateral arrangements in the international security system. For some democracies these principles are enshrined in a Constitution. As the EU has developed as a hybrid system of power, with no formal constitution at the time of writing, and because of the ad hoc piecemeal nature of the development of the ESDP, the EU does not have already agreed political and strategic visions of its role in the world. Although the High Representative for CFSP has recently developed Strategies to define its role toward certain regions, these strategies do not form an overall Grand Strategy. They cannot be used to evaluate or provide guidelines for specific policies adopted at a lower level of policy-making.

Given that the military rely on a clear chain of command and need to have military concepts (sometimes also referred to as doctrines) for different levels of command, the military in the EU require clear political leadership. In fact, in an 'ideal' type of democracy in which a high level of transparency and accountability exists in the policy-making process, the Chiefs of Staff should develop military concepts that are derived from the Grand Strategy laid down by political leaders. This type of procedure was not pursued in the development of ESDP.

This has occurred because there were a number of competing national and institutional agendas driving the consensus behind the Helsinki, Feira and Nice EU Summits (Bono 2002a, pp. 32-38; Bono 2002b, pp. 14-21). As a consequence, the defence ministries of EU member states and the various working groups set up by the Capabilities Commitment Conference have defined some of the political goals of the Rapid Reaction Force. This was done partly involuntarily: out of a need to have clear guidelines for deployment.

---

29 For an overview of its current activities see their web site: http://www.assemblee-ueo.org/
30 For a review of the history and role of the Assembly see: Lotter, 1997. For an overview of its current activities see their web site: http://www.assemblee-ueo.org/

Even if a mandate has been given for the first ESDP operation, Concordia, it is not clear whether the military doctrine that shapes the operation is simply 'borrowed from NATO' or follows a different vision of security engagements.

This lack of clarity in the political-military relationship creates problems for democratic accountability in that without agreed strategies and established and transparent principles, it is more difficult for parliamentarians to judge whether EU governments are justified in making decisions with regard to external crises.

External Accountability

Will future EU external military engagements adhere to established norms of international law? Will the ESDP be based on the traditional principles of peacekeeping (neutrality, impartiality and the need for consensus)? Or will it be based on the new set of principles outlined in the Brahimi Report (United Nations, 2000)? Only nebulous answers are available on these crucial matters.[31]

The issue of Western nations' democratic accountability vis-à-vis the governments and citizens of countries in which they intervene is pivotal because of changes in the nature of the relationship between developed and developing nations. Since the end of the Cold War there has been an intensified trend toward Western military intervention in less developed countries based on arguments of the supremacy of international humanitarian law,[32] and more recently on the doctrine of 'pre-emptive action'. Both of these doctrines challenge basic principles of non-intervention in the affairs of sovereign nation states. Some critics argue that these doctrines mask the reality of a return to forms of Western domination over less developed countries, reminiscent of Western colonial intervention of the 19th century (Chandler 2002; Chomsky 1999; Hardt and Negri 2000).

Although EU member states have officially stated that their external military engagements will respect the rules of international law, there remains some ambiguity in their positions and marked differences of opinion. These differences have recently emerged in the debate over the necessity of a UN mandate for the US- and British-led war against Iraq, Rules of Engagement and the command structure of peacekeeping operations in Afghanistan (International Security Assistance Force).[33]

Internal Accountability

As Chapter Eleven explains, national parliaments have difficulties in supervising ESDP because they have different methods of scrutinising foreign, security and defence policies. The EP has slightly more powers but these are still very limited in comparison to the traditional role of national parliaments. Hence, at present, EU

---

31 For a critique of the Brahimi Report, see Chandler, 2001.
32 For an overview of the debate, see Ortega, 2001; Mayall, 2000; Adam, 1999.
33 For the debate about the mandate of the NATO force in Macedonia, see Dempsey 2001; For the debate about the mandate of ISAF and the extent to which ISAF should work under US command and link itself to US combat activities: Connolly, 2001; Hoge, 2001.

citizens cannot rely on either their legislatures or the EP to scrutinise ESDP. Moreover, since the EU Council is not directly elected, representatives of member states in EU countries are not able to penalise the EU Council if they disagree with their decisions to send armed forces into a conflict situation.

The role of civil-society and pan-European parties in shaping the policy-making process in Brussels in the area of ESDP is also extremely limited. Some NGOs are included as part of the working groups that discuss conflict prevention but these NGOs are self-selected and do not represent all of strands available in European public opinion (Warleigh, 2001).

Moreover, Article 46 of the TEU excludes the European Court of Justice (ECJ) and the European Court of First Instance (CFI) from playing any role in scrutinising CFSP and ESDP. There have, however, been some exceptions to this rule. For example, since the ECJ plays a role in the delimitation of competences between the Community and the Union, when a member state takes decisions in CFSP that conflict with the obligations to ensure the development of the Community, actions can be taken to court. Some cases were referred to the ECJ by national courts in relation to the Yugoslav and Iraqi sanctions. There have also been isolated attempts to take the Council to the CFI over the disclosure of documents in the area of arms exports. Other potential actions could arise when the implementation of CFSP obligations by national authorities is in contradiction to Community law or when member states want to complain about the misuse of certain EC funds for CFSP purposes (Wessels, 1999, pp. 223-229).[34]

Despite these cases and potential usage of the European courts, limits exist to the extent an EU citizen can rely on the EU courts to make governments accountable for CFSP and ESDP decisions. The juridical system of the European Union is perceived by the EU judges as being a guarantor of the appropriate application of European law, that is, as a service to the objective of European integration, rather than as an instrument for the protection of individuals from the excesses of the system or as a means to allow EU citizens to participate in the decision-making process (Costa, 2001).

Conclusions

Whilst allowing the EU to assume a role in external military engagements, the new development of the ESDP has created challenges for democratic accountability. Five arguments have been advanced. Firstly, the developments have worsened the already existing lack of *administrative accountability* within the EU so far as it has resulted in the creation of a great number of new working groups that cut across the EU pillars structure and have links with NATO and non-EU member states. Secondly, the developments have exacerbated the problem of *parliamentary accountability*, since EP, the EU Interim European Security and Defence

---

34 For the case of access to documents in the area of armaments, see the case brought by Council of the European Union v. Heidi Hautala, 2001. For background on this case, see Bauer, 2001.

Assembly, and national parliaments in EU member states have not been given any new powers of scrutiny over ESDP. Thirdly, the manner in which the initial decisions to establish the Headline Goal were taken, has inverted the nature of the military-political relationship which, in democracies, is normally based on elected politicians issuing political guidelines to the military. In fact, EU political leaders have not agreed on a Strategic Concept for the ESDP. By so doing, they have failed, at least until recently, to provide clear political guidelines to their military staff. Hence, in 2000-2001 EU military staff and officials located in the lower-echelon of the EU and NATO defence ministries have been forced to take decisions regarding the Headline Goal that implicitly contained *political* assumptions about the geographical scope and mandate of the Rapid Reaction Force and the EU international police force. Fourthly, there is the problem of *external* democratic accountability in the ESDP because it is unclear what type of national, European and international laws will be followed when the EU becomes involved in external conflicts. Finally, there is the problem of *internal* democratic accountability because the current national and European legislatures, including the European judiciary system, are incapable of scrutinising the ESDP. Civil society is not organised in such a manner as to represent the various opinions present in the EU. The debate about the reform of the EU calls for changes in the transatlantic security relationship and offers an opportunity to resolve some of the challenges of making the EU's external military and police operations democratically accountable.

Chapter 11

Parliamentary Accountability and ESDP: The National and the European Level

Catriona Gourlay

Introduction

Decisions concerning defence and security implications are increasingly made in an EU framework. Recent policy and institutional developments to create a common European Security and Defence Policy (ESDP) have underscored this trend (see Chapter Ten). While the EU has long coordinated and implemented decisions having significant security implications, in 1999 its member states decided to develop an autonomous EU military capability to undertake 'Petersberg tasks' ranging from humanitarian intervention to peace-enforcement. The ESDP will require many aspects of national defence policy to be decided on in the relatively opaque context of intergovernmental and interinstitutional negotiation in Brussels. Within this framework national parliaments can, in principle, hold their executives accountable for decisions reached by unanimity but, in practice, it is extremely difficult for national parliamentarians to acquire the necessary oversight and expertise to judge these decisions effectively. The transfer of decision-making from the national to European level is therefore seen by many to exacerbate the problem of democratic scrutiny in an area of policy-making in which parliaments in any case enjoy relatively few formal powers.

As the ability of national parliaments to scrutinise EU security and defence policy becomes increasingly strained, many argue that this role should be taken up by the European Parliament (EP). However, despite the gradual strengthening of the Common Foreign and Security Policy (CFSP) and the development of the ESDP, the European Parliament's formal powers in this area remain extremely weak. In short, whereas the EP has better access to information on the development of CFSP and ESDP, it lacks the relevant legal competencies to formally scrutinise or hold governments to account for decisions on ESDP taken within the Council.

This chapter aims to unpack the specific challenges that national parliaments and the European Parliament face with regard to the scrutiny of ESDP. It will outline the scope of parliamentary control of this sector at a national level and at the European level and will end by exploring potential remedies, some of which may be born out of the on-going EU institutional reform debate and the

2004 Inter-governmental Conference (IGC), that might help bridge the accountability gap in EU security and defence policy.

Frameworks for Analysis

The task of comparing the effectiveness of parliaments in scrutinising and influencing policy is a challenging one. Some comparative studies have focused purely on the legal framework, rather than analysing its operation in practice.[1] This offers clear results but little insight into the parliament's *ex-post* ability, in practice, to hold executives to account.[2] On the other hand, those studies that have sought to develop general taxonomies by comparing functional activities, also encounter problems of comparison since the same procedures can have different meanings and a different impact in diverse national contexts.[3] Such broad comparative analyses are also ill-equipped to account for the relationship between the legislatures and their environments.[4]

With regard to the specific challenge of comparing European Union member states' parliaments and the European Parliament's role in the oversight of ESDP, it is therefore necessary to take a narrower, policy-specific approach, but one that is open to drawing on the explanatory potential of a broad range of variables. The key variables that influence a parliament's general ability to exert influence over the executive should be taken into consideration, while particular emphasis is placed on a limited number of factors that are most relevant to this policy sphere.

With regard to the ability of parliaments to influence and scrutinise ESDP, however, there are a number of factors which relate to the European Union's institutional configuration and the politics of enlargement that complicate the task of parliamentary oversight of ESDP. This chapter will first identify these challenges to the oversight and scrutiny of ESDP before exploring the key factors that influence parliaments' potential to influence and scrutinise ESDP, in particular. These are:

- Access to relevant information and internal capacities to process it;
- Involvement in the decision to deploy forces;
- Budgetary powers and involvement in armaments policy (defence procurement and arms exports).

---

1   See, for example, Henkin and Rosenthal, 1990. This study concludes that the parliaments of European Union member states, with the exception of Denmark, do not have the power to supervise CFSP.
2   However, various parliaments in democracies in the Euro-Atlantic area have the legal power of prior authorisation of peace support operations (PSOs) (see Chapter Four).
3   For broad comparative studies across the policy spectrum see Menzy, 1979; Blondel, 1973.
4   This has been argued by Norton, 1995 and Patzelt, 1995.

It is beyond the scope of this chapter to conduct a thorough comparative analysis of EU national parliaments and the European Parliament to scrutinise security and defence policy in general and even ESDP in particular.[5] Rather it will seek to outline the range of types and levels of parliamentary involvement in scrutinising ESDP in relation to these factors, with a view to exploring the concrete constitutional and procedural options that might enhance national and European-level parliamentary scrutiny of ESDP in the future.

The Challenge of Parliamentary Scrutiny of ESDP

At first sight, the democratic logic of parliamentary oversight of the ESDP is straightforward. As ESDP is formally an intergovernmental or 'second pillar' activity, the relevant executive organs remain the member states. Since decisions on ESDP are made at a European level within the General Affairs Council and the crisis management decision-making bodies that service it, however, it follows that national parliaments must also oversee their national executives in the intergovernmental decision-making context of the Council.

This is likely to be an enduring reality of ESDP. There is a clear trend towards 'multi-nation'-alising security and defence. Yet, given that matters of security and defence are the most jealously guarded areas of national sovereignty, decision-making in this area is likely to remain strictly intergovernmental. It is highly improbable, for example, that qualified majority voting will be extended to decisions to launch an EU-led crisis management operation in the foreseeable future.

So what are the particular challenges that this picture poses for parliamentary oversight? Where is the democratic deficit? ESDP poses at least two distinct challenges for parliamentary oversight: the gap between national responsibility for ESDP and the challenge of a mixed executive.

The Gap between the National and the European level

While national parliaments have the competence to scrutinise national security and defence policies, even where these are exercised within the framework of ESDP, they currently lack the information to carry out this task effectively. Each national parliament experiences difficulty in obtaining a European overview of ESDP. They have no way of adequately reflecting on decisions taken (by consensus) in the Council in the absence of a comparative and broader overview of the intergovernmental dynamics of the decision-making process. National parliaments are currently informed on the issues of ESDP by their national governments on a bilateral basis and the only way that a national parliament comes to hear directly about the opinion-forming process in, and perceptions of, other governments is through occasional individual contacts on an *ad hoc* basis.

---

5   For comparative research on national parliamentary oversight of peace support operations, see Chapter Four.

In contrast, the European Parliament is privileged vis-à-vis national parliaments as regards the provision of information. Article 21 of the Treaty on European Union 1992 (TEU) obliges the EU Presidency and the Commission to consult the European Parliament on the development of the CFSP. In recent practice, this has been extended to include ESDP, a fact that is likely to be codified in the 2004 Inter-Governmental Conference. Article 21 of the TEU also states that the Presidency shall ensure that 'the views of the European Parliament are duly taken into consideration'. However, the Council is under no contractual obligation to reply to EP recommendations or resolutions relating to CFSP or ESDP and, in practice, its consultation of the EP involves occasional public briefings to the EP on the latest developments in CFSP and ESDP and does not extend to involving the EP in policy-making. Nevertheless, negotiations are under way to extend the EP's provision with information by allowing a limited number of Members of the European Parliament (MEPs) access to relevant classified information and the Presidency is also obliged to provide the EP with timely financial information relating to the ESDP budget.[6] Thus, the EP enjoys better access to information on the development of CFSP and ESDP, but it does not have the relevant legal competencies to formally hold governments to account for decisions on ESDP taken within the Council. Hence effective democratic control of ESDP risks falling between the two stools of the European Parliament and national parliaments.

The Challenge of a Mixed Executive

The second challenge for the oversight of ESDP relates to the fact that there is, in practice, a mixed executive when it comes to implementing European security policy, with competencies shared between the Commission and the Council and exercised through the distinct decision-making frameworks of the first, second and increasingly even third pillars of the EU institutional structure. These are as follows:

- The first pillar consists of the European Communities, providing a framework within which the member states, through the Community Institutions, can jointly exercise their sovereignty in the areas covered by the Treaties. Under the first pillar, decisions are made by qualified majority voting in accordance with the *acquis communitaire* and implemented by the Commission.
- The second pillar is the common foreign and security policy laid down in Title V of the TEU. This 'CFSP' pillar is purely intergovernmental and decisions with security or defence implications must be unanimous. There are, nevertheless, options for constructive abstention in many areas of CFSP which do not have direct military implications.
- The third pillar is cooperation in the fields of justice and home affairs laid down in Title VI of the TEU.

---

6 See the following section on the role of the European Parliament for a full description of the EP's rights with regard to the provision of information and budgetary oversight.

Titles V and VI provide for intergovernmental cooperation using the common institutions, with certain supranational features such as associating the Commission and consulting parliament. Decisions made within the second and third pillars are therefore implemented by member states, although in practice the Commission often helps implement common decisions in accordance with the Community's legal framework (first pillar).

The distribution of policy areas which are relevant to European security and defence do not, however, neatly conform to these institutional distinctions. While ESDP is considered to fall under the second pillar, in practice a number of actions with relevance to the implementation of CFSP and ESDP will also fall under first and third pillar competencies.

The modern demands of an effective conflict prevention, crisis management, armaments and anti-terrorism policy involves the use of a panoply of national and Community instruments with a complex mix of executive responsibilities. This presents an additional challenge for parliamentary scrutiny, whereby democratic accountability runs the risk of falling between the 'pillars' of Community and Council competence. Bridging this accountability gap will require national parliaments to develop capacities to provide them with a broad overview of these intergovernmental and inter-pillar links. It will also require close cooperation with the European Parliament, the body with the principal responsibility for overseeing the Commission's execution of decisions made within the first pillar.

The Present Roles of the European Parliament and National Parliaments

The European Parliament

Since 1979, the European Parliament has been the only international parliament directly elected by universal suffrage. Broadly speaking, its powers have been linked to its role of supervising the institutions of the EU and have therefore been increased over time in keeping with the increased competencies of the European Community.

A brief history of an extension of the European Parliament's powers is as follows.[7] Replacement of member state contributions by the Community's own resources led to a first extension of the parliament's budgetary powers under the Treaty of Luxembourg, signed on 22 April 1970. These powers were later extended in the Treaty of Brussels on the same subject, agreed in 1975. The Single European Act, which entered into force in 1987, strengthened the parliament's powers by making Community agreements on enlargement and association agreements subject to its assent. For the legislative process it introduced a procedure for cooperation between the parliament and the Council which gave the parliament

---

7   For references to the legal basis of the EU and a more detailed account of the history of the EU and the European Parliament in particular, see the website of the European Union (www.europa.eu.int) and the European Parliament (www.europarl.eu.int).

real, if limited, legislative powers. Later, in 1993 when the Maastricht Treaty entered into force, the co-decision procedure was introduced into certain areas of legislation and the cooperation procedure was extended to others. This marked the beginning of the parliament's role of co-legislator. It also gave it the power of final approval over the membership of the Commission, an important step in the parliament's political control over the European executive. The Treaty of Amsterdam further amended the Treaty on the European Union (TEU) when it entered into force in 1999. It extended the co-decision procedure to all the areas of legislation where the Council may decide by qualified majority excepting only agriculture and competition policy and reformed the procedure, putting parliament as co-legislator on an equal footing with the Council. With the appointment of the President of the Commission being made subject to parliament's approval (after nomination by the member states), parliament further increased its control over the executive power.

Hence today the European Parliament enjoys powers of co-decision with the Council under most aspects of Community competence, under the first pillar, and has principal responsibility for holding the European executive – the European Commission – to account. This ensures that the European Parliament has the principal responsibility for the scrutiny and control of those aspects of EU security and defence which fall under the first pillar including many aspects of conflict prevention, civilian crisis-management and anti-terrorism. With regard to its oversight and scrutiny of CFSP and ESDP in the second pillar, however, its powers are far more limited to rights of consultation and indirect influence through budgetary controls. In keeping with the comparative methodological approach set out at the beginning of this article, the European Parliament's powers and capacities to scrutinise CFSP and ESDP will be analysed in relation to its (1) access to relevant information and internal capacity to process it; (2) involvement in the decision to deploy forces; and, (3) budgetary powers and involvement in armaments policy.

(1) Access to information and internal capacities to process it There is evidence that the obligation to consult the European Parliament in the area of CFSP under the terms of Article 21 of the TEU is being taken increasingly seriously. The Presidency now regularly addresses the Foreign Affairs Committee, as does the High Representative for CFSP, Javier Solana, the Commissioner for External Relations, Chris Patten, and the Secretary General of NATO.[8] The EP also has the right to call the High Representative for CFSP and EU special representatives to appear before the parliament's Foreign Affairs, Security and Defence Committee in order to give evidence concerning their appointment and mandate.[9] The

---

8 In the current parliamentary term each Presidency, represented at ministerial level, has addressed the Foreign Affairs Committee at least twice and the High Representative for CFSP, the Commissioner for External Relations Chris Patten and the Secretary General of NATO have addressed the Committee or the plenary session at least twice a year.

9 Articles 18 and 21 of the Treaty of the European Union 1992 provide the legal basis for this.

European Parliament therefore undoubtedly enjoys greater opportunities to question ministers directly on matters of CFSP than it did before the development of ESDP and than do its national counterparts.

Nevertheless, the European Parliament's access to relevant information on ESDP is still subject to the discretion of the Presidency. Moreover, in July 2000 EU Ambassadors in the Council voted to introduce new rules denying public access to classified, secret or top-secret documents containing information on military or non-military crisis-management, or to documents that could enable 'conclusions to be drawn' regarding the content of classified information. The decision also made an entire class of documents invisible to the public by withdrawing all references to classified documents for the Council's public register (Council of the European Union, 2000a, 2000b, 2000c).[10] The decision clearly undermined the parliament's ability to oversee ESDP by restricting public and parliamentary access to information across the board. It remains controversial and is being challenged by the European Parliament in the European Court of Justice (ECJ).[11] However, on 19 March 2001, the Council passed a new decision on adopting the Council's security regulations (Council Decision 2001/264/EC; Official Journal L 101), which superseded its decisions of the year 2000. This was nevertheless similar in substance to the aforementioned decisions taken in 2000 and is therefore being challenged, on the same grounds, by the European Parliament in the ECJ.

Since the 2000 decisions, a number of initiatives have been introduced to redress the balance and secure the European Parliament the right to access to relevant information on ESDP, including classified information. One example is the introduction into Community law in December 2001 of Article 9(7) of regulation 1049/2001 which provides that '(t)he Commission and the Council shall inform the European Parliament regarding sensitive documents in accordance with arrangements agreed between the institutions'.[12] This is commonly interpreted as implying that, in order for the European Parliament to be able to exercise its rights and duties under the Treaties, it needs access to the information on the basis of which decisions on the CFSP are taken.

Moreover, in September 2002, the European Parliament, represented by the Chair of the Foreign Affairs Committee, Elmar Brok (MEP), and the Council's Committee of Permanent Representatives (COREPER) negotiated a '*Decision on the implementation of the Inter-institutional Agreement governing European*

---

10 For a deeper analysis of these decisions see Jensen, 2000.
11 On 23 October 2000, the European Parliament brought an action against the Council in the Court of Justice in which it sought the annulment of these two decisions. The European Parliament argued that the legal basis chosen by the Council (Article 207 EC) is incorrect and, since the entry into force of the Treaty of Amsterdam, decisions which lay down the 'principles' and 'limits' of the right to access to Council documents should be adopted under the co-decision procedure pursuant to Article 255 EC.
12 Sensitive documents are defined in paragraph 1 of Article 9 as documents classified in order to protect essential interests of the Union or its member states in the areas covered by Article 4(1)(a) of the regulation, '*notably public security, defence and military matters.*'

Parliament access to sensitive Council information in the sphere of security and defence policy'. This Agreement provided for the Council, represented by the High Representative for CFSP to brief a small Committee of five members of the European Parliament (MEPs), *in camera,* and to provide them with classified information relevant to ESDP. The Agreement does not, however, confer rights on the parliament to receive access to classified information but rather gives the Council the right to share classified information 'where this is appropriate and possible in the light of the nature and the content of the information'. Thus, it does not extend the European Parliament's 'right' to access classified information but rather increases the likelihood that a few MEPs are granted privileged access to some classified information. This decision has not been universally welcomed within the European Parliament, and MEPs such as Heidi Hautala, have argued that it might undermine the parliament's right to be informed on CFSP in accordance with existing Community law.[13] In any case, the European Parliament's access to information on ESDP remains limited and is granted at the discretion of the Council. In addition, the post-11 September 2001 international climate is less conducive to sharing information freely and this may lead, in practice, to a very conservative interpretation of the Council's obligation to consult the European Parliament in the area of ESDP.

Whether or not the European Parliament can effectively scrutinise ESDP depends not only on its access to relevant information but also on its ability to process it. There is, however, no trend to increase the internal resources and capacities of the European Parliament to match the transfer of decision-making to the European level in ESDP. On the contrary, after the Amsterdam Treaty extended the legislative role of the European Parliament in areas of Community competence (first pillar), the European Parliament prepared for its entry into force by reorganising its work and reallocating its resources so as to prioritise its legislative work. This did not lead to greater resources being allocated to the oversight of decision-making in the intergovernmental (second) pillar of security and defence. Rather, the decision was taken to abolish the two sub-committees of the Committee of Foreign Affairs, Security and Defence. Consequently, in the current parliamentary term (1999-2004) the ability of the European Parliament to scrutinise ESDP has been limited by the fact that a single Committee – the Committee on Foreign Affairs, Human Rights, Common Security and Defence Policy – is responsible for the oversight of all aspects of foreign affairs, including human rights, EU enlargement, CFSP and ESDP. Consequently, in practice, the European Parliament therefore has relatively fewer resources (including Committee research staff and number of authorised reports) to dedicate to the scrutiny of CFSP and ESDP than in it did in the past.[14] Despite its privileged access to information on ESDP *vis-à-vis* national parliaments, the quality of the

---

13 Heidi Hautala, MEP, reported to the Committee on Legal Affairs and the Internal Market, recommending that the Council's decisions be challenged in the ECJ. Her objections to the negotiated Inter-institutional Agreement were quoted in European Voice, 2002.

14 For more detailed analysis of parliamentary restructuring in 1999, see Gourlay, 1999.

European Parliament's scrutiny of and expertise in ESDP still suffers from its inadequate provision with information and limited Committee resources.

(2) Involvement in the decision to deploy force Given that the decision to engage in a military operation must be taken by consensus within the second intergovernmental pillar, the European Parliament has no formal involvement in a decision to deploy force. If there is parliamentary involvement in these decisions, it is strictly at the national level. Nevertheless, the European Parliament has provided post-hoc scrutiny of multinational operations in the past and will undoubtedly see that it is within its supervisory mandate to monitor and scrutinise the implementation of EU-led operations in the future.

(3) Budgetary powers and involvement in armaments policy. The European Parliament has important co-decision rights with regard to individual budget lines for civilian crisis-management under the first pillar, including, for example, approval of the budget for the Rapid Reaction Mechanism, and the approval of the entire annual budget for CFSP which is charged to the Community budget according to the Article 28 of the TEU.[15] The CFSP budget is used to support the second pillar, CFSP activities (excluding those with military or defence implications) and the EP's co-decision rights, as elaborated in the Inter-Institutional Agreement between the EP, Council and Commission in 1997 (Inter-institutional Agreement, 1997). The powers are limited to disagreeing with the total size of the CFSP budget and potentially freezing it at the size of the past year's budget or the current year's draft budget, whichever is the lower. While this co-decision power is crude and not tailored to specific expenditure, it is currently being used to exert pressure on the Council to provide the parliament with greater budgetary oversight.

The Inter-institutional Agreement also provided the European Parliament with additional budgetary information. It states that the Presidency will consult the EP on a yearly basis and provide it with a document on the financial implications of CFSP for the Community budget. Moreover, whenever the Council adopts a decision in the field of CFSP requiring expenditure (for example, appointing a new special representative), it will immediately send the EP an estimate of the costs envisaged. The European Parliament therefore has important rights to information about how Community funds are spent, including those allocated to the CFSP budget line. While it cannot determine how funds are spent within this broad budget, its co-decision rights provide it with the threat of sanction should the parliament object to the political orientation of ESDP.

With regard to the oversight of armaments policies, the European Parliament has no formal powers but has nevertheless routinely responded to Commission Communications on the European Defence Industry and to the Council's consolidated annual reports on the implementation of the EU Code of Conduct on Arms Exports. The parliament's reports have consistently called for loopholes in the EU Code to be addressed i.e. to establish control over arms

---

15 This budget is commonly referred to as the B8 chapter of the Community budget.

brokering agents and for the quantity and quality of information provided by member states to be enhanced and be presented in comparable form. The European Parliament also supports bringing armaments cooperation such as the Framework Agreement within the EU framework so that it has a role in their oversight.

Recognising that the scrutiny of the military aspects of ESDP will continue to be the prerogative of national parliaments, however, the European Parliament has sought to improve the overall oversight of ESDP by increasing its cooperation with national parliaments by holding bi-annual meetings between the Foreign Affairs Committee and the chairs of its national counterparts. Similarly, recognising the need to associate non-EU NATO countries with ESDP, the EP Foreign Affairs Committee has strengthened its relationship with the NATO Parliamentary Assembly. It now invites representatives of the Assembly to the meetings at which the High Representative of CFSP and the Presidency report to the EP on the developments in the field of CFSP and ESDP. These initiatives are nevertheless seen to fall short of the goals of providing national parliaments with an adequate overview of ESDP and ensuring meaningful involvement and cooperation with parliamentarians from non-EU NATO countries and candidate countries.

According to Armin Laschet (MEP), the European Parliament would like to extend its cooperation with national parliaments in the future in order to collectively review the development of ESDP (Laschet, 2002, pp. 6-7). To this end, it proposes that a parliamentary conference on ESDP be held on a regular basis, to be convened jointly by the parliament of the member state holding the Presidency and the European Parliament's Committee on Foreign Affairs, Human Rights, Common Security and Defence Policy. The conference would bring together the Council Presidency, the High Representative for CFSP and the Commissioner for External Relations with the chairs and selected members of all member states', applicant states' and European parliamentary committees responsible for foreign affairs, defence, and EU affairs. Parliamentarians from non-EU NATO countries, candidate countries and the NATO Parliamentary Assembly could also be invited to attend as observers. With this view, a regular conference on ESDP would effectively fill the role of providing national and European parliamentarians with multinational oversight of ESDP through information exchange in a multinational setting. In the past this role has been played by the WEU Assembly, a consultative body that oversaw the functions of the WEU, but the European Parliament believes that since the core functions of the WEU have now been integrated into the EU, the WEU Assembly has lost its *'raison d'être'* and should be discontinued.

The European Parliament's ambitions with regard to improving its scrutiny of ESDP will be made clear by its representatives to the Convention on the future of Europe. As of yet there is no common European Parliament position, but in general terms, most MEPs would prefer to see greater communitarisation of CFSP and some aspects of ESDP which would, in turn, extend the parliament's role in the oversight of ESDP. For example, some parliamentarians, including Armin Laschet (2002), would like to see the common costs of EU-led military operations funded from the Community budget and some representatives of the Socialist (PSE) and Conservative (PPE) groups would also like to see the defence industry brought within the single market. This would make it subject to EU competition rules and eligible for potential research and development funding grants. More specifically, the European Parliament is likely to press for greater formal powers of consultation with regard to ESDP by strengthening Article 21 of the TEU and making its applicability to ESDP explicit. With regard to increasing its internal capabilities to oversee ESDP, there are no formal proposals to bolster the resources and role of the Committee on Foreign Affairs or to create another Committee dealing with ESDP. However, such internal reorganisation would only be possible in the next parliamentary term in 2005 and therefore the debate is expected to follow the conclusion of the 2004 Intergovernmental Conference and enlargement decisions.

The Role of the National Parliaments

If the EU's democratic deficit in ESDP relates to the lack of effective controls over the executive functions of crisis management that have been transferred to the European level, the weakness of parliamentary oversight over governments at a national level can be viewed as a 'double democratic deficit'. The specific historical, constitutional and cultural contexts of national parliamentary systems mean that no single, constitutional or procedural fix is likely to deliver a minimum standard of national parliamentary scrutiny of ESDP. However, in cases where parliaments have few powers to hold their executives to account and minimal access to information on ESDP, their role in exercising democratic oversight will be fundamentally limited. It is beyond the scope of this chapter to address the question of how to enhance national parliamentary controls, but it is relevant to ask whether the centralisation of decision-making at an EU level is an obstacle to parliamentary oversight or might, in time, lead to a narrowing of the national divergences in parliamentary control of ESDP and a raising of the minimum standard.

Within the EU, the relationships between national executives and their parliamentary counterparts are diverse. They range from relationships of relative equality where the legislature is a partner in government and the executive cannot function effectively without its cooperation (Germany), to a starkly unequal relationship where the executive effectively functions as an 'elected dictator', subject only to ex-post oversight (the United Kingdom or Canada – see Chapter Six). EU member states occupy different positions along this continuum and their ability to influence decision-making in national security and defence policy varies accordingly. The following analysis seeks only to define the range of relevant parliamentary powers and capacities within the European Union in regard to the three key criteria identified above.

(1) Access to information and internal capacities to process it The provision of information on EU affairs to national parliaments has generally improved since the Protocol on the role of National Parliaments (PNP) was inserted into the Amsterdam Treaty (1997). However, this excludes all documents in the CFSP pillar and in July 2000, the entire category of Council working documents relating

to ESDP was ruled beyond public access.[16] As a result, the information flow to parliaments from governments is on a strictly bilateral basis and varies widely across the EU. In Belgium, Greece, Spain, Italy, Portugal and France all information on CFSP and ESDP is given to national parliaments at the government's discretion. In most other countries, including Sweden, Finland, Denmark, the UK and Austria, arrangements for the provision of information on CFSP are similar to those for the first pillar. This usually means that the Foreign Affairs committees are provided with all CFSP texts agreed in the Council as well as Commission Communications to the Council and European Parliament resolutions. In some cases (Denmark) this is also accompanied by explanatory information provided by the government (Maurer, 2001, p. 14). Although some parliaments routinely receive publicly-available information on CFSP and ESDP, in recent gatherings of the WEU Assembly, national parliamentarians have consistently called for more information on ESDP to be made available to national parliamentarians and for more opportunities for information exchange in a multinational context.

The degree to which national parliaments are able to effectively utilise these (limited) information resources to scrutinise ESDP, depends on the capacities of the relevant committees and parliamentarians to process the information. This, in turn, depends on factors such as the length and frequency of committee meetings, their level of specialisation, their access to internal research support and external expertise, and the level of research support that individual parliamentarians have at their disposal. Some parliaments, notably in Denmark, Sweden and Germany are generally well endowed in these respects (Bennett and Pullinger, 1991; Chapter Four), but this does not always result in a culture of critical scrutiny. For example, while some parliaments such as the German Bundestag have highly developed procedures for accountability, this parliamentary power is directed more at the process of policy making than post-hoc scrutiny. Given that the Bundestag has a serious role in policy-making, it dedicates relatively fewer resources to the post-hoc scrutiny of the implementation of policy. This suggests that even if all parliaments received public Council and Commission documents of relevance to CFSP and ESDP, there is no guarantee that this would necessarily endow a legislature with a culture of critical scrutiny necessary to hold the executive to account for its decisions made and implemented in the framework of ESDP.

(2) Involvement in the decision to deploy force Some countries, for example Germany, Sweden, as well as (according to current political practice) Denmark and the Netherlands, require parliamentary authorisation for the decision to deploy forces in an international military operation.[17] In some countries such as France, parliamentary approval for the engagement of troops in foreign operations is only required when there are formal war operations. French involvement in the Gulf War is the only example of their parliament being consulted. In other countries,

---

16 Council of the EU, 2000e, Committee of Permanent Representatives Decision, 27 July 2000.

17 Assembly of the WEU, 2001a; and see Chapter Four.

governments are not obliged to consult the parliament before making decisions about the deployment of troops. In the UK, for example, such decisions are regarded as matters of Royal Prerogative and the Defence of the Realm is the sole responsibility of the executive. Nevertheless, even where parliaments have no formal powers in this decision-making process, the threat of parliamentary censure including the tabling of a 'no confidence motion' makes it practically impossible for the government to take a decision that is not supported by a majority of parliamentarians.

(3) Budgetary powers and involvement in armaments policy Once again, there is a range of parliamentary powers with regards to the budgetary control of security and defence. The member states with the most intrusive powers include Germany where decisions on procurement programmes with a value of more than 50 million DM (approximately 25 million Euros) are taken on a case by case basis rather than in a single budget agreement. In France, the parliament authorises defence bills that determine long-term resources for defence as well as military funds for specific military operations. The UK is, once again, at the other end of the spectrum with no formal ability to check government spending on defence. There are nevertheless systems of informal scrutiny in place and House of Commons Defence Select Committee, supported by the National Audit Office regularly scrutinises (post hoc) the expenditure of the Ministry of Defence (Born, 2003a, p.143).

Parliamentary oversight of armaments policies is generally greater in legislatures that have a greater formal role in decision-making (e.g. Germany and Sweden). But, even in these contexts, it is made more difficult by the trend to agree armaments policies in various multinational contexts outside the EU framework (Framework Agreement, 2000). In contrast, the implementation of the EU Code of Conduct on Arms Exports has generally resulted in greater transparency at the national level, with more member states publishing increasingly detailed national export reports. In this policy area, the gradual 'Europeanisation' of policy-making therefore appears to have enhanced national parliamentary scrutiny of arms exports.

When comparing intrusive, decision-making legislatures (such as Germany) with those whose power is limited to post-hoc scrutiny of the executive (the UK), it has been noted that:

> To some extent all legislatures in the West face a dilemma: either they try to equip themselves in terms of knowledge ... to keep pace with the executive, and thus run the risk of losing political colour and popular interest, or they stick to the notion of parliament as a debating arena and place of challenge to the executive, with the concomitant risk of being hopelessly ill-informed and ill-equipped to understand or impede what the executive proposes (Johnson, 1983, p. 224).

This suggests that the national-level challenge for the oversight of ESDP is not to simply increase formal parliamentary powers vis-à-vis national executives but to pursue the more limited and subtle goal of strengthening the scrutinising role of parliaments. This nevertheless requires that all national parliaments have access to a minimum level of information and the internal resources to critically debate it. It also requires a multinational overview to assess the decision-making context and policy options. Moreover, cross-national exposure to critical scrutiny can provide the added benefit of increasing the standard of national scrutiny and narrowing the corridor of national divergence.

Prospects for the Future: the Convention, the IGC and Beyond

Governments are increasingly involved in institutional networks, which dilute lines of accountability, and the trend towards the 'Europeanisation' of decision-making with regard to ESDP appears to be irreversible. Yet national assemblies and the European Parliament are not structurally well suited to coordinating their activities. Addressing the democratic deficit in ESDP therefore requires structural change.

In an effort to enhance the democratic legitimacy of the EU, the Council of the European Union in Laeken (2001a) raised the issue of the role of national parliaments, and highlights three key questions that emerge from the on-going EU institutional reform debate:

- 'Should [national parliaments] be represented in a new institution, alongside the Council and the European Parliament?
- Should they have a role in areas of European action in which the European Parliament has no competence? and,
- Should they focus on the division of competence between the Union and member states, for example, through the preliminary checking of compliance with the subsidiary principle?' (Council of the European Union, 2001a, Annex 1, p 24).

There is no common position in response to these questions from parliamentarians engaged in the scrutiny of ESDP, but members of the WEU Assembly and European Parliament did agree on a number of common principles as early as May 2001.[18] These underpin the current discussions on how parliamentary scrutiny of ESDP can be enhanced but their practical and institutional interpretation may still take a number of forms. They include:

- Certain crucial decisions within ESDP (i.e. defence budgets and deployment of forces) should continue to be the prerogative of national parliaments;
- The parliamentary dimension should reflect the aim for EU security arrangements to be elaborated through cooperation with non-EU European NATO members and EU-candidate countries;

---

18 These principles were agreed by an inter-parliamentary seminar hosted by the Netherlands section of the European Movement at the Dutch Parliament in The Hague on 14 May 2001.

- To perform parliamentary scrutiny more effectively at the national level, national parliaments need a structure to allow them to gain a coherent overview of ESDP;
- National parliaments and the European Parliament should cooperate in finding an appropriate way for effective parliamentary scrutiny of ESDP, ideally in an inter-parliamentary forum; and that
- The TEU should be amended to ensure that this inter-parliamentary assembly is provided with an annual written report on all ESDP activities.

While there is widespread support for increased opportunities for multinational scrutiny, this is tempered in many member states by the reluctance to erode the current institutional structure of the Union or add a further complicating layer. The democratic logic of the Union's present institutional arrangements has the advantage of being relatively clear: the directly-elected European Parliament represents the peoples of the Union and the Council of Ministers represents the member states through elected governments. Many argue that there is little democratic benefit in adding an additional layer by creating a body involving some members of the European Parliament and some members of national parliaments. The form that any multinational and multi-level body for parliamentary oversight should take is, however, inextricably linked to the broader institutional reform debates and to what extent CFSP and ESDP will remain purely intergovernmental or be 'communitarised'.

On one side of the institutional reform debate are those who argue for a more 'communitarised' CFSP and ESDP, with an extended use of qualified majority voting in non-military matters of CFSP and its concomitant potential for extension of co-decision procedures in the EP. This position is often combined with support for merging the position of High Representative for the CFSP with that of Vice-President of the Commission and with suggestions to use the Community budget to cover all civilian crisis management costs and even common costs incurred in military operations. These proposals would strengthen the executive role of the Commission, ensure that it maintains its monopoly over EU funding and would, in turn, imply a greater role for the European Parliament in the scrutiny of ESDP. Consequently those in favour of strengthening the role of the European Parliament with regard to ESDP note that the principal way to achieve this is through its communitarisation.

On the other side of the debate are those who argue for Europe *à la carte*, using 'enhanced cooperation' between willing member states to develop CFSP/ESDP without undermining its inter-governmental form. This view tends to favour a stronger role for the Council and Presidency and many see this as compatible with suggestions to strengthen CFSP by giving more weight to the High Representative, reforming the General Affairs Council to improve its decision-making effectiveness with regard to CFSP and reforming the rotating Presidency system to improve continuity. The United Kingdom has even floated the idea that the only way to ensure effective decision-making in CFSP is to create a restricted 'Security Council' of the Union including the largest and most militarily-active member states. With regard to the funding of ESDP, the protagonists of the intergovernmental approach generally favour the direct payment by member states of costs related to military operations on a 'costs lie where they fall' basis. Nevertheless, to ensure that the principle of solidarity can be reconciled with the intergovernmental nature of ESDP, some suggest that a separate budget should be established and controlled by the Council, to partially fund military and civilian ESDP operations.

It is likely that some compromise will be found between the two positions and this may well lead to a mixture of the above proposals and a mixed Commission-Council executive in the area of CFSP and ESDP. The consequences for the parliamentary scrutiny of ESDP will be that both national parliaments and the European Parliament will have to share the responsibility and power to scrutinise ESDP. Whether their formal competencies to fill this role will be extended at either the European level or the national level remains unclear.

Aside from the issue of whether the Convention on the 'Future of Europe' and the 2004 Intergovernmental Conference will deliver a formal extension of powers to the European Parliament, is the issue of whether a multinational, Inter-parliamentary Assembly with expertise in ESDP will survive and, if so, what legal and institutional form it will take. One option is that the Inter-parliamentary Assembly be based on the WEU Assembly[19] model – a proposal that is evidently favoured by the current WEU Assembly (Assembly of the WEU, 2001b). The WEU Assembly meets twice a year, involving at least two representatives of each member state parliament, and has a committee structure serviced by a bureau of experts similar to the structure of the NATO Parliamentary Assembly. This structure could simply change its name and continue to serve as a body for inter-parliamentary information exchange operating outside the EU framework. Alternatively, in the past the European Parliament has favoured (European Parliament, 2002) the model of the Conference of Community and European Affairs Committees of the Parliaments of the EU (*Conférence des Organes Spécialisés dans les Affaires Communitaires [COSAC]*). However, this position has since been developed into the proposal to host regular conferences on ESDP, providing opportunities for national parliamentarians and European parliamentarians to collaborate in the scrutiny of ESDP (see above).

Whatever the outcome of the 2004 IGC and the structural changes that it may deliver, parliamentarians will be required to constantly inject new life into their institutions at national and multinational level if they are to prevent parliamentary democracy from becoming an outmoded institution, overtaken by technological imperatives and rapid decision-making in a globalised world, with the media and interest groups increasingly taking over the role of executive scrutiny.

---

19 Following the transfer of WEU's operational activities to the EU in 2000, it acts as the Interim European Security and Defence Assembly.

Conclusions

In conclusion, neither the national parliaments, nor the European Parliament, currently have sufficient capacities to perform their respective scrutinising roles effectively. The democratic dimension of ESDP has lagged far behind the rapid construction of an institutional infrastructure for ESDP. Nor is it certain that this democratic deficit will be clearly resolved in favour of any one institution during the next Intergovernmental Conference, since potential formal solutions are so entangled in the politics of European integration. It is therefore likely that there will continue to be a mixed executive governing CFSP and ESDP and that the role of democratic oversight will be shared between national parliaments and the European Parliament for the foreseeable future. In any case, the level of transparency of ESDP can and should be improved, and the capacities of the European and national parliaments to scrutinise ESDP enhanced. This chapter concludes with some recommendations of how this might be achieved. These recommendations serve two objectives: increasing transparency and enhancing the capacity of the European Parliament and national parliaments. As to the former objective, the following recommendations may be considered:

- The rules on public access to documents should be revised in accordance with Article 255 of the Amsterdam Treaty. The new decision must be made using the co-decision procedure and public access to ESDP documents should be decided on a case by case basis.
- The Protocol (No. 9) on the role of National Parliaments to the TEU should be revised to include the clear obligation on the Council to transmit all public documents in the fields of CFSP and ESDP to the EU Affairs, Foreign Affairs and Defence committees in all member states.
- Council deliberations on matters requiring co-decision must be made public. This includes decisions on development cooperation and civilian crisis management under the first pillar.
- The Presidency should produce, in cooperation with the Commission, public reports of how the Union's external relations instruments, including CFSP and ESDP, have been used on a regional basis. These reports should include a statement of the financial implications of these actions for the Community budget.
- The Presidency should produce, in cooperation with the Commission, a public annual consolidated programme for future priorities in the areas of CFSP, ESDP and conflict prevention.

As to enhancing the capacity of the European Parliament and national parliaments, the following recommendations may be considered:

- Article 21 of the TEU, which obliges the Presidency and Commission to inform the European Parliament on CFSP, should be amended to explicitly include ESDP and to oblige the Presidency, Commission and the High

Representative of CFSP to respond, in writing, to questions on ESDP put by the European Parliament.

- The resources of the European Parliament and the Foreign Affairs Committee in particular should be increased to enable it to hold more hearings and inquiries on the implementation of the Union's conflict prevention, foreign, security and defence policies. This should include resources for the Foreign Affairs Committee to commission experts to provide written and oral evidence, and conduct independent studies evaluating the implementation of EU policy.

- To improve the European Parliament's budgetary scrutiny of civilian crisis management, all civilian crisis-management funding should be under the first pillar and subject to co-decision. The use of the CFSP budget line should be limited to administrative expenditure for diplomatic actions. The Commission's mechanisms for funding civilian crisis management should be revised so that they are more flexible and rapid.

- Cooperation between the European Parliament and OSCE, Council of Europe and NATO parliamentary assemblies should be enhanced through cross-representation and through the European Parliament soliciting the opinion of these parliamentary assemblies on European Parliamentary reports on the implementation of CFSP and ESDP.

- Inter-parliamentary cooperation should be improved through the adoption of a joint annual report reviewing the development and implementation of CFSP and ESDP and the Presidency's programme of action with a view to strengthening the conflict prevention capacities of the Union. This could be drafted, jointly by a rapporteur from the parliament of the country holding the Presidency and a rapporteur from the European Parliament. All parliaments would be invited to submit amendments and the final draft would be approved (by a majority) at a conference of the chairs of the foreign affairs and defence committees of national parliaments and the European Parliament (as proposed by the European Parliament).

ESDP is part of a broader trend towards multi-nationalising security and defence. Due to growing interdependencies, states have to cooperate in the field of security and transfer powers from the national to the international level. This is a trend which can be witnessed in Europe among NATO and EU member states. However, without strengthening the capacity of national and European parliaments to oversee the ESDP, the transfer of decision-making power results in uneven checks and balances between the legislative and the executive. A polity that is out of balance cannot provide a secure and legitimate basis for ESDP, which is in the interest of neither the executive, nor the legislative nor its citizens.

PART VI

CONCLUSIONS

Chapter 12

The Use of Force under International Auspices: Strengthening Parliamentary Accountability

Hans Born

Introduction

Within the context of the growing interdependence and cooperation between states, two points of departure may be used for drawing up conclusions: firstly, the considerable growth of the use of force under international auspices in the post Cold-War period and, secondly, the increasing concern about the lack of democratic accountability of the international use of force. This concern is expressed by various authors regarding the democratic accountability of international cooperation in general. In this volume the focus is on *parliaments'* involvement in the use of force under international auspices, a topic that has received only sporadic attention so far. The oversight of the international use of force poses a serious challenge for parliaments, particularly as parliaments already have a full workload in taking care of domestic priorities and maintaining contact with their electorate. The main conclusion of this book is that the democratic and especially parliamentary accountability of the use of force under international auspices is problematic at both the national and the international level. This leads to the 'double democratic deficit', within and outside the nation state (see Chapter One).

In this concluding part the main research findings are brought together, discussing what can be learnt from the role, experiences and critiques of the parliamentary accountability of the use of international force. First, an overview is given of the main points of analysis and findings, as brought forward by the contributors to this volume. Secondly, the main concerns and recommendations are identified, grouped around the three aspects of parliamentary accountability, being authority, ability and attitude, in Chapter One referred to as the triple-A criteria of parliamentary accountability.

Taking Stock of Parliamentary Accountability

Parliaments and the Use of Force under International Auspices

Since the end of the Cold War, the process of internationalisation of security policies and institutions has intensified in the Euro-Atlantic area. This is not per se an undesirable development, since international security benefits from de-nationalising security. The United Nations (UN), the European Union (EU), the North Atlantic Treaty Organisation (NATO) and the Organisation for Security and Cooperation in Europe (OSCE) have, for example, been institutionally strengthened and re-oriented towards new security challenges. As Owen Greene indicates, these transformation processes are taking place within the context of more fundamental political, economic and societal transformation processes associated with 'globalisation' (see Chapter Two). Regarding the use of force under international auspices, tension exists between international cooperation that is both effective and democratically legitimate. The need for timely and sometimes confidential decision-making on the use of force does not always go along with the need for 'deep' democratic processes on the use of force. According to Owen Greene, the challenge is to develop democratic systems that involve parliaments, stakeholders and citizens, in balance with the requirements of executive decision-making and the professional autonomy of armed forces.

Charlotte Ku's study (Chapter Three) shows that the lack of transparency confounds democratic accountability by limiting possibilities for understanding the bases and purposes of military operations, as authorised by the UN or by NATO. This precludes an informed debate and opportunity for oversight that are important for democracies. Charlotte Ku concludes that debates in the national parliaments are more extensive and deeper when the operations involve more force and when the international legal basis for action becomes murkier. National parliamentary oversight is more effective if it includes formal authorisation to deploy troops abroad, the right to hold inquiries on peace support operations (PSOs), and if it is backed up by political consensus.

Use of Force under UN Auspices

After the end of the Cold War, PSOs became an important instrument for maintaining international peace and for the protection of human rights, in which the UN played the leading role. During the last 10 years, two times more PSOs were carried out than during the Cold War. In 2002, 15 UN peacekeeping operations were carried out, in which 45,145 military personnel, civilian police and staff were involved at a total cost of 2,77 billion dollars (United Nations, 2002). In addition to this growing number, PSOs became a varied phenomena, ranging from monitoring missions to peace enforcing operations.

Since the UN is an intergovernmental organisation, it does not have an executive or legislature which is directly elected by the people. The UN derives its democratic legitimacy only via its member states through the democratically elected representatives at the national level, at least, if those member states are democratic themselves. It is not easy for the general public and the national Members of Parliament to keep track of what happens at the UN level. The distance between the UN and the people is large, the Security Council often convenes behind closed doors and the complex command and control structure of PSOs impede democratic accountability at the international level. Due to the lack of democratic accountability at the level of the UN, national parliaments are the sole providers of democratic accountability.

Hans Born and Marlene Urscheler (Chapter Four) put parliamentary oversight of the international use of force in a comparative perspective. The findings of their analyses of 16 states in the Euro-Atlantic area demonstrate that substantial differences exist in the nature and functioning of the parliaments of the countries. They identify three groups of parliaments, depending on their power of giving prior authorisation to deployment of troops abroad: (1) parliaments without power to give prior authorisation; (2) parliaments with prior authorisation power; and (3) parliaments with prior authorisation powers plus follow-up powers to oversee the deployment in more detail. Parliaments without prior authorisation power can still influence government policy for at least two reasons. Firstly, they can organise public debate and, in doing so, render or withhold public support for the pending PSOs. Secondly, those parliaments which enjoy power over the purse, are capable of withholding funds for ongoing PSOs.

Jan Hoekema's case-study (Chapter Five) focuses on the parliamentary accountability of the deployment of troops to the UN Protection Force (UNPROFOR in Bosnia-Herzegovina), which was unable to protect the civilian population of Srebrenica in 1995. One of the main conclusions of Hoekema's study is that parliaments can become too much involved in governments' decision-making, as the Dutch parliament did when it committed Dutch troops to UNPROFOR in 1992. Under pressure from public opinion and the international community, the parliament urged the government to send troops to the UN force in Bosnia and therefore became co-responsible for this decision. From this conclusion it appears that if parliament is unable to maintain a sufficient distance from the government's decisions, it becomes rather difficult to control the government objectively. This situation becomes exacerbated by close ties and networks between the government and the government's parties in parliament.

Donna Winslow's and Christ Klep's (Chapter Six) research demonstrates that even parliaments in consolidated democracies (like Canada) have great difficulty in overseeing the government's decisions on the use of force under international auspices. Parliamentary oversight seems to be seriously stalled by party discipline, which de-motivates members of parliament, preventing them from putting forward questions or launching inquiries that are too critical of their fellow party-members in government. Winslow and Klep's analysis and case-study of the official inquiry into the gross misconduct of Canadian military servicemen during the UN peace support operation 'Provide Hope' in Somalia in 1993 makes clear how difficult it is to hold those in authority accountable, due to the government's majority in parliament, the civil-military gap (general disinterest in military affairs by politicians and public) as well as the tactics of the government to disarm parliament and truncate the inquiry committee.

However, the picture concerning the status quo of parliamentary oversight of multinational peace support operations is not totally grim. The comparative research of Ku and Born/Urscheler as well as the case-studies of Winslow/Klep and Hoekema also illustrate some positive points. Since 1950, when US President Harry Truman could authorise use of international force in the Korean War without Congressional authorisation, the use of international force without parliamentary approval has become rare. Parliaments are regarded as indispensable for building up public support and legitimacy for multinational peace support operations. The case-studies on the parliaments of Canada and the Netherlands illustrate that parliaments are adjusting to the post Cold War political reality of PSOs. Parliaments are developing new tools of oversight such as amendments to the constitution, developing criteria for systematic parliamentary decision-making, appointing special Ombudsmen, as well as developing new rules of procedure for parliamentary inquiries. This results in parliaments not only applying lessons learned to peace operations, but also maintaining parliamentary oversight of those operations.

Use of Force under NATO Auspices

NATO is an intergovernmental organisation, consisting of sovereign states, providing collective defence for its members. There is no oversight exercised by an international parliamentary body; only national parliaments oversee the governments of the NATO member states. The main characteristics of NATO decision-making are: US leadership, a strong emphasis on multilateral procedures as well as a well-functioning military and political bureaucracy. NATO member states, in the need for rapid decision-making during crisis, have mandated relevant decision-making powers to the North Atlantic Council (NAC) which exercises political control over major military commanders. The international parliamentary dimension of NATO is shaped by the NATO Parliamentary Assembly (NATO PA). It has no formal oversight powers and is formally independent from NATO. The Assembly attempts to foster a dialogue between parliamentarians of the member states and to assist in the development of parliamentary democracy throughout the Euro-Atlantic area, especially Eastern Europe and the Commonwealth of Independent States (CIS). According to Willem Van Eekelen (Chapter Seven), the Assembly did not play a role in the Kosovo intervention or in the adaptation of NATO's new strategic concept in 1999. Only in the case of NATO enlargement was the NATO PA relevant for consensus and as a dialogue network between members of parliament of NATO member states and applicant states.

In so far as NATO has a democratic deficit, according to some, the cause has to be found in the capitals of NATO member states. National parliaments are supposed to oversee how their government's permanent representatives operate in the NAC. Here we see that democratic accountability becomes rather problematic because the decisions have been made confidentially, and/or decisions have to be taken so quickly, as in the Kosovo intervention, that there is not always sufficient time for deliberations. Additionally, since parliamentary control of NATO rests with national parliaments, a major drawback is the uneven national practice. In some countries, accountability to parliament in foreign affairs as well as defence and security policy is very powerful and active and in other countries not, leading to the 'double democratic deficit'.

The contribution of Lori F. Damrosch (Chapter Eight) discusses the parliamentary accountability of NATO as a collective defence organisation *in action* during NATO's Kosovo intervention. Her study concentrates on the control of the United States Congress and the German Parliament over the decision to apply military force in Kosovo. The US Congress, overseeing US military force in the Kosovo intervention, stayed mostly on the sidelines throughout the operation. Whereas the Congress was confused about its own constitutional role and unable to speak with a clear voice, according to Lori F. Damrosch, the Bundestag, by contrast, carried out its constitutionally mandated responsibility to give affirmative authorisation for committing troops to an international military deployment. In both countries, individual members of parliament went to court in order to contest the decision to deploy troops abroad. However, the role of the judiciary in both countries was different. In the US, the Supreme Court declined to clarify contested constitutional responsibilities between the executive and the legislative. In Germany, the Constitutional Court ruled and confirmed the power of the Bundestag. The consequence was that President Bill Clinton was able to engage US armed forces in military conflict without direct approval from the legislative branch. In Germany, however, the parliament was able to have a 'long, earnest and searching' public debate before approving the sending of troops abroad. The author concludes that parliamentary deliberations provide a level of transparency and a potential for consensus-building that would be lacking if the executive could take such a decision alone. In that regard, Lori F. Damrosch concludes the German model, under which parliament must openly debate and decide before armed forces can be used for purposes other than self-defence, may hold attractions for newly-democratising states which want to become NATO member.

Being part of an integrated military organisation poses national parliaments with a specific set of problems, notably the stationing of foreign troops and armaments on its territory, contributing troops to the NATO operations and the integration of military units in permanent multinational NATO formations. Roman Schmidt-Radefeldt (Chapter Nine) gives a close-up view of how the German parliament deals with these three issues. The German Constitutional Court, which played an important role in clarifying the constitutional competences of the parliament and the government, ruled in 1984 that the stationing of troops and (nuclear) weapons on German territory has to be considered as a consequence of being part of NATO. By ratifying the NATO Treaty in 1955, the German parliament was supposed to have been delegating the resulting military decisions to the government. However, the decision to deploy troops abroad under NATO command is regarded as an 'essential matter' which has to be approved by parliament. Also in this case, the German Constitutional Court clarified the responsibilities and competences of the parliament and the government. More specifically, the Court conceives the armed forces not as a tool exclusively in the hands of the executive, but rather as a 'parliamentary army'. The parliament has the task of securing the integration of the armed forces in the democratic order by controlling both the establishment and the use of the armed forces. With regard to multinational military integrated units, for example the German-Netherlands' army corps, Roman Schmidt-Radefeldt concludes that the political legitimacy is to be derived from national parliaments only, as no international control bodies exist and because the Constitution does not permit sovereign power over the use of force to be handed over to foreign states and multinational units.

Use of Force under EU Auspices

The European Union is unique among international organisations because it constitutes a hybrid organisation in the sense that it combines intergovernmental cooperation and supranational integration. The Common Foreign and Security Policy (CFSP) and the European Security and Defence Policy (ESDP) fall mainly in the former category.

Giovanna Bono's analysis (Chapter Ten) gives an overview of the history and current state of affairs of ESDP. She concludes that the ESDP has resulted in a deepening of the EU's policy on security and defence, without at the same time strengthening parliamentary institutions. Rather than removing, the EU has been adding opacity to the decision-making process by creating more institutions and ad hoc working groups, therefore making the ESDP less accessible for members of national parliaments and the EU parliament. It is difficult for parliamentarians to exercise oversight over the ESDP because of the hybrid character of decision-making, the major role of civil servants who are unsupervised by national parliaments, and a network of ad hoc groups of experts between the various EU institutions. Accountability to the EU electorate is problematic. The Council and the Commission are not directly elected and therefore the people cannot sanction the EU executive by not re-electing them. The national parliaments face difficulties because each parliament has its own method and viewpoint of oversight, they lack access to EU documents on ESDP and national MPs are not part of the very influential informal policy networks in Brussels. Additionally, the European parliament has very limited powers to oversee ESDP.

In addition to democratic accountability, Catriona Gourlay's contribution (Chapter Eleven) deals specifically with the parliamentary accountability of ESDP. While ESDP is considered to be an intergovernmental issue (Second Pillar), in practice many ESDP-related activities belong to the First Pillar (eg civilian aspects of crisis management) and to the Third Pillar (eg anti-terrorism cooperation). The consequence is that for different policy fields related to ESDP, different decision mechanisms and institutions are active, which leads to one of the core problems of accountability. There is not one executive to be controlled, but a mixed executive consisting of the Commission, Council and the governments at national level. Additionally, there is not one parliament but 16 parliamentary bodies responsible for oversight (15 national parliaments plus the European Parliament).[1] National

---

1   One might add the interim European Security and Defence Assembly, formerly the Assembly of the Western European Union.

parliaments can hold their executive to account for their decisions reached in the Council by unanimity, but in practice, oversight is difficult to exercise. The main problem is that the EU member states' national parliaments are responsible for ESDP oversight and that there are examples of weak and strong parliamentary oversight of the security sector, leading to the so-called 'double democratic deficit' because of both weak national and European parliamentary oversight. Most of the challenges and recommendations for parliamentary oversight of ESDP depend on one main underlying question: will the EU become an integrated (federal) EU or remain an intergovernmental organisation with regard to security and defence policy?

Strengthening Parliamentary Accountability

What are the main concerns and problematic aspects of overseeing the use of force under international auspices and which options are available for improving the situation? This is the central issue of this closing section. Table 12.1 gives an overview of the main results regarding this question. The concerns and recommendations can be clustered around the three factors determining the effectiveness of parliamentary accountability: authority, ability and attitude (see Chapter One).

Table 12.1   Parliamentary oversight of the international use of force: main concerns and possible recommendations

	Main Concerns	Possible Recommendations
Authority	• Democracy at the international level.	• People's representation at international level.
	• Lack of adequate powers.	• Adjusting national constitution to new situation.
	• Uneven national practice.	• Coordination among national parliaments.
Ability	• Resources.	• Defence committee, budget.
	• Expertise.	• External expertise, information-sharing among parliaments, hearings, inquiries.
	• Confidentiality, secrecy.	• Post accountability, confidentiality measures in parliament.
Attitude	• Civil-military gap.	• Public debates in parliaments.
	• Party discipline.	• Role of opposition, independent audits and inquiries.

Authority

Authority refers to the power which parliament uses to hold government accountable. These powers are derived from the constitutional and legal framework as well as customary practices. Parliaments need these powers to fulfil their functions such as the legislative, budgetary, elective, representative and scrutiny function (see Chapter One).

A first concern is democracy at the international level and, more precisely, the absence of assemblies with oversight powers over the executive at international level. Since the UN and NATO are intergovernmental, they are accountable to the governments of their member states only. The UN does not have an elected assembly; the NATO Parliamentary Assembly is appointed (consisting of national parliamentarians) and has no formal powers in relation to NATO. Concerning the EU, the European Parliament is the only international assembly in the world that is directly elected. However, it has only very marginal powers to oversee ESDP. One has to keep in mind that a truly international 'demos' or political community does not exist but is an emerging phenomenon including international think tanks and advocacy organisations which are playing an increasingly important role (see Chapter Two). The existence of a 'demos' is important for without public support, demands and feedback from citizens and civil society organisations, a parliament lacks democratic legitimacy and can hardly perform its functions. The most far-reaching solution, within the cosmopolitanism school of thought, would be to create new representative bodies related to these international organisations, for example creating a UN People's Chamber. A more modest option would be to improve the functioning of existing representative bodies, either by improving their representation through adding national parliamentary delegations to the assemblies, by giving those international assemblies more oversight powers, e.g. budget scrutiny of the European Parliament (see Chapter Eleven), or by improving their procedures, e.g. the NATO Secretary General delivering a yearly State of the Alliance message to the NATO PA (see Chapter Seven). A third option would be not to improve parliamentary oversight at the international level, but to focus entirely on the national level.

Concerning parliamentary oversight powers at the national level, two problems were raised in this volume. Firstly, the lack of sufficient powers and secondly the uneven oversight practice in the various states. Whilst analysing the functioning of parliament in this regard, a preliminary remark about the different types of political systems is essential. We may distinguish three types of political democratic systems: presidential, parliamentary and parliamentary Westminster. In general, the following distinction can be made (acknowledging that exceptions to the general rule exist). In a presidential system, the president has large autonomy in decisions on the international use of force. The president is not elected by the parliament and therefore the parliament has few formal powers (for example in France), or has contested powers (such as in the US – See Chapters Three, Four and especially Chapter Eight). More specifically, Hans Born and Marlene Urscheler's contribution shows that none of the parliaments in a presidential system (nor in a Westminster type of system, see below) have the power of authorising PSOs in advance (Chapter Four). Nevertheless, parliaments in these systems are potentially able to obstruct executive policies, for example, by granting less or no budget for PSOs or by delaying votes on adopting relevant laws. The chance of an obstructing parliament is larger when the opposition has a majority in parliament.

In a parliamentary system, however, the head of the executive is elected by the parliament. Therefore, executive decisions about the use of force under international auspices are dependent on the consent of parliament. This is the case in, for example, Germany and the Netherlands, where the cabinets have to ensure parliamentary approval when sending troops abroad (see Chapters Five, Eight and Nine). In some parliamentary systems, the parliament has a strong involvement in deciding on the international use of force. Jan Hoekema (Chapter Five) calls this the 'co-government' role of parliament. In these parliaments, in the very early phase before a formal decision has been made, the parliamentary committee on defence discusses with the government relevant aspects of PSOs, such as the mandate, rules of engagement, budget, risks for military personnel, and the duration of the mission. The studies in this volume show that a form of 'co-government' between parliament and government exists in Germany, the Netherlands and Denmark (Chapters Four, Five and Nine). The downside of a strong parliamentary involvement in decisions on the international use of force is that parliaments become committed and therefore co-responsible for executive decision-making.

In Westminster type of political systems, the government dominates the parliament since the government is part of parliament and, due to party discipline, has a firm grip on its (majority) party in parliament. This is illustrated by the Canadian case-study where the government truncated the official independent Royal Commission of Inquiry into the Somalia peacekeeping scandal, just as the inquiry's commissioners were starting to investigate the role of the top level government and military officials (Chapter Six). Therefore, Donna Winslow and Christ Klep qualify the Canadian political system as an 'elected dictatorship', in which the parliament is quite powerless to change the course of government.

Therefore, since parliaments are embedded in different political systems, they fulfil different roles, sustained by different instruments, practices and legal powers, leading to a situation that the use of force under international auspices is overseen by strong and weak parliaments. One has to bear in mind that strong parliaments did not automatically become strong in the field of overseeing the use of force under international auspices. The case studies of the Netherlands and Germany (Chapters Five and Nine) show that these parliaments did not posses such a favourable position from the outset. In the German case, the Court had to rule a few times to confirm the powers of parliament. The powers of the Dutch parliament slowly grew in the last two decades, resulting in a change of the constitution in favour of parliament. Also in other countries, such as France, the urge was felt to amend the constitution. The main reason is that the constitutions were drafted in times that PSOs were not a prominent feature in the management of international security. Therefore, the constitution mainly addresses the issue of the role of parliament in declaring and ending a war, but not the role of parliament in sending troops for PSOs.

In terms of lack of adequate powers, the strongest element of parliamentary oversight is the right of prior authorisation of PSOs. Amendment of the constitution is a point of departure for reinforcing parliamentary oversight powers. However, since these powers are rooted in the framework of a political system, changing those powers implies a modification of the constiution. This is a long process, full of long struggles with the executive, as the case of the Netherlands shows. Before strengthening parliamentary oversight in this respect, one has to answer the question of why parliaments should be given a more powerful position. Answers to this question will differ in the context of presidential, parliamentary and Westminster types of political systems. Another viewpoint when answering the 'why' question is democratic governance. In representative democracies, all essential matters should be subject to democratic decision-making processes, that is, representatives of the people have the opportunity to influence government policy. If we agree that despatching troops abroad in conflict situations is an essential matter, then parliaments should play a role. From a more practical point of view, the contributions to this volume show that national parliaments and international assemblies can play a meaningful and influential role, before, during and after troops have been sent abroad. PSOs, as such, do not prohibit parliamentary oversight. The political will of both parliamentarians and government executives plays a role as well, an issue that will be discussed below.

With regard to parliamentary powers, another relevant finding is the uneven national oversight practice, resulting in a major drawback in the parliamentary oversight of the use of force under international auspices. Such a situation is complex when it comes to the ESDP, which is overseen by 15 national parliaments within the member states' polity and partly by the European Parliament (and one might add the Interim European Security and Defence Assembly). Catriona Gourlay (Chapter Eleven) points out that inter-parliamentary cooperation could be enhanced by guaranteeing that all parliaments have the disposition of the same information, by producing joint annual reports on the state of affairs and by having regular conferences of the chairs of the foreign affairs and defence committees of the national parliaments involved. Solutions in this direction suggest that international assemblies like the European Parliament and the NATO PA play and could play an increasing coordinating role between national parliaments.

Ability

A second factor that determines parliamentary accountability is their ability or capacity to fulfil oversight functions. Based on a comparative research on the power and resources of the 19 NATO member states' parliaments to oversee peace operations, Hans Born and Marlene Urscheler come to the conclusion that a specialised defence committee, parliamentary staff attached to the defence committee, a sufficient working budget, as well as the opportunity to consult experts in civil society are all conducive for exercising oversight (Chapter Four). Though all parliaments have a defence committee with a support staff, it appears that some parliaments have more resources than others in terms of information and research infrastructure as well as libraries, specialised parliamentary committees, committee staff and budgets for the defence committee. Having resources is one issue that may facilitate or hinder oversight. A second issue is having expertise on

PSOs, zones of conflict where PSOs operate, and knowledge about the complex functioning of international organisations. The contributions in this volume on the UN and EU reveal that both national parliaments and European Parliament lack the capacity to obtain sufficient information about international security policy and peace operations. The flow of information between international organisations and parliaments is hindered by restrictive classification and confidentiality procedures. The UN Security Council, the North Atlantic Council and the Council of the European Union often convene behind closed doors and the procedures of their meetings are often confidential. The case of the EU shows that foreign affairs, as well as security and defence policy, is a more difficult area to oversee than other governmental areas; for example, the EU institutions are obliged to send all their documents directly to national parliaments, except for documents related to foreign and defence policy (Chapter Eleven).

The short time-frame in which crisis decision-making on PSOs takes place is another factor limiting the ability for public or parliamentary deliberations. In some cases, for example during the Kosovo campaign, decisions have to be taken so quickly that there is little time for deliberations in parliament.

How could this disadvantageous situation be alleviated? Concerning decision-making in crisis situations, some states, in order to involve parliaments even in the most urgent decisions, have a constitutional or legal obligation that obliges the executive to seek parliament's consent as soon as possible afterwards (Chapters Five, Eight and Nine). As far as confidentiality is concerned, some parliaments choose the option that, if needed, parliamentarians convene behind closed doors and are cleared to see confidential documents. The disadvantage is that parliamentarians can be compromised and silenced because they possess confidential knowledge. Another option is that, according to freedom of information laws, parliamentarians and the public have the possibility of asking for declassification of documents, after the necessity for secrecy is past. In doing so, post-accountability becomes possible, that is keeping the government accountable after the PSO is terminated. In terms of expertise, the Dutch and Canadian case study in this volume (Chapters Five and Six), provide good examples of how parliaments, especially when a PSO is characterised by failure or scandals, can make use of external and independent expertise to scrutinise the use of force under international auspices, provided that external experts have unrestrained access to documents and to decision-makers in government and in the military.

Attitude

The attitude or willingness to hold the executive to account is relevant too, because strong powers are of no avail if parliament is not willing to perform its oversight function. The willingness of parliamentarians to exercise oversight seems to depend on public pressure and party discipline. As far as public opinion is concerned, especially at the beginning of the 1990s, there was a great enthusiasm to 'do something', mostly propelled by media reports about the horrible aspects of civil wars and other zones of conflict Chapters Four and Five). In the second half of the 1990s, the impulse to do something was no longer only driven by enthusiasm, but also by realism and the feasibility of PSOs as a tool for intervening in conflicts. Today this is especially evident: the more risky and dangerous a PSO is, the deeper and more intense the parliamentary debates will be (Chapter Three). Another factor of public opinion is the 'civil-military gap', which stems from a lack of interest by society in military and defence affairs due to the absence of an immediate military threat. The civil-military gap may result in, as Donna Winslow and Christ Klep point out, that defence and military issues have a low political and media value. Even if a major scandal occurs, as happened in 1993 when Canadian peacekeepers severely mistreated and killed Somalian people, parliament was only moderately interested in the Somalia Affair and its consequences for Canadian defence policy (Chapter Six). Parliaments have to find a balance between too much and too little attention and pressure from public opinion and the media, that is between the drive to 'do something', to act in specific cases of conflicts abroad on the one hand, and, the general lack of interest in foreign and defence policy on the other hand. Public debates in parliament and public hearings attended by experts in society may be a way to address too much or too little public and media interest. During public hearings, experts can point out the advantages and disadvantages of complex issues like dispatching troops to zones of conflict. They can lead to an informed and balanced decision-making in parliament, independent from government. Public debates and hearings may be also a tool for creating interest in society for foreign and defence issues and, therefore, a tool for bridging the 'civil-military gap'.

Party-discipline refers to informal networks between party leaders, parliamentary faction leaders, and government ministers that limit the freedom of individual parliamentarians to vote or to raise critical questions against the government, as could be witnessed in the German, Netherlands and Canadian case-studies (Chapters Five, Six, Eight and Nine). The level of party discipline differs from country to country but seems to be especially strong in parliamentary (Westminster type) models. The importance of party-discipline for the use of force under international auspices lies in the fact that most parliamentary powers can be applied only if a majority in parliaments backs its use. The legal power to approve or reject a government's decision to dispatch troops abroad, the budget of PSOs as well as the power to start an independent inquiry can be used only if a majority in parliament endorses its use. The negative influence of party discipline on parliamentary accountability is difficult to reduce as it is partly caused by the power structures and procedural features of the political system. A way to improve this situation is to give more power to the opposition party in parliament, e.g. by giving members of the opposition a leading role in defence committees or in ad-hoc committees of inquiry. This is particularly relevant if sending troops abroad requires a two thirds majority in parliament. In such a situation, it is very likely that government has to cooperate with the opposition parties in order to get parliamentary approval. Hungary is a case in point, where a two-thirds majority is required. However, the Hungarian situation also shows that a two-thirds majority leads to long and complex negotiations between majority and opposition parties and that domestic issues heavily influence the vote.

Conclusions

The previous discussions have shown that elements of the democratic deficit are present both at the international and national level, hence the notion of a 'double democratic deficit'. The deficit can be caused by lack of constitutional and legal powers as well as insufficient abilities and willingness of parliamentarians to hold the executive accountable. Research on parliaments is available in abundance as well as research on the functioning of PSOs. However, more research is required that addresses the link between parliamentary accountability and use of force under international auspices. In particular, in-depth case studies on the willingness of parliamentarians to be involved in security policy and comparative research on parliamentary accountability of the use of force under international auspices is in high demand. This volume focused on democracies in the Euro-Atlantic area. It would be challenging and meaningful to conduct a comparative research on parliamentary accountability and the use of force under international auspices in other parts of the world as well as in transitional democracies.

Concerning the national level or internal dimension of the 'double democratic deficit', parliamentary oversight can be developed and improved only with a particular role for parliament in mind. Some parliaments have a relatively strong role ('co-government') whereas in most cases the government claims the dominant role in foreign and security policy. The issue is: where to draw the 'dividing line' between the parliament and government? From a democratic governance point of view, i.e. 'government of, by, and for the people', the bottom line is that democratic accountability is indispensable. It is difficult to imagine that such an important issue as the use of force under international auspices is excluded from democratic decision-making processes, since parliaments are the sole providers of democratic legitimacy to the use of force under international auspices.

At the international level, the external dimension of the 'double democratic deficit' is strongly within the UN, NATO and to a lesser extent, the EU. Ambitious revolutionary solutions, such as the creation of new parliaments at the international level, may reduce this 'double democratic deficit'. However, the authors to this volume have shown that the democratic deficit can be reduced within the present boundaries of the international system. Nevertheless, it is not to be expected that these deficits will be transformed into a democratic surplus in the near future.

Bibliography

Adam, B. (1999), 'Après la Guerre du Kosovo, quelles Leçons pour la Sécurité Européenne?', *La Guerre du Kosovo. Eclairages et Commentaire*, Complexe/GRIP, Bruxelles.

Aksu, E. and Camilleri, J. (eds) (2002), *Democratizing Global Governance*, Palgrave Macmillan, Houndmills and New York.

Albright, M.K. (1998), 'The Right Balance will Secure NATO's Future', *Financial Times*, 7 December, p. 12.

Allen, M. and Vanderhei, J. (2002), 'Bush: Unity soon on Iraq: Democrats see more Negotiation on War Resolution', *The Washington Post*, 27 September, p. A1 and p. A18.

American Journal of International Law (1999), 'Editorial Comments: NATO's Kosovo Intervention', *American Journal of International Law*, Vol. 93, No. 4, October.

Amsterdam Treaty (1997), *Consolidated Version of the Treaty on the European Union*, (incorporating the changes made by the Treaty of Amsterdam, signed on 2 October 1997) Official Journal C 340, 10.11.1997, pp. 145-172.

Anderson, J (ed) (2002), *Transational Democracy: Political Spaces and Border Crossings*, Routledge, London and New York.

Armed Forces and Society (1997), *Special Issue on Peacekeeping*, Spring 1997, Vol. 23, No. 3.

Assembly of the WEU (2001a), *National Parliamentary Scrutiny of Intervention Abroad by Armed Forces Engaged in International Missions: the Current Position in Law*, Report submitted on behalf of the Committee for Parliamentary and Public Relations by Mrs Troncho, Rapporteur Document A/1762, 4 December.

Assembly of the WEU (2001b), *The Parliamentary Dimension of the ESDP*, Document A/1752, 18 October.

Basic Law (Grundgesetz) (1949), *The Constitution of the Federal Republic of Germany*, May 23.

Bauer, S. (2001), 'L'Européanisation des Politiques d'Exportation d'Armements', in S. Sur and J.-J. Roche (eds), *Annuaire Français de Relations Internationales*, Bruylant, Brussels.

BBC News (2002), World Edition, 1 July.

Beaudoin, L.I. (1998), 'Les Commissions d'Enquête', *Le Journal du Barreau*, Vol. 30, No. 16, 1 October.

Beek, R. ter (1996), *Manoeuvreren*, Balans, Amsterdam.

Behn, R. (2001), *Rethinking Democratic Accountability*, Brookings Press, Washington DC.

Bennett, P. and Pullinger, S. (1991), *Making the Commons Work: Information Analysis and Accountability*, Paper of the Institute of Public Policy Research, London.

Bercusson, D.J. (1997), *A Paper Prepared for the Minister of National Defence*. 25 March.

Beyme, K. von (2000), *Parliamentary Democracy: Democratization, Destabilisation, Reconsolidation, 1789-1999*, Macmillan, Houndmills and New York.

Bienen, D., Rittberger, V., and Wagner, W. (1998), 'Democracy in the United States System. Cosmopolitan and Communitarian Principles', in D. Archibugi, D. Held and M. Köhler (eds), *Re-Imaging Political Community. Studies in Cosmopolitan Democracy*, Polity Press, Cambridge, pp. 287-308.

Bland, D.L. (2000-2001), 'Parliament's Duty to Defend Canada', *Canadian Military Journal*, Vol.1, No.4, Winter.

Blondel, J. (1973), *Comparative Legislatures*, Prentice-Hall, New Jersey.

Board of Inquiry Chaired by Major General Tom De Faye (1993), *Report*. 19 July.

Bono, G. (2002a), *European Security and Defence Policy: Theoretical Approaches, the Nice Summit and Hot Issues*, Research and Training Network, Bradford and Brussels, February.

Bono, G. (2002b), *European Security and Defence Policy: the Rise of the Military in the EU*, Peace Studies, Working Papers. Bradford University, Peace Studies Department, March 2002.

Bono, G. (2002-2003), 'L'Ambiguïté des Relations OTAN-PESD: Faux Débat ou Enjeu Réel?', *La Revue Internationale et Stratégique*, No. 48, Winter.

Bono, G. (2003), *NATO's Peace-Enforcement Tasks and 'Policy Community': 1990-1999*, Ashgate, Aldershot.

Born, H. (ed.) (2003a), *Parliamentary Oversight of the Security Sector: Principles, Practices and Mechanisms. Handbook for Parliamentarians No. 5*, DCAF/IPU, Geneva.

Born, H. (2003b), 'Democratic Control of Armed Forces: Relevance, Issues and Research Agenda', in G. Caforio (ed.), *Handbook of the Sociology of the Military*, Kluwer Academic/Plenum Publishers, New York.

Born, H., Caparini, M., and Fluri, P. (eds) (2002), *Security Sector Reform and Democracy in Transitional Societies*, Nomos, Baden-Baden.

Boyer, Sur Y.S. and Fleurence, O. (2003), 'France: Security Council Legitimacy and Executive Primacy', in C. Ku and H. Jacobsen, *Democratic Accountability and the Use of Force in International Law*, Cambridge University Press, Cambridge, p. 280-299.

Brodeur, F.D. (1998), 'Les Travaux d'une Commission d'Enqête-2. Amateurs de Procès s'Abstenir', *Le Journal du Barreau*, Vol. 30, No. 17, October 15.

Bronstone, A. (2000), *European Security into the Twenty-Forst Century. Beyond Traditional Theories of International Relations*, Ashgate, Aldershot.

Brühl, T. and Rittberger, V. (2001), 'From International to Global Governance: Actors, Collective Decision-Making, and the United Nations in the World of the Twenty-First Century', in V. Rittberger (ed.), *Global Governance and the United Nations System*, United Nations University, Tokyo, pp. 1-47.

Brunner, G. (1979), *Vergleichende Regierungslehre*, Vol. 1, UTB Schöningh, Paderborn.

Brussels Treaty (1948), *Treaty of Economic, Social, and Cultural Collaboration and Collective Self-Defence*, Brussels Treaty, 17 March 1948, as amended by the Paris Agreements 23 October 1954.

Brzoska, M. (2002), *The Framework Agreement – Accountability Issues*, BICC, Bonn. Paper presented at the ESDP Democracy Project, June.

Bulletin Quotidien Europe (2002), 'EU/Balkans: Council Reaches Agreement on Mission, Arrangements and Funding for a Police Force to take over from UN in Bosnia-Herzegovina from 1st January 2003', *Bulletin Quotidien Europe*, 18 and 19 February (No. 8153), pp. 4-5.

Bundestag (2000), Protocols of the Plenary Session of 8 June 2000, 14th Legislature Period/108th Session.

Burk, J. (1995), *Public Support for Peacekeeping in Lebanon and Somalia*, Paper prepared for the Inter University Seminar on Armed Forces and Society, Baltimore, 22-25 October.

Bush, G.W. (2002), 'Address to the United Nations General Assembly in New York City', *Weekly Compilation of Presidential Documents*, Vol. 38, No. 37, pp. 1529-1533.

Butler, N. (2000), 'NATO: From Collective Defence to Peace Enforcement', in A. Schnabel and R. Thakur (eds), *Kosovo and the Challenge of Humanitarian Intervention*, United Nations University Press, Tokyo, pp. 273-290.

Campbell v. Clinton (1999), District Court for the District of Columbia, 52 f. Supp. 2d 34, D.D.C. 1999.

Campbell v. Clinton (2000), Supreme Court of the United States 52 F.Supp.2d 34, D.D.C., 1999, *affirmed*, 203 F.3d 19, D.C. Cir. 2000, *cert. denied*, 531 U.S. 815.

Canadian News Digest (1997), *Canadian Press*, 15 April.

Canadian Senate Debates (Hansard) (1997a), *National Defence: Deployment of Canadian Airborne Regiment in Somalia*, 2nd Session, 35th Parliament, Vol. 136, Issue 70, 12 February, p. 1550.

Canadian Senate Debates (Hansard) (1997b), *Establishment of Special Committee to Examine Activities of Canadian Airborne Regiment in Somalia*, 2nd Session, 35th Parliament, Vol. 136, Issue 85, 20 March, p. 1440.

Caparini, M. (2003), 'Security Sector Reform and NATO and EU Enlargement', in *SPRI Yearbook 2003: Armaments, Disarmament and International Security*, Oxford University Press, Oxford, pp. 233-256.

CBC News (1997), *The National Online*, Transcripts, 20 March.

CBC News (2000), 9 February.

CBC Television News (1997), *Transcripts*, 10 January.

CBS News Online (2002), *Mistaken-Bombing Pilots Face Charges*, 13 September.

Centa, R. and Macklem, P. (2001), 'Securing Accountability through Commissions of Inquiry: a Role for the Law Commission of Canada', *Osgoode Hall Law Journal*, Vol. 39, No. 1, Spring.

Centre for Defence Studies (2001), *Achieving the Helsinki Headline Goals*, Centre for Defence Studies, London, November.

Certain Expenses of the United Nations Case (1962), International Court of Justice, Advisory Opinion, 20 July.

Chandler, D. (2001), 'The People-Centred Approach to Peace Operations: the New UN Agenda', *International Peacekeeping*, Spring, Vol. 8, No. 1.

Chandler, D. (2002), *From Kosovo to Kabul: Human Rights and International Intervention*, Pluto Press, London.

Charter of the United Nations (1945), San Francisco, 26 June 1945.

Chomsky, N. (1999), *The New Military Humanism: Lessons from Kosovo*, Pluto Press, London.

Chryssochoou, D.N. (2000), *Democracy in the European Union*, Tauris Publishers, London and New York.

Clark, I. (1999), *Globalization and International Relations Theory*, Oxford University Press, Oxford.

Clark, W.K. (2001), 'Waging Modern War', *Public Affairs*, New York.

Clinton, B (1995), 'Letter to Senate Democratic Leader Thomas Daschle on Implementation of the Balkan Peace Process', *United States Weekly Compilation of Presidential Documents*, Vol. 31, p. 2177, 1 December.

Cohen, R. (1998), 'NATO Opens Way to Start Bombing in Serb Province', *New York Times*, 13 October, pp. A1, A10.

Coker, C. (2002), *Globalisation and Insecurity in the Twenty-first Century: NATO and the Management of Risk*, Adelphi Paper 345, The International Institute for Strategic Studies, June.

Commission of Inquiry into the Deployment of Canadian Forces to Somalia (1995), *Transcripts of Procedural Hearings*, 24 May 1995, Vol.1P, p. 3.

Commission of Inquiry into the Deployment of Canadian Forces to Somalia (1997a), 'The Need for a Vigilant Parliament', in *Dishonored Legacy: The Lessons of the Somalia Affair*, Ottawa: Minister of Public Works and Government Services Canada, Vol. 5, Ch. 44.

Commission of Inquiry into the Deployment of Canadian Forces to Somalia (1997b), *Dishonored Legacy: The Lessons of the Somalia Affair*, Ottawa: Minister of Public Works and Government Services Canada, Vol. 1-5.

Commission of Inquiry into the Deployment of Canadian Forces to Somalia (1997c), 'Executive Summary', in *Dishonored Legacy: The Lessons of the Somalia Affair*, Ottawa: Minister of Public Works and Government Services Canada, Vol. 1-5, p. ES-3.

Commission of Inquiry into the Deployment of Canadian Forces to Somalia (1997d), 'The Inquiry's Unfinished Mandate', in *Dishonored Legacy: The Lessons of the Somalia Affair*, Ottawa: Minister of Public Works and Government Services Canada, Vol. 5, pp. 1403-1406.

Committee on Military Affairs and Justice of the Association of the Bar of the City of New York (1999), 'Congressional Control of the Military in a Multilateral Context: A Constitutional Analysis of Congress's Power to Restrict the President's Authority to place United States Armed Forces under Foreign Commanders in United Nations Peace Operations', *Military Law Review*, Vol. 162, pp. 50.

Conaughton, R. M. (2001), *Military Intervention and Peacekeeping: The Reality*, Ashgate, Aldershot.

Connolly, K. et al (2001), 'Berlin Opens Rift over Peace Force', *The Guardian*, 20 December 2001, pp. 8.

Constitution of the Kingdom of Denmark (1992).

Constitution of the Kingdom of Netherlands (2002), Published by the Ministry of the Interior and Kingdom Relations, Constitutions Affairs and Legislation Department, in collaboration with the Translation Department of the Ministry of Foreign Affairs.

Constitution of the Kingdom of Sweden (1975).

Constitution of the Republic of Hungary (1949).

Constitution of the Republic of Poland (1997).

Costa, O. (2001), 'La Cour de Justice et le Controle Démocratique de l'Union Européenne', *Revue Française de Science Politique*, Vol. 51, No. 6, December, pp. 881-902.

Cottey, A. (1998), *The European Union and Conflict Prevention: The Role of the High Representative and the Policy Planning and Early Warning Unit*, International Alert/Saferworld, London, December.

Cottey, A., Edmunds, T. and Forster, A. (eds) (2002), *Democratic Control of the Military in Post-communist Europe: Guarding the Guards*, Palgrave, Basingstoke.

Council of the European Union (2000a), *On Measures for the Protection of Classified Information Applicable to the General Secretariat of the Council*, Council Decision adopted on 27 July 2000, Official Journal 2000/C 239/01.

Council of the European Union (2000b), Council Decision 2000/527/EC of 14 August.

Council of the European Union (2000c), *Presidency Report on the European Security and Defence Policy*, Press Release No. 14056/2/00, 4 December 2000.

Council of the European Union (2000e), Committee of Permanent Representatives Decision, OJ 2000/C 239/01, 27 July.

Council of the European Union (2001) v. Heidi Hautala Case, Court of First Instance of the European Community, Decision 93/731/EC, 19 July 1999.

Council of the European Union (2001a), 'Draft Presidency Report on European Security and Defence Policy', COSDP 333 (annexed to the Laeken Declaration), EU Council, Brussels, 11 December.

Council of the European Union (2003), 'Council Joint Action on the European Union Military Operation in the Former Yugoslav Republic of Macedonia', Brussels, COSDP 56, Relex 35, No. 5794/03, 4 February.

Cowell, A. (1995), 'Germany to Send Forces to Balkans to Support U.N.', *New York Times*, 27 June, p. A3.

Cowell, A. (1996), 'Germans plan Combat Troops outside NATO, a Postwar First', *New York Times*, 14 December, p. A3.

Dahl, R.A. (1994), 'A Democratic Dilemma: System Effectiveness and Citizen Participation', *Political Science Quarterly*, 109 (I), pp. 32-34.

Dahl, R. A. (1998), *On Democracy*, Yale University Press, New Haven.

Damrosch, L.F. (1995), 'Constitutional Control over War Powers: a Common Core of Accountability in Democratic Societies?', *University of Miami Law Review*, Vol. 50, pp. 181-199.

Damrosch, L.F. (1996), 'Is there a General Trend in Constitutional Democracies toward Parliamentary Control over War-and-Peace Decisions?', in *Proceedings of the 90th Annual Meeting of the American Society of International Law*, ASIL, Washington, D.C., pp. 36-40.

Damrosch, L.F. (1997), 'Use of Force and Constitutionalism', *Columbia Journal of Transnational Law*, Vol. 36, pp. 449-472.

Damrosch, L.F. (2000), 'The Clinton Administration and War Powers', *Law and Contemporary Problems*, Vol. 63, pp. 125-141.

Damrosch, L.F. (2003), 'The Interface of National Constitutional Systems with International Law and Institutions on Using Military Forces: Changing Trends in Executive and Legislative Powers', in C. Ku and H. Jacobsen (eds), *Democratic Accountability and the Use of Military Force in International Law*, Cambridge University Press, Cambridge, pp. 39-60.

Dau, K. (1989), 'Rechtliche Rahmenbedingungen einer Deutsch-Französischen Brigade', 31 *Neue Zeitschrift für Wehrrecht – NZWehrR*.

Dempsey, J. (2001), 'EU Calls for Nato-Led Force to Protect Observers in Macedonia', *Financial Times*, 10 September 2001, pp. 3.

Desbarats, P. (1997), *Somalia Cover-Up: A Commissioner's Story*, McClelland and Stewart, Toronto, p. 221.

Desch, M. (2001), *Civilian Control of the Military: The Changing Security Environment*, Johns Hopkins University Press, London.

Deutsche Presse-Agentur (1996), 'Germany Approves Sending Tornado Jets to East Slavonia', 9 February.

Diehl, P.F. (1993), *International Peacekeeping*, Baltimore, Johns Hopkins University Press, London.

Diehl, P.F. (1995), *International Peacekeeping: With a New Epilogue on Somalia, Bosnia and Cambodia (Perspectives on Security)*, Johns Hopkins University Press, London.

Diehl, P.F. (ed.) (2001), *The Politics of Global Governance: International Organizations in an Interdependent World*, Lynne Rienner, Boulder.

Docherty, D. (1997), *Mr. Smith goes to Ottawa. Life in the House of Commons*, UBC Press, Georgetown.

Dombey, D. (2002), 'EU to Go Ahead with Satellite System', *Financial Times*, pp. 3, 27, March.

Dryzek, J. (1995), 'Political and Ecological Communication', *Environmental Politics*, Vol. 4, No. 4, pp. 49-68.

Duke, S. (2000a), *From Elusive Quest for European Security: from EDC to CFSP*, Martin's Press, New York.

Duke, S. et al. (2000b), 'The Major European Allies: France, Germany, and the United Kingdom', in A. Schnabel and R. Thakur (eds), *Kosovo and the Challenge of Humanitarian Intervention*, United Nations University Press, Tokyo, pp. 128-148.

Dunne, T. and Schmidt, B. (2001), 'Realism', in J. Baylis and S. Smith (eds), *The Globalisation of World Politics*, Oxford University Press, Oxford, pp. 141-161.

Durch, W.J. (ed.) (1996), *UN Peacekeeping, American Policy, and the Uncivil Wars of the 1990s*, St. Martins Press, New York.

Economist, The (2000), *Phoney Democracies*, 22 June.

Economist, The (2002), *A Nastase Shock for NATO?*, 4 April.

Economist, The (2003), *The European Union going Military in Macedonia*, p. 34.

Eekelen, Van, W.F. (2002), *Democratic Control of Armed Forces: the National and International Parliamentary Dimension*, DCAF Occasional Paper No. 2, October.

Elster, J. (ed.) (1998), *Deliberative Democracy*, Cambridge University Press, Cambridge.

Ely, J.H. (1993), *War and Responsibility*, Princeton University Press, Princeton.

Ely, J.H. (1988), 'Suppose Congress Wanted a War Powers Act that Worked', 88 *Columbia Law Review*.

Eriksen, E.O. and Fossum, J.E. (eds) (2000), *Democracy in the European Union: Integration through Deliberation?*, Routledge, London.

European Commission (2003), *Towards an EU Defence Equipment Policy: Commission Proposal*, IP/03/05, Brussels, 11 March.

European Convention (2002), Working Group on Defence (16 December 2002), Final report of Working Group-Defence, Brussels.

European Defence Meeting (2003), *European Defence Meeting: Conclusion (Egmont Palace Brussels)*, Meeting of Heads of State and Government of Germany, France Luxembourg and Belgium on European Defence, Brussels, 29 April.

European Parliament (2002), *Report on Relations Between the European Parliament and the National Parliaments in European Integration*, Committee on Constitutional Affairs, 2032 InI, 23 January.

European Union (2002), 'Council Joint Action of 11 March 2002 on the European Union Police Mission', *Official Journal*, Vol. 45, 13 March, Brussels.

European Union (1992), 'Treaty of the European Union', in *Europe Documents*, No. 1759/60, 7 February, Agence Europe, Brussels.

European Voice (2002), *Row over MEPs: Restricted Access to Security Files*, Vol. 8 No. 28, 18 July.

Evans, G. (1993), *Cooperating for Peace: The Global Agenda for the 1990s and Beyond*, Allen and Unwin, St. Leonards.

Everts, P. (2002), *Democracy and Military Force*, Palgrave, Houndmills and New York.

Fawcett, L., and Hurrell, A. (eds) (1995), *Regionalism in World Politics: Regional Organization and International Order*, Oxford University Press, Oxford.

Fink, U. (1999), 'Verfassungsrechtliche und verfassungsprozessrechtliche Fragen im Zusammenhang mit dem Kosovo-Einsatz der Bundeswehr', *Juristenzeitung*, Vol. 21, pp. 1016-1022.

Fischer, L. (1995), 'The Korean War: on what Legal Basis did Truman act', in *American Journal of International Law*, Vol. 89, No. 1, pp.21-39.

Fisher, L. (1999), 'Congressional Abdication: War and Spending Powers', *St. Louis University Law Journal*, Vol. 43, pp. 931-1012.

Fleck, D. (ed.) (2001), *The Handbook of the Law of Visiting Forces*, Oxford University Press, Oxford.

Framework Agreement (2000), *Framework Agreement between the French Republic, the Federal Republic of Germany, the Italian Republic, the Kingdom of Spain, the Kingdom of Sweden and the United Kingdom of Great Britain and Northern Ireland*

Concerning Measures to Facilitate the Restructuring and Operation of the European Defence Industry, Farnborough, 27 July.

Franck, T. and Rodley, N. (1973), 'After Bangladesh: the Law of Humanitarian Intervention by Force', *American Journal of International Law*, Vol. 67, pp. 275-305.

Franck, T. (1992), *Political Questions/Judicial Answers: Does the Rule of Law Apply in Foreign Affairs?*, Princeton University Press, Princeton.

Freedom House (2003), *Freedom in the World: The Annual Survey of Political Rights and Civil Liberties 2001-2002*, Transaction Publishers, Sommerset.

Friesenhahn, E. (1985), 'Parlament und Regierung im modernen Staat', *Veröffentlichungen der Vereinigung Deutscher Staatsrechtslehrer*, Vol. 16, p. 29.

Fursdon, E. (1980), *The European Defence Community: a History*, The Macmillan Press Ltd., London.

Gallis, P. (2003), *NATO's Decision-Making Procedure*, CRS Report for Congress, RS 215/0, Congressional Research Service/The Library of Congress, Washington DC.

General Framework Agreement for Peace in Bosnia and Herzegovina (1995), *International Legal Materials* (I.L.M.), Vol. 35, 1996.

George, B. and Morgan, J. (1999), *Parliament and National Security*, Paper presented at conference on 'Redefining Society-Military Relations from Vancouver to Vladivostok', Birmingham, 16-18 April.

German-Netherlands Corps Agreement (1997), *Agreement between the Government of the Kingdom of the Netherlands and the Government of the Federal Republic of Germany on the Organisation and the Activities of the 1 (German-Netherlands) Corps and the Air Operations Coordination Centre*, 6 October.

German-Netherlands Corps Convention (1997), 'Convention between the Government of the Federal Republic of Germany and the Government of the Kingdom of the Netherlands on the General Conditions for the 1 (German-Netherlands) Corps and Corps-related Units and Establishments', BGBl. 1998 II, p. 2438, 6 October.

Ghébali, V.Y. (2003), *The OSCE Code of Conduct on Politico-Military Aspects of Security (3 December 1994). A Paragraph-by-Paragraph Commentary on Sections VII and VIII (Democratic Control and Use of Armed Forces)*, Geneva Centre for the Democratic Control of Armed Forces, Document No. 3, February.

Glennon, M.J. (2003), 'The United States: Democracy, Hegemony, and Accountability', in C. Ku and H. Jacobson, *Democratic Accountability and the Use of Force in International Law*, Cambridge University Press, Cambridge, pp. 323-348.

Gourlay, C. (1999), 'The European Parliament's Role in Scrutinising Defence and Security: an Uncertain Future', *ISIS Europe Briefing Paper*, No. 21, Brussels.

Gourlay, C. and Monaco, A. (2001), 'The Rapid Reaction Force: the EU takes stock', *European Security Review*, No. 9. December.

Governance Commission (1995), *Commission on Global Governance, Our Global Neighbourhood*, Oxford University Press, Oxford.

Granatstein, J.L. (1997), *A Paper Prepared for the Minister of National Defence*, March 25.

Greene, Owen (2003), 'International Standards and Obligations: Norms and Criteria for Democratic Control in EU, OSCE and OECD Areas', in Germann, Wilhelm N., Edmunds, Timothy (eds.) *Towards Security Sector Reform in Post Cold War Europe: A Framework for Assessment*, Nomos, Baden-Baden (forthcoming).

Guardian, The (2002), *Cold War Enemies Warm to Joint Task*, 13 May.

Guardian, The (2003), *Europe Tests its Military Rings*, 13 June.

Hague, R., Harrop, M., and Breslin, S. (eds) (1998), *Comparative Government and Politics. An Introduction*, 4th edition, Macmillan, Houndmills and London.

Haltiner K.W. and Klein, P. (eds) (2002), *Europas Armeen im Umbruch*, Nomos, Baden-Baden, S. 235-258.

Hampson, F.O. (2003), 'Canada: Committed Contributor of Ideas and Forces, but with Growing Doubts and Problems', in C. Ku and H. Jacobsen (eds), *Democratic Accountability and the Use of Force in International Law*, Cambridge University Press, Cambridge, p. 141.

Hardt, M. and Negri, A. (2000), *Empire*, Harvard University Press, Cambridge.

Harlow, C. (2002), *Accountability in the European Union*, Oxford University Press, Oxford.

Haushaltskontrolle der Nachrichtendienste (1986) Bundesverfassungsgericht. German Federal Constitutional Court, Judgement of 14 January 1986. BVerfGE Vol. 70, pp. 324, at 358 ff.

Heintschel von Heinegg, W. and Haltern, U.R. (1994), 'The Decision of the German Federal Constitutional Court of 12 July 1994 in Re: Deployment of the German Armed Forces 'out of area'', *Netherlands International Law Review*, Vol. 41.

Heisbourg, F. (1999), 'Les Prémices d'une Convergence des Objectifs', *Défense Nationale*, Vol. 55, March, pp. 18-23.

Held, D. (1987), *Models of Democracy*, Polity Press and Blackwell Publishers, Cambridge.

Held, D. (1995), *Democracy and the Global Order*, Polity Press, Cambridge.

Held, D. (1996), *Models of Democracy*, 2nd edition, Polity Press, Cambridge.

Henkin, L. (1990), *Constitutionalism, Democracy and Foreign Affairs*, Columbia University Press, New York.

Henkin, L. (1996), *Foreign Affairs and the United States Constitution*, Oxford University Press, Oxford.

Henkin, L. and Rosenthal, A. (1990), *Constitutionalism and Rights: the Influence of the United States Constitution Abroad*, Columbia University Press, New York.

Herzog, R., et al. (eds) (2001), *Grundgesetz Commentary*, Beck-Verlag, München.

Hewson, C.W. (1985), *Mobile Command Study – Report on Disciplinary Infractions and Anti-Social Behaviour with Particular Reference to the SSF and the Canadian Airborne Regiment*, 26 September.

Heywood, A. (1997), *Politics*, Palgrave Macmillan, Houndmills and New York.

Hillen, J. (1998), *Blue Helmets: The Strategy of U.N. Military Operations*, Brassey's, London.

Hix, S. (1999), *The Political System of the European Union*, Macmillan Press Ltd., London.

Hoge, W. (2001), 'U.K. Presses Plan for Afghan Force', *International Herald and Tribune'*, 20 December, p. 1.

Hopkinson, W. (2001), *Enlargement: a New NATO*, Chaillot Paper 49, WEU Institute for Security Studies, Paris.

Hoskyns, C. and Newman, M. (eds) (2000), *Democratizing the European Union*, Manchester University Press, Manchester and New York.

House of Commons (1995a), *Debates*, 12 May, Ottowa, Canada.

House of Commons (1995b), *Oral Question Period*, 22 March, Ottowa, Canada.

House of Commons (1996a), *Debates*, 28 March, Ottowa, Canada.

House of Commons (1996b), *Debates*, 8 October, Ottowa, Canada.

House of Commons (2000), 'Fourth Report', *Foreign Affairs Select Committee*, 7 June. London, United Kingdom.

House of Lords (2002), Select Committee on the European Union, (29 January 2002), *The European Policy on Security and Defence*, Session 2001-2002, 11th Report, HL Paper 71(1), House of Lords, London.

Hunt, G. (1906), *The Writings of James Madison*, G.P. Putnam's Sons, New York.

Immigration and Naturalization Service v. Chadha (1983), Supreme Court of the United States 461 U.S. 919.

Independent International Commission on Kosovo (2000), *Kosovo Report*, Oxford University Press, Oxford.

International Crisis Group (2001), *EU Crisis Response Capabilities: Institutions and Processes for Conflict Prevention and Management*, IGC Issues Report No. 2. ICG, Brussels, 26 June.

International Crisis Group (2002), *EU Crisis Response Capabilities: an Update*, ICG, Brussels, 29 April.

International Institute for Strategic Studies (IISS) (2001), *Strategic Survey 1999-2000*, Oxford University Press, Oxford.

International Military Deployments Case (1994), Federal Constitutional Court of the Federal Republic of Germany, 90 BverfGE 286. An English version can be found at International Law Reports (I.L.R.), 1997, Vol. 106, pp. 318-352.

Jensen, F. (2000), 'Military Secrecy in the EU Council Provokes Legal Challenges', *European Security Review*, Issue 2, p.1.

Jett, D.C. (2000), *Why Peacekeeping Fails?*, St. Martins Press, New York.

Johnson, N. (1983), *State and Government in the Federal Republic of Germany*, 2nd Edition, Pergamon Press, Oxford.

Justizverwaltungsakt (1975), Bundesverfassungsgericht, German Federal Constitutional Court, Judgement of 28 October 1975. BVerfGE, Vol. 40, p. 237 (at 248 ff).

Kalkar I. (1978), Bundesverfassungsgericht, Judgement of 8 August 1978. BVerfGE, Vol. 49, p. 89 (at 126 f).

Karatnycky, A. and Piano, A. (eds) (2002), *Freedom in the World: The Annual Survey of Political Rights and Civil Liberties, 2001-2002*, Rowman and Littlefield, Lanham, US.

Katz, R.S. (2001), 'Models of Democracy: Elite Attitudes and the Democratic Deficit in the European Union', *European Union Politics*, Vol. 2, No 1.

Kay S. and Binnendijk, H. (1997) *After the Madrid Summit: Parliamentary Ratification of NATO Enlargement*, INSS, NDU, Washington D.C.

Kenny, C. (1998), 'Parliamentary Control and National Defence: the Canadian Experience', Canadian Institute of Strategic Studies Strategic, Toronto, *Strategic Datalink*, No. 70.

Khan, D.E. and Zöckler, M. (1992), 'Germans to the Front? Or Le Malade Imaginaire', *European Journal of International Law*, Vol. 3, p. 163.

Kinsella, W. (1994), *Web of Hate: Inside Canada's Far Right Network*, HarperCollins, Toronto.

Klang, K. (1986), 'NATO-Mitgliedschaft und Verteidigungsfall', 28 *Neue Zeitschrift für Wehrrecht – NZWehrR*, p. 103.

Knowlton, B. (2002), 'Bush Cheers Support of Congress Leaders for Swift Vote on Iraq', *International Herald Tribune*, 19 September, pp. 1, 4.

Koh, H.H. (1990), *The National Security Constitution*, Yale University Press, New Haven.

Kokott, J. (1996), 'Kontrolle der Auswärtigen Gewalt', 111 *Deutsches Verwaltungsblatt – DVBl*.

Kommers, D.P. (1997), *The Constitutional Jurisprudence of the Federal Republic of Germany*, Duke University Press, North Carolina, Durham.

Kostakos, G. (2000), 'The Southern Flank: Italy, Greece, Turkey' in A. Schnabel and R. Thakur, (eds), *Kosovo and the Challenge of Humanitarian Intervention*, United Nations University Press, Tokyo, pp. 166-180.

Kress, C. (1995), 'The External Use of German Armed Forces – the 1994 Judgment of the Bundesverfassungsgericht', *International and Comparative Law Quarterly*, Vol. 44, pp. 414-415.

Ku, C. and Jacobson, H. (2003a), 'Toward a Mixed System of Democratic Accountability', in C. Ku and H. Jacobsen (eds), *Democratic Accountability and the Use of Force in International Law*, Cambridge University Press, Cambridge, pp. 349-383.

Ku, C. and Jacobson, H. (eds) (2003b), *Democratic Accountability and the Use of Force in International Law*, Cambridge University Press, Cambridge.

Kuperman, A. (2001), *The Limits of Humanitarian Intervention: Genocide in Rwanda*, Brookings, Washington.

Laird, R.F. (1991), *The Europeanization of the Alliance*, Westview Press, Boulder, Colorado.

Lamy, F. (2000), *Le Contrôle Parlementaire des Opérations Extérieures*, Rapport 2237, Onzième Legislature, Paris.

Landmanns, G.P (eds) (2002), *Der Peloponnesische Krieg* (German translation), Artemis & Winkler Verlag, München.

Laschet, A. (2002), *Parliamentarisation of the European Security and Defence Policy*, Geneva Centre for the Democratic Control of Armed Forces, Working Paper Series, No. 82, pp. 6-7.

Legault, A. (1997), *A Paper Prepared for the Minister of National Defence*. 1 March.

Leurdijk, Dick and Zandee, Dick (2001), *Kosovo: From Crisis to Crisis*, Ashgate, Aldershot.

Lewis, F. (1999), 'A Clash with Russia in Kosovo came too Close for Comfort', *International Herald Tribune*, 1 October.

Lijphart, A. (ed.) (1992), *Parliamentary versus Presidential Government*, Oxford University Press, Oxford.

Lijphart, A. (1999), *Patterns of Democracy: Government Forms and Performance in Thirty-Six Countries*, Yale University Press, New Haven and London.

Limpert, M. (2002), *Auslandseinsatz der Bundeswehr*, Dunckler and Humblot, Berlin.

Linklater, A. (1998), *The Transformation of Political Community*, Polity Press, Cambridge.

Linz, J. (1992), 'The Perils of Presidentialism', in A. Lijphart (ed.) *Parliamentary versus Presidential Government*, Oxford University Press, Oxford.

Lobel, J. and Ratner, M. (1999), 'Bypassing the Security Council: Ambiguous Authorizations to Use Force, Cease-fires and the Iraqi Inspection Regime', *American Journal of International Law*, Vol. 93, No. 1, pp. 124-54.

Lodge, J. (1996), *The European Parliament*, in S.S. Anderson and K.A. Eliasssen (eds), *The European Union: How Democratic Is It?*, Sage Publication, London, pp. 187-214.

Lord, C. (1998), *Democracy in the European Union*, Sheffield Academic Press, Sheffield.

Lord, C. (2001), 'Assessing Democracy in a Contested Polity', *Journal of Common Market Studies*, Vol. 39, No. 4, November, pp. 641-661.

Lotter, C. (1997), *Die Parliamentarische Versammlung der Westeuropäischen Union*, Nomos, Baden-Baden.

Lunn, S. (2000), 'Defence and Security Policy: the Role of Parliaments and the Evolution of the NATO Parliamentary Assembly', in NATO Parliamentary Assembly, *Defence and Security for the 21st Century*, Atalink, London.

Lunn, S. (2002), *Secretary General's Annual Report*, NATO PA Document AV 37, SC (02) b, March.

Mace, C. (2003), 'Putting the "Berlin Plus" into Practice: Taking Over from NATO in FYROM', *European Security Review*, No. 16, 2-4 February.

Majone, G. (1994), 'The Rise of the Regulatory State in Europe', *West European Politics*, No. 17.

Majone, G. (1999), 'Europe's 'Democratic Deficit': the Question of Standards', *European Law Journal*, Vol. 4, No 1, pp. 5-28.

Martin, L. (2000), *Democratic Commitments: Legislatures and International Co-operation*, Princeton University Press, Princeton.

Mattson, I. and Stroem, K. (1996), 'Parliamentary Committees', in H. Döring (ed.), *Parliaments and Majority Rule in Western Europe*, St. Martin's Press, New York.

Maurer, A. (2001), 'National Parliaments after Amsterdam: Adaptation, Re-Calibration and Europeanisation by Process', Paper for Working Group Meeting, XXIVth COSAC, 8-9 April.

Mawdsley, J. (2002), *Arms, Agencies and Accountability: the Case of OCCAR*, BICC, Bonn. Paper presented at the ESDP Democracy Project, BICC, Bonn. June.

Mayall, J. (2000), 'The Concept of Humanitarian Intervention Revisited', in A. Schnabel and R. Thakur, *Kosovo and the Challenge of Humanitarian Intervention*, United Nations University Press, Tokyo, New York.

McGrew, A. (2002), 'Democracy Beyond Borders?', in D. Held and A. McGrew (eds), *The Global Transformation Reader: and Introduction to the Globalisation Debate*, Polity Press, Cambridge, pp. 405-419.

Mearsheimer, J. (1990), 'Back to the Future: Instability of Europe after the Cold War', *International Security*, Vol. 15, Summer, pp. 5-57.

Menzel, E. (1963), 'Nationale und internationale Strukturreform der NATO', 18 *Europa Archiv*.

Menzy, M.L. (1979), *Comparative Legislatures*, Duke University Press, Durham.

Miller, D. (1995), *On Nationality*, Clarendon Press, Oxford.

Miller, J. (2002), 'Reflections on National Security and International Law Issues during the Clinton Administration', *Chicago Journal of International Law*, Vol. 4, Spring.

Mingst, K. (2003), 'Domestic Political Factors and Decisions to Use Military Forces', in C. Ku and H. Jacobson, *Democratic Accountability and the Use of Force in International Law*, Cambridge University Press, Cambridge, pp. 61-80.

Minister of Defence (1997), *A Commitment to Change. Report on the Recommendations of the Somalia Commission of Inquiry*, Ottawa, October.

Minister's Monitoring Committee on Change in the Department of National Defence and the Armed Forces (1999), *Final Report*, Ottawa.

Mitchell, A. (1998), 'House Signals Backing for a Kosovo Force', *New York Times*, 12 March, p. A6.

Mitchell, A. (1999), 'Deadlocked House Denies Support for Air Campaign', *New York Times*, 29 April, p. A1.

Morton, D. (1997), *A Paper Prepared for the Minister of National Defence*, 25 March.

Morton, D. (1999), 'Reflecting on Ten Years', Defence Associations National Network, *National Network News*, Vol. 6, No.1, Spring.

Morvacsik, A. and Nicolaidis K. (1999), 'Explaining the Treaty of Amsterdam: Interests, Influence, Institutions', *Journal of Common Market Studies*, Vol. 37, No. 1, March.

Moussis, N. (2002), 'Aeronautical Industries', *Access to European Union*, Euroconfidential, Brussels, April.

Mueller, J. (1989), *Retreat from Doomsday: The Obsolescence of Major War*, Basic Books, New York.

Muench, I. and Kunig, P. (eds) (2002), *Basic Law, Commentary*, Publisher, Munich.

Muller-Wille, B. (2002), 'EU Intelligence Cooperation. A Critical Analysis', *Contemporary Security Policy*, Vol. 23, No. 2, August, pp. 61-86.

Multinational Corps Northeast Agreement (1998), 'Agreement between the Government of the Federal Republic of Germany the Government of the Kingdom of Denmark and the Government of the Republic of Poland on the Multinational Corps Northeast (MNC NE)'. 5 September 1998, Bundesgesetzblatt 1999, Vol. II,p. 675.

Multinational Corps Northeast Convention, 1998. 'Convention between the Government of the Federal Republic of Germany the Government of the Kingdom of Denmark and the Government of the Republic of Poland on the Multinational Corps Northeast (MNC NE)', 5 September 1998, Bundesgesetzblatt 1999, Vol. II.

Murphy, S. (1999a), 'Contemporary Practice of the United States Relating to International Law', *American Journal of International Law*, Vol. 93, pp. 161-170.

Murphy, S. (1999b), 'Contemporary Practice of the United States Relating to International Law', *American Journal of International Law*, Vol. 93, pp. 470-479.

NATO (1990), *London Declaration*, 6 July 1990. Reprinted in Bulletin of the German Government No. 90 of 10 July 1990, p. 777.

NATO (1999), *The Alliance's Strategic Concept*, approved by the Heads of State and Government participating in the meeting of the North Atlantic Council in Washington D.C.on 23rd and 24th April 1999.

NATO (2001), *NATO Handbook*, NATO Office of Information and Press, Brussels.

NATO (2002), *EU-NATO Declaration on ESDP, NATO*, NATO Press Releases (2002) 142, 16 December.

NATO Parliamentary Assembly (1998), *NATO in the 21st Century*, NATO PA, September.

NATO Parliamentary Assembly (1999a), *Declaration on Kosovo*, 10 May.

NATO Parliamentary Assembly (1999b), *The Warsaw Plenary Declaration on Kosovo*, 31 May.

NATO Parliamentary Assembly (2001), *Declaration on NATO Enlargement*.

NATO Parliamentary Assembly (2002a), *Declaration 322: Istanbul Declaration on NATO Transformation*.

NATO-Russian Founding Act (1997), *Founding Act on Mutual Relations, Cooperation and Security between NATO and the Russia Federation*, Paris, 27 May.

NATO-Ukraine Charter (1997), *Charter on a Distinctive Partnership between the North Atlantic Treaty Organisation and Ukraine*, Madrid, 9 July.

Nederlands Instituut Voor Oorlogsdocumentatie (NIOD) (2002), *Srebrenica, een 'veilig' gebied. Reconstructie, achtergronden, gevolgen en analyses van de val van een Safe Area*. ('Srebrenica – a Safe Area: Reconstruction, Background, Consequences and Analysis of the Fall of a Safe Area'), in 3 Volumes, Boom Publishers, Meppel.

New York Times (1990), *Germany Pledges $1.87 Billion to Aid Gulf Effort*, 16 September p. A16.

New York Times (1999), *In Clinton's Words: Speak with a Single Voice*, 29 April, p. A14.

Nice Treaty (2001), 18 March.

Nincic (1988), *United States Foreign Policy, Choices and Tradeoffs*, Congressional Quarterly Press, Washington DC.

Nolte, G. (1994), "Die neuen Aufgaben' von NATO und WEU', 54 *Heidelberg Journal of International Law* – ZaöRV, p. 652.

Nolte, G. (2002), *Vergleich Europäischer Wehrrechtssysteme*, Nomos, Baden-Baden.

Nolte, G. (2003), 'Germany: Ensuring Political Legitimacy for the Use of Military Forces by Requiring Constitutional Accountability', in C. Ku and H. Jacobson, *Democratic Accountability and the Use of Force in International Law*, Cambridge University Press, Cambridge, pp. 231-256.

North Atlantic Treaty, The (1949), Washington D.C. 4 April.

Norton, P. (1995), 'Special Issue on National Parliaments and the European Union', *The Journal of Legislative Studies*, Vol. 1, No. 3.

Norton, P. (ed.) (1998), *Parliaments and Governments in Western Europe*, Frank Cass, London.

Norton, P. (2002), *Parliaments and Citizens in Western Europe*, Frank Cass, London.

Nustad, K. G. and Thune, H. (2003), 'Norway: Political Consensus and the Problem of Accountability', in C. Ku and H. Jacobson, *Democratic Accountability and the Use of Force in International Law*, Cambridge University Press, Cambridge, p. 154-175.

Olson, D. (1994), *Democratic Legislative Institutions: a Comparative View*, M.E. Sharpe, Armonk, New York and London.

Olson, D. and Norton, P. (eds) (1996), *The New Parliaments of Central and Eastern Europe*, Frank Cass, London.

Omaar, R. and Waal, De, A. (1993), *Somalia. Human Rights Abuses by the United Nations Forces*, Africa Rights Report, London, July.

Order in Council (1995), 1995-442, March 20, in Commission of Inquiry into the Deployment of Canadian Forces to Somalia (1997), *Dishonored Legacy: the Lessons of the Somalia Affair*, Ottawa: Minister of Public Works and Government Services Canada, Appendix, Vol. 5, pp.1503-1507.

Order in Council (1997), P.C. 1997-456, April 3, in Commission of Inquiry into the Deployment of Canadian Forces to Somalia (1997), *Dishonored Legacy: the Lessons of the Somalia Affair*, Ottawa: Minister of Public Works and Government Services Canada, Appendix, Vol. 5.

Organisation for Security and Cooperation in Europe (1994), *Code of Conduct on Politico-Military Aspects of Security*, Budapest, 5-6 December.

Organstreit Case (2001), Federal Constitutional Court of the Federal Republic of Germany, 6/99, 22 November.

Ortega, M. (2001), *Military Intervention and the European Union*, Chaillot Papers 45, WEU Institute for Security Studies, Parism March.

Parliamentary Assembly of the Council of Europe (2002), *Resolution 1289 on Parliamentary Scrutiny of International Institutions*.

Patterson, S.C. and Copeland, S.W. (1994), 'Parliaments in the Twenty-First Century', in G.W. Copeland and S.C. Patterson (eds), *Parliaments in the Modern World*, Ann Arbor, The University of Michigan Press, Michigan.

Patzelt, W.J. (1995), 'Vergleichende Parlamentarismusforschung also Schluessel zum Systemvergleich. Vorschläge zu einer Theorie – und Forschungsdebatte', in W. Steffani and U. Thaysen, *Demokratie in Europa: Zur Rolle der Parlamente*, Westdeutscher Verlag, Bonn.

Perlez, J. (1998), 'NATO Raises its Pressure on the Serbs', *New York Times*, 12 October, p. A8.

Pfaff, T. (2000), *Peacekeeping and the Just War Tradition*, Strategic Studies Institute Monographs, US Army War College.

Pierre, A. (1999), 'De-Balkanizing the Balkans: Security and Stability in Southeastern Europe', *U.S. Institute of Peace Special Report*, United States Institute of Peace, Washington.

Polsby, N. (1975), 'Legislatures', in Greenstein, F. and Polsby, N. (eds), *Governmental Institutions and Processes: Handbook of Political Science*, Vol. 5, Addison-Wesley, Reading, Mass.

Raap, C. (1999), *Deutsches Wehrrecht*, Heidelberg.

Radio Free Europe/Radio Liberty (1997), *Rumania/Slovenia: NATO Membership Debate Continues*, 3 June.

Raines v. Byrd, (1997), Supreme Court of the United States, 521 U.S. 811.

Reuters World Service (1995), *Parliament approves German Troops for Bosnia Mission*, 6 December.

Reveley, W.T. III (1981), *War Powers of the President and Congress: Who Holds the Arrows and Olive Branch*, University Press of Virginia, Charlottesville.

Roberts, A. (1999), 'NATO's Humanitarian War over Kosovo', *Survival*, Volume 41, No. 3, Autumn.

Rosamond, B. (2000), *Theories of European Integration*, Palgrave, New York.

Royal Commission (1870), 'The Improvement of the Water Communications and the Development of Trade with the Northeastern United States', *Order-in-Council*, No. 17, 16 November.

Rühe, V. (1993), 'Shaping Euro-Atlantic Policies: A Grand Strategy for a New Era', *Survival*, Vol. 35, No. 2, Summer, pp. 129-137.

Rutten, M. (2001), *From St-Malo to Nice: European Defence: Core Documents*, Chaillot Paper No. 47, Institute for Security Studies, Western European Union, Paris, May.

Rutten, M. (2002), *From Nice to Laeken: European Defence: Core Documents*, Vol. 2, Chaillot Paper No. 51, Institute for Security Studies, European Union, Paris, April.

Sarooshi, D. (1999), *The United Nations and the Development of Collective Security: the Delegation of the UN Security Council of its Chapter VII Powers*, Oxford University Press, Oxford.

Savoie, D. (1999), *Governing from the Centre: the Concentration of Power in Canadian Politics*, University of Toronto Press, Toronto.

Scharpf, F. (1994), 'Community and Autonomy: Multi-Level Policy Making in the European Union', *Journal of European Public Policy*, Vol. 1, pp. 219-242.

Scharpf, F. (1999), *Governing in Europe: Effective and Democratic?*, Oxford University Press, Oxford.

Schmidt, M. (2000), *Demokratietheorien (Theories of Democracy)*, 3rd edition, UTB Leske and Budrich, Opladen.

Schmitt, B. (2000), *From Cooperation to Integration: Defence and Aerospace Industries in Europe*, Chaillot Paper No, 40, July, WEU Institute for Security Studies, Paris.

Schmitt, E. (2000a), 'Senators Refuse to Set a Deadline on Kosovo Troops', *New York Times*, 19 May, p. A1.

Schmitt, E. (2000b), 'Bush on Spot as G.O.P. Pushes to Pull Out G.I.'s from Kosovo', *New York Times*, 15 September, p. A12.

Schmitter, P. (2000), *How to Democratise the EU...And Why Bother?*, Rowman and Littlefield Publishers, Inc., Boston.

Scholte, J.A. (1997), 'Global Trade and Finance', in John Baylis and Steve Smith, *The Globalisation of World Politics: an Introduction to International Relations*, Transaction Publisher, Sommerset

Scholte, J.A. (2000), *Globalisation: a Critical Introduction*, Palgrave, Basingstoke.

Scholte, J.A. (2001), 'The Globalisation of World Politics', in John Baylis and Steve Smith, *The Globalisation of World Politics: an Introduction to International Relations*, Oxford University Press, Oxford.

Schulentlassung (1981), Bundesverfassungsgericht, German Federal Constitutional Court Judgement of 20 October 1981. BVerfGE vol. 58, pp. 257 (at 268 f.)

Sexualkundeunterricht (1977), Bundesverfassungsgericht, German Federal Constitutional Court Judgement of 21 December 1977, BVerfGE vol. 47, pp. 46 (at 78 f).

Shibata, A. (2003), 'Japan: Moderate Commitment within Legal Strictures', in C. Ku and H. Jacobson, *Democratic Accountability and the Use of Force in International Law*, Cambridge University Press, Cambridge, p. 207-230.

Simeon, R. (1972), *Federal-Provincial Diplomacy. The Making of Recent Policy in Canada*, University of Toronto Press, Toronto.

Simma, B., et al. (1995). *The Charter of the United Nations: a Commentary*, Oxford University Press, Oxford.

Simma, B. (1999), 'NATO, the UN and the Use of Force: Legal Aspects,' *European Journal of International Law*, Vol. 10, pp. 1-22.

Sloan, S. R. (2000), *The United States and European Defence*. WEU Institute for Security Studies, Paris, April.

Sloan, S. R. (2001), *A Perspective on the Future of the Transatlantic Bargain*, Presentation to the Political Committee of the NATO Parliamentary Assembly, Ottawa, 7 October.

Special Advisory Group on Military Justice and Military Police Investigation Services (Dickson Committee) (1997), Report, Ottawa, March 25.

Stationing Case (1984), Bundesverfassungsgericht, German Federal Constitutional Court, BVerfG, Collected Judgements, Vol. 68.

Stationing Treaty (*Aufenthaltsvertrag*) (1954), 'Treaty on Foreign Armed Forces in the Federal Republic of Germany', 23 October 1954, BGBl. II 1955, p. 253.

Strategisches NATO-Konzept (2001), Bundesverfassungsgericht, German Federal Constitutional Court, 2 BvE 6/99, Judgement of 22 November 2001, in Deutsches Verwaltungsblatt, 2002, p. 116

Streek, W. (ed.) (1998), *Internationale Wirtschaft, Nationale Demokratie? Herausforderungen für die Demokratietheorie*, Campus, New York.

Stromseth, J.E. (1996), 'Understanding Constitutional War Powers Today: Why Methodology Matters', *Yale Law Journal*, Vol. 106, No. 3, December.

Sutterlin, J. (1995), *The United Nations and the Maintenance of International Security: A Challenge to be Met*, Praeger, Westport.

Tálas, P. and Valki, L. (2000), 'The New Entrants: Hungary, Poland, and the Czech Republic', in A. Schnabel and R. Thakur (eds), *Kosovo and the Challenge of Humanitarian Intervention*, United Nations University Press, Tokyo, pp. 201-212.

Thakur, R. and Schnabel, A. (eds) (2001), *UN Peacekeeping Operations: Ad Hoc Mission/ Permanent Engagement*, United Nations University Press, Tokyo.

Thakur, R. and Thayer, C.A. (eds) (1995), *A Crisis in Expectations: UN Peacekeeping in the 1990s*, Westview, Boulder.

Tiefer, C. (1999), 'War Decisions in the Late 1990s by Partial Congressional Declaration', *San Diego Law Review*, Vol. 36, No. 1, Winter.

Toetsingskader (White Paper) (1995), *Criteria for Deployment of Forces Abroad*, Kamerstukken 1995-1996, 23 591, No. 6, and 2000-2001, 23 591 No. 7.

Tomuschat, C. (1978), 'Der Verfassungsstaat im Geflecht der internationalen Beziehungen', 36 *Veröffentlichungen der Vereinigung Deutscher Staatsrechtslehrer* – VVDStRL.

Toronto Star, (1994), *Editorial*, 17 July.

Trapans, J., and Fluri, P. (2003), *Defence and Security Sector Governance in South East Europe: Insights and Perspectives. A Self-Assessment Study*, Vol. I and II, Geneva Centre for the Democratic Control of Armed Forces, Geneva, and Centre for Civil-Military Relations, Belgrade.

Troncho, M. (2001), *National Parliamentary Scrutiny of Intervention Abroad by Armed Forces Engaged in International Missions: The Current Position in Law*, Assembly of Western European Union – Committee for Parliamentary and Public Relations, 22 October, Doc. A/WEU/CRP, p. 9

Tuzmukhamedo V.B. (2003), 'Russian Federation: the Pendulum of Powers', in C. Ku and H. Jacobsen, *Democratic Accountability and the Use of Force in International Law*, Cambridge University Press, Cambridge, pp. 257-279.

UNDP (2002), *Human Development Report 2002: Deepening Democracy in a Fragmented World*, published for the United Nations Development Programme, Oxford University Press, Oxford.

United Nations (1999a), 'Observance by United Nations Forces of International Humanitarian Law', *Secretary-General's Bulletin*, United Nations, New York, (ST/SGB/1999/13).

United Nations (1999b), *Report of the Secretary-General Pursuant to General Assembly Resolution 53/35: The fall of Srebrenica*, New York: United Nations, 15 November, A/54/549.

United Nations (2000), *Report of the Panel on United Nations Peace Operations*, United Nations, New York, 21 August, A/55/305, SC/2000/809.

United Nations (2002), *Background Note: United Nations Peacekeeping Operations*, New York: United Nations, 1 June.

United Nations Association (UK) (2003), *The Financial Cost of Peacekeeping Briefing Paper*, London.

United Nations Security Council (1999), *Report of the Independent Inquiry into the Actions of the United Nations During the 1994 Genocide in Rwanda*, 16 December, United Nations, New York, (S/1999/1257).

United Nations Security Council (2002), *Security Council welcomes European Union offer to provide Police Mission in Bosnia-Herzegovina from 1 January 2003, Resolution 1396 (2002) Adopted Unanimously*, 5 March 2002, UN Security Council Press Release SC/7319.

United States Congress (1973), *War Powers Resolution*, Pub. L. No. 93-148, 87 Stat. 555, 1973, codified at 50 U.S.C. sections 1541-1548, 1998.

United States Congress (1995), S.J. Res. 44, in *Congressional Record*, Vol. 141, p. S18552, 13 December.

United States Congress (1996a), *Congressional Record*, Vol. 142, p. H12, Daily Ed. 3 January.

United States Congress (1996b), 'Memorandum from Walter Dellinger, Assistant Attorney General', 8 May. *Congressional Record*, Vol. 142, pp. H10061-62, Daily Ed. 5 September 1996.

United States Congress (1999a), H.R. Res. 130, 106th Cong., in *Congressional Record*, Vol. 145, No. 47, pp. H1660-1669.

United States Congress (1999b), S. Con. Res. 21, 106th Cong., in *Congressional Record*, Vol. 145, No. 53.

United States Congress (1999c), H.R. J. Res. 44, 106th Cong., in *Congressional Record*, Vol. 145, No. 59, pp. H2427-2441.

United States Congress (1999d), H.R. Con. Res. 82, 106th Cong., in *Congressional Record*, Vol. 145, No. 59, pp. H2376-2400.

United States Congress (1999e), H.R. 1569, 106th Cong., in *Congressional Record*, Vol. 145, No. 59, pp. H2400-2414.

United States Congress (1999f), Pub. L. No. 106-31, title 11, ch. 3, 113 Stat. 57 (1999), codified at 7 U.S.C. section 1427(a).

United States Senate (1950), *Memorandum of July 3*. Prepared by the U.S. Department of State on the Authority of the President to Repel the Attack in Korea' in *Military Situation in the Far East: Hearings before the Senate Committee on Armed Services and the Committee on Foreign Relations*, Government Printing Office, Washington, 82nd Congress, 1st session, Pt. 5, pp. 3373-81.

United States Weekly Compilation of Presidential Documents (1973), Vol. 9, pp. 1285-86, 24 October.

United States Weekly Compilation of Presidential Documents (1999), *Letter to Congressional Leaders Reporting the Deployment of United States Military Personnel as part of the Kosovo International Security Force*, Vol. 35, p. 1107, 12 June.

Vancouver Sun, (1994), June 3.

Walker, R.B.J. (1988), *One World, Many Worlds: Struggle for a Just World Peace*, Lynne Rienner, Boulder.

Walt, S. (1998), 'The Ties that Fray: Why Europe and America are Drifting Apart', *National Interest*, No. 54, Winter 1998/9, pp. 3-11.

Warleigh, A. (2001), 'Europeanizing' Civil Society: NGOs as Agents of Political Socialization', *Journal of Common Market Studies*, Vol. 39 No. 4, November, pp. 619-39.

Washington Post, The (1999), 'NATO Embraces Three from Warsaw Pact', p. A1.

Weber, M. (1978), *Economy and Society*, Vol. II, University of California Press, Berkeley.

Wehrbeauftragtengesetz (1982), Gesetz über den Wehrbeauftragten des Deutschen Bundestages' of 16 June 1982, BGBl. III 50-2.

Weiler, A. and M. Netwich (eds) (1998), *Political Theory and the European Union. Legitimacy, Constitutional Choice and Citizenship*, Routledge, LondonNew York.

Weimar Constitution (1919), *Constitution of the German Federation of 11 August 1919*.

Wessels, R. A. (1999), *The European Union's Foreign and Security Policy*, Kluwer Law International, Hague and Boston.

Western European Union Council Of Ministers (1992), *Western European Union Council of Ministers Petersberg Declaration*, 19 June 2002. WE, Brussels.

White, N. D. (2003), 'The United Kingdom: Increasing Commitment Requires Greater Parliamentary Involvement' in C. Ku and H. Jacobsen, *Democratic Accountability and the Use of Force in International Law*, Cambridge University Press, Cambridge, pp. 300-322.

Whitney, C. (1998), 'Allies Inch toward Action against Serbs' *New York Times*, 25 September.

Wieland, J. (1999), 'Ausländische Vorgesetze deutscher Soldaten in multinationalen Verbänden', 41 *Neue Zeitschrift für Wehrrecht – NZWehrR*, p. 133.

Wild, M. (2000), 'Verfassungsrechtliche Möglichkeiten und Grenzen für Auslandseinsätze der Bundeswehr nach dem Kosovo-Krieg', *Die Öffentliche Verwaltung –* DÖV.

Wolfrum, R. (1997), 'Kontrolle der auswärtigen Gewalt', *VVDStRL* 56.

Woodbridge, J. (2001), 'Pledging Police for Crisis Management', *European Security Review*. No. 9, December, pp. 4-5.

Woodbridge, J. (2002a), 'Tackling Terrorism within EU Borders', *European Security Review*, No. 12, May, pp. 5-6.

Woodbridge, J. (2002b), 'Combating Terrorism outside the Borders of the Union', *European Security Review*, No. 13, July, pp. 3-4.

Woodbridge, J. (2002c), 'Breakthrough in ESDP Funding', *The European Security Review*, No. 13, July, pp. 5-6.

Wulf, H. (2003), 'Demokratische Kontrolle der Streitkräfte bei Militärischen Interventionen: Eine Herausforderung für Global Governance', in Th. Fues, and J. Hippler (eds), *Globale Politik. Entwicklung und Frieden in der Weltgesellschaft*, Logo Dietz-Verlag, Bonn.

Yost, D. (1999), *NATO Transformed: The Alliance's New Roles in International Security*, United States Institute of Peace, Washington DC.

Zöckler, M. (1995), 'Germany in Collective Security Systems – Anything goes?', *European Journal of International Law*, Vol. 6, p. 274.

Zürn, M. (2000), 'Democratic Governance beyond the Nation-State: the EU and other International Institutions', *European Journal of International Relations*, Vol. 6 (2), pp. 183-221.

Zur Zulässigkeit von Anträgen im Organstreitverfahren (1999), Bundesverfassungsgericht, German Federal Constitutional Court, BVerfG – 2 BvE 5/99, Judgement of 25 March 1999.

Index